LLOYD GEORGE

PROFILES IN POWER
General Editor: Keith Robbins

. . . .

LLOYD GEORGE

Martin Pugh

LONGMAN
London and New York

Longman Group Limited,
Longman House, Burnt Mill, Harlow,
Essex CM20 2JE, England
and Associated Companies throughout the world.

Published in the United States of America
by Longman Inc., New York

First published 1988
Third impression 1994

British Library Cataloguing in Publication Data

Pugh, M. D.
Lloyd George.——(Profiles in power)
1. Lloyd George, David 2. Prime ministers
——Great Britain——Biography
I. Title II. Series
941.083′092′4   DA566.9.L5
ISBN 0-582-02387-4 CSD
ISBN 0-582-55268-0 PPR

Library of Congress Cataloging-in-Publication Data

Pugh, Martin.
Lloyd George/M. D. Pugh.
p.   cm.——(Profiles in power)
Bibliography: p.
Includes index.
ISBN 0-582-02387-4
ISBN 0-582-55268-0 (pbk)
1. Lloyd George, David, 1863–1945. 2. Prime ministers ——Great
Britain——Biography. 3. Great Britain ——Politics and
government–1837–1901. 4. Great Britain——Politics and
government——1901–1936. 5. Great Britain——Politics and
government——1936–1945. I. Title. II. Series: Profiles in power
(London, England)
DA566.9.L5P78 1988
941.083′092′4——dc19
[B]   87-26360
CIP

Set in 10½/12pt AM Comp Edit Baskerville

Produced by Longman Singapore Publishers (Pte) Ltd.
Printed in Singapore

CONTENTS

PREFACE

The seventh of December 1986 marked the seventieth anniversary of David Lloyd George's accession to the premiership. This event, however, did not appear to arouse much attention, let alone inspire celebration, amongst the politically aware in this country. Despite the fact that any of the three main parties in Britain could, conceivably, have taken Lloyd George as its leader – and one of them did – each of them has, in the decades since 1922, generally thought it prudent to distance itself from him. It is not without significance that the association during the 1980s between Social Democrats and Liberals has awakened some sympathetic interest in him. But, with this exception, Lloyd George has been allowed to slip unimpeded into history, and his reputation into the hands of historians. Unlike the politicians, they have, especially during the last twenty years, gone a long way to establishing him as the greatest constructive statesman of twentieth-century Britain.

It is, therefore, a pleasure to be asked to write on such a figure for a wide audience and to acknowledge the help and encouragement of the series editor, Keith Robbins, as well as the efficiency of Longman in seeing the book through. The target they set proved to be a more difficult one than it had seemed at first. Lloyd George was, after all, involved in almost every major political question in twentieth-century Britain up to the Second World War. To contain him and his career within the space of 70,000 words was to try to squeeze a particularly lively genie into his bottle. However, this volume is intended as a synthesis not as a work of fresh research, though the book does reflect a good deal of work done over the years on the Lloyd George papers at the House of Lords Record Office (and previously at the Beaverbrook Library), and in the National Library of Wales.

The mass of published work on Lloyd George from which the author has benefitted is proceeding at several levels. We have had a number of detailed monographs and essays analysing particular aspects of Lloyd George's career. On the biographical front John Grigg began to put Lloyd George in a fresh and challenging light in 1973 with the first of three volumes which have, so far, taken his life to 1916. More recently Bentley Gilbert has begun to publish another multi-volume biography. Obviously the present work is on an entirely different scale. The last short biography of Lloyd George was Kenneth Morgan's which, over the 14 years since it was published, has been a blessing to many students of the subject. Clearly a good deal of work has been done both on Lloyd George and on the issues with which he was involved since then; and in any case the present author takes a different view of his subject to Dr Morgan.

As is only appropriate in a series entitled *Profiles in Power* I have devoted some attention to the methods and techniques employed by Lloyd George when in office for an unusually long and uninterrupted period from 1905 to 1922. I have also attempted to interpret his politics and his career in terms of a coherent political tradition stretching from Joseph Chamberlain to the present day. Nor, since this is a biography, have I neglected his personal life; indeed, I would regard both his childhood experience and his married life as being of considerable significance for his public career, though, again, I have not approached these aspects in the same way as many other writers. Even as this manuscript was being completed the Lloyd George family was in the process of placing more personal material concerning Lloyd George with the National Library of Wales, and it seems safe to conclude that he will continue to be a fascinating subject for revision and debate for years to come.

Martin Pugh
Slaley, Northumberland

FOR HANNAH AND ALISTAIR

Chapter 1

ESCAPING FROM WALES
1863 – 1898

From the perspective of late-twentieth-century Britain, David Lloyd George is a difficult man to place in social terms. His life's progress from Davy Lloyd, the 'cottage-bred boy', to the titled magnificence of 'Earl Lloyd George of Dwyfor' makes a fascinating story; but such labels sit uncomfortably upon him. It was an unusual cottage that nurtured Lloyd George, and an unlikely hereditary peerage to which he attained in old age. If we are to understand the youth climbing the social ladder in late-Victorian Wales we must surely put aside the simplicities of English social class; for he can hardly be fitted neatly into any obvious category.

David's father, William George, who died when David was only 17 months old, was by profession an elementary-school teacher who rose to become a headmaster at schools in Pwllheli and Manchester. However, in 1864 ill health forced him to abandon teaching in Lancashire to return to Pembrokeshire where he adopted his family's traditional occupation of farming. Argumentative, politically aware, latitudinarian in his religion, and perennially attracted by the opportunities offered by England, William George had much in common with his elder son. But he differed in being of a sombre, thoughtful turn of mind, and he displayed a far less buoyant personality.

William died in 1864 leaving a widow, Elizabeth, a daughter, Mary, and a son, David. Elizabeth was also pregnant with a third child who was to be named William. Elizabeth's brother, Richard Lloyd, came to her assistance by taking the family to live with him and his mother at Llanystumdwy in south Caernarfonshire. There, at the cottage known as Highgate, at the eastern end of the village street, was David's boyhood home.

1

In the context of rural Wales, it was by no means a humble home. Highgate was, in fact, a solid double-fronted stone house with three rooms downstairs, two up, a workshop to one side, and a large garden behind. Here Richard Lloyd pursued his father's trade, shoemaking, assisted by his mother who had managed the business since her husband's death. The work involved skilled manual labour on Richard's part, but he also employed several assistants in the workshop. He was thus both working man *and* entrepreneur. Consequently the young David grew up in modest material comfort. At Llanystumdwy the children were always well fed and better clothed than most of their contemporaries in the village. Not until the period in which both David and his brother William were serving their articles did the family suffer financial hardship.

This home provided a stable, loving base for the future statesman. With his mother, grandmother, and elder sister on hand to pander to his needs, David grew up without learning how to look after himself. The notion that he was destined for higher things was powerfully reinforced by the father-figure of his uncle. For Richard Lloyd the prospect of a childless old age had suddenly evaporated before the reality of a ready-made family. A deeply religious man, he served as unpaid minister to the Campbellite Baptist Chapel near Criccieth until his death in 1917. Richard's Christianity was not merely cerebral, it expressed itself in deeds; and the heavy responsibility of his sister's children must have been profoundly satisfying to him. Moreover, he was a well-read, intellectually alert person, immersed in the Welsh cultural revival of the late nineteenth century, a keen student of politics and an ardent Liberal. But for the circumstances of his birth, he might easily have become more than a respected but parochial figure. In his intelligent, precocious nephew he quickly discerned the man who might translate his own unrealised dreams into proud reality. Thus David, in brother William's words, became 'the apple of Uncle Lloyd's eye ... [he] could do no wrong in Uncle Lloyd's estimation'.[1] Even allowing for the natural chagrin of the brother whom the family took for granted, this is not an unjust view. Though not a spoilt child, David was cocooned in affection and fully aware of his own importance in the family. He thus grew up self-confident, easy in handling his fellow men, and sure of winning their loyalty and love.

This secure Welsh background has encouraged most of

Lloyd George's biographers, from the early days of Edwardian hagiography to the scholarly studies of more recent times, to present him as essentially the great *outsider* in modern British politics; radical, rebel, Welshman, Nonconformist, his whole career unfolds in a struggle with the might of the British Establishment. But if this is to be more than a platitude, Lloyd George must be compared with the many outsiders of the late Victorian and Edwardian period, whose attitude to the system ranged from defiance and parochialism on the one hand to sycophancy and immersion on the other. Where does Lloyd George stand in this continuum? Obviously, he was less of an outsider than a William Abraham or a Keir Hardie; but he maintained his radicalism and detachment far better than John Burns; and he resisted the charms of the Establishment far more effectively than Ramsay MacDonald. While undeniably outside the social stratum from which most politicians were then drawn, Lloyd George proved himself remarkably adaptive to the British system; yet, in adapting successfully, he always remained quite free of snobbery and side, which is surely one of his most attractive qualities. However, the very fact of his easy transition into British national politics – a rare accomplishment for a Welshman at this time – tells us something about his Welshness. The usual view of him tends to simplify what was really a most ambivalent and complicated relationship between Lloyd George and the society from which he sprang. Indeed, it seems essential to a balanced appreciation of him to recognise that from an early age he became acutely conscious of the conflicting pressures – Welsh and English – bearing upon him. As he learned to cope with these forces his very distinctive personality gradually developed.

Even as a boy, he showed a capacity for keeping a foot in two camps. For example, he attended the 'National' school in Llanystumdwy, an Anglican institution catering for a predominantly Nonconformist population. Welsh parents often resented their dependence on such schools since the brightest boys might be lured into Anglicanism by the offer of a pupil-teachership. At Llanystumdwy Lloyd George flourished under the excellent instruction and encouragement provided by his headmaster, David Evans – doubtless a source of mingled pride and anxiety for Uncle Lloyd. The most famous incident of these years was David's attempt to incite his schoolfellows to refuse to recite the Anglican catechism on the annual visitation of the governors and clergy. Though thwarted on the day, his effort was apparently rewarded subsequently by the abandonment of the ritual. However, the significance of the episode is invariably missed. It is easy enough for a schoolboy to play the role of rebel; and almost as easy to be a diligent, model pupil. But to be *both*, which David contrived to be, indicates unusual qualities. For his acts of rebellion never led him to recoil from school work or schoolmasters; in due course he received the offer of a pupil-teachership, and continued to enjoy the support of David Evans in pursuing his career. In this way, the keynote of his whole life manifested itself at an early stage: he was the rebel who understood how to make the system work for him.

. . .

THE LAW, MARRIAGE AND POLITICS

The rejection of a teaching career raised the problem of David's future. Family aspiration pointed away from manual occupations, but it was not clear where. Uncle Lloyd favoured the Nonconformist ministry, but his own small sect had no paid ministry. Medicine seemed attractive, but David was squeamish and shrank from the sight of blood. That left the law, to which they were encouraged by Thomas Goffey, a solicitor and family friend. Accordingly, David sat the Preliminary Law Examination in November 1877, began work for Messrs Breese, Jones, and Casson, solicitors of Porthmadog, in 1878, and was articled to Randall Casson in 1879 at the age of 16 at a cost of £100. By 1880 Uncle Lloyd had given up shoemaking through ill-health and the family moved to a small house in Criccieth. For several years, very little money came in, and they managed only by drawing upon the modest investments left to Elizabeth by William George, by borrowing from friends, and by taking lodgers in the summer.

These first steps towards his career intensified the conflicting pressures on David as represented by the Welsh Nonconformity of Uncle Lloyd and Criccieth on the one hand, and the English influence personified by Randall Casson on the other. When he began work David took lodgings in Porthmadog, which immediately offered an escape route from the strictness of village life. Finding his feet planted in two camps he relied upon all his natural charm and nimbleness to avoid a fall. For

4

example, his uncle was a strict non-smoker and teetotaller, and David learned how to deliver a temperance lecture. But in the company of Casson he also learned to enjoy a drink – not an untypical accomplishment for the Victorian Liberal politician! It was doubtless through Casson's example that he participated in the Porthmadog Volunteers, though apparently without telling the family. He sometimes covered his tracks skilfully. On Sundays he might go to Penmachno to preach – a perfect excuse to be out of Uncle Lloyd's sight on the Sabbath – which gave the opportunity for youthful flirtations with the girls of another village!

Yet the demands of religion taxed David's patience severely. He was known to refer privately to Uncle Lloyd as 'the Bishop'; and even an innocent spot of gardening on a Sunday would cause an argument with his mother. While Nonconformity united the Welsh people against the English, it also divided them in their daily lives. The Lloyds were the only members of the 'Campbellites' or 'Disciples of Christ' in Llanystumdwy, and therefore had to tramp 4 miles to their chapel at Criccieth three times each Sunday. While David undoubtedly enjoyed vigorous hymn-singing and a powerful sermon, his religion was neither spiritual nor doctrinal. In fact, Sundays palled dreadfully for him. He complained of being obliged to sit through the 'mumbling of musty prayers', and could be driven to sarcasm by predictably pious sermonising:

> Who raved most deliriously about the agonies of the wicked's doom and about the bliss of every true Calvinist's predestination?[2]

Nonconformist sectarianism even complicated his marriage prospects. The family of his future wife, Margaret Owen, were Calvinistic Methodists and thus, to a Campbellite, not far removed from Anglicanism. This resentment at being trapped explains his comment in his diary after his last night at Llanystumdwy that he left 'without a feeling of regret, remorse or longing'.

Consequently, from an early age, Lloyd George took a very detached view of Welsh Nonconformist society. If in due course he became one of its spokesmen, he tended to regard himself as its *victim* too. Obliged to champion certain radical causes, he could never share the strict sectarian approach to education, temperance, or disestablishment. He could scarcely have imagined a worse fate than a lifetime spent in the obscurity of a country solicitor's office and the committees of Caernarfonshire County Council, which was to be his brother's lot. From his first visit to London in 1881 he revealed an almost physical longing for the South which, in later life, manifested itself in Mediterranean holidays and houses in Surrey. Complaining of the incessant damp, rain, and mist of north Wales, he responded exuberantly to the sun, warmth, and bright light of southern climes. Lloyd George's love for his Welsh homeland was of a kind that waxed strong when he was safely removed from it, and deflated with physical proximity.

For some years, however, the exciting world of London remained but a distant prospect briefly glimpsed. Meanwhile he put in just enough work to pass his law examinations in 1884 with third-class honours, whereupon the firm offered him a post as managing clerk in their office in Dolgellau. He was only 21, and the position would have brought a regular income to his family, now supporting brother William's legal training with some difficulty. But David had no desire to be tied to humdrum work in Dolgellau. Instead, he left promptly to open his own office in Criccieth, and subsequently in Blaenau Ffestiniog, Porthmadog, and Pwllheli. Consequently William came under severe pressure to qualify so that he, too, could abandon Breese, Jones, and Casson to join the new firm of 'Lloyd George and George'.

By the early 1880s it was becoming clear that for David the law was less a career in itself than a springboard into politics. Since Mr Breese acted as the Liberal Agent for Merioneth and parts of Caernarfonshire, David soon gained experience of canvassing and parliamentary registration work, and appeared in the Revision Courts for the Liberals. Once he became a practising solicitor in his own right, he won attention by his outspoken and impertinent treatment of the local magistrates, especially when acting in cases involving landlords, poachers, and the clergy. By the late 1880s he had earned himself a reputation as a combative lawyer ready to stand up for the rights of the small man.

For an ambitious young radical, the general elections of 1880, 1885, and 1886 formed an exciting period. It began with Gladstone's triumphant return to office after the Midlothian campaigns, it saw the emergence of Irish nationalism as a dominant element at Westminster, and it brought a trebling of the electorate in the Welsh counties. The new voters enhanced the prospects of success for Welsh radical causes, notably the disestablishment of the Church, the abolition of the tithe, and temperance reforms such as the local option and Sunday closing. Land reformers looked to the Irish precedent in the form of rent tribunals and security of tenure; while educationists agitated for university colleges in Wales, the provision of secondary education, and the training of Nonconformist teachers.

It was against this background that the young Lloyd George developed his political strategy; between 1880 and 1886 he changed from an enthusiastic 17-year-old to a mature and single-minded 23-year-old politician. In 1880 he began to write letters in the *North Wales Express*; he made his mark in the Porthmadog Debating Society, on temperance platforms, and as a lay preacher; and he gained prominence as secretary to the Anti-Tithe League in south Caernarfonshire.

His youthful speeches provide rather mixed evidence of the political ideas of the future statesman, and it would be rash to attribute too much significance to them. In his first published letter in the *North Wales Express* he loftily rebuked Lord Salisbury for reneging on the liberal Tory tradition of Canning in foreign affairs:

> Toryism has not been barren of statesmen – real not charlatan – statesmen who prized the honour of England above the interests of party – who really hated oppression and demonstrated their detestation of it, not by pleading immunity from condign punishment for the instigation of foul and atrocious crimes, but by the laudable assistance which they rendered in the name of England to weak nationalities in their desperate struggles for Liberty – for freedom from the yoke of unhuman despots – for very existence.

Now throughout his life Lloyd George almost never spoke like this. The stilted language and convoluted sentences are quite out of character. His words reveal a precocious boy of 17 constructing his letter with immense care because it is his first communication to a newspaper and written in a foreign language! This perhaps minimises its significance. Yet it does give a tantalising glimpse of his breadth and subtlety. It hardly seems the work of a simple Welsh radical, but suggests one alive to wider concerns. The reference to the honour of *England*, rather than Britain, is particularly striking. Like all adolescent politicians, Lloyd George was posing, but his *choice* of pose is not what one would expect; already he is up above mere party interests on a cloud with English national statesmen.

On the other hand, his inaugural effort at the Porthmadog Debating Society showed the more familiar Welsh radical when, in an 'argumentative and nervous speech', he attacked the notion of paying compensation to Irish landlords who had suffered under the Land Act. Similarly, in 1882, when the society tackled the question of Britain's recent occupation of Egypt, Lloyd George, now 19, denounced the wickedness of the enterprise and the injustice to a peasant people. Yet this preview of the anti-war radical is qualified by a good deal of inconsistency. With the advantage of William George's notebooks and diary W. R. P. George reported that Lloyd George showed *no* opposition to the occupation of Egypt, and even declared, 'I am rather glad of the splendid practice of our guns.'[3] It is worth noting that the Debating Society voted its approval of the invasion by a large majority. Even in radical Wales it was difficult for a boy to grow up immune to the glamorous cause of empire and its military heroes, as Lloyd George's own involvement with the Volunteers suggests. If he had mixed feelings about Egypt – taking pride in the success but regretting that it had occurred – then this should not be interpreted as insincerity, but as a typical reaction. A 19-year-old cannot be expected to have a consistent strategy for imperial development, and what seems a firm opinion one week may easily be jettisoned the next.

None the less, by 1885, when Lloyd George was beginning to be referred to as a future MP, a consistent party line had become a necessity for him. Although all but four of the Welsh seats were Liberal by 1880, Liberals felt some tension between Gladstone's politics and those of his foremost critic, Joseph Chamberlain, who left the Cabinet in 1885 to campaign for his 'Unauthorised Programme' prior to his dramatic rupture with Gladstone over Irish Home Rule the following year. The young Lloyd George was evidently torn between the two leaders, but he greatly admired Chamberlain and enthusiastically espoused his programme, especially graduated taxation, death duties, and land reforms. On the Liberal victories of 1885 he observed: 'Am convinced that this is all due to Chamberlain's speeches.

Gladstone had no programme that would draw at all.' On the other hand, when Gladstone committed himself to Irish Home Rule in January 1886, he was difficult to resist. In February, Lloyd George appeared locally on a platform with Michael Davitt of the Irish Land League to whom he gave an eloquent vote of thanks. He was undoubtedly impressed by the dual strategy of the Irish in using their voting strength in Parliament while maintaining an extra-parliamentary movement in the country. Their example offered lessons for the Welsh. In spite of this, however, he was unwilling to subordinate all questions to the cause of Home Rule as Gladstone demanded. Indeed, Lloyd George planned to attend the inaugural meeting of Chamberlain's new Radical Union in May 1886; but he apparently missed the train! If this was a genuine accident it was an extremely fortunate one, for it had the effect of leaving his options open. Undoubtedly Lloyd George regarded Chamberlain as the future leader of Liberalism, and expected his withdrawal from the party to be temporary. However, it soon became clear that there was not much future in Chamberlainism, in that most rank-and-file radicals remained loyal to Gladstone. Welsh Liberals, who might have been expected to share Lloyd George's impatience with Gladstone, felt grateful for the reforms already achieved under his aegis. By 1885 Gladstone had clearly begun to reconcile himself even to Welsh disestablishment; after the 1886 split he would be more dependent upon Welsh support and thus open to pressure from them.

Chamberlain never returned to the Liberal Party, but for his part, Lloyd George never lost his taste for the Chamberlainite formula in domestic and external politics. Having avoided the split in 1886, albeit narrowly, he was well placed to capitalise on the resurgence of Gladstonian Liberal fortunes in the late 1880s. Moreover, he enjoyed a considerable personal boost from his role in the famous Llanfrothen Burial Case of 1888. Under the Burials Act of 1880 Nonconformists had been granted the right to be buried in parish churchyards according to their own religious rites. This would have resolved the issue but for the obduracy of a handful of Anglican clergymen. One such was the Rector of Llanfrothen near Porthmadog. After the death of a Nonconformist quarryman in 1888 he believed he had found a way of circumventing the law, and he locked the gates of the churchyard against the dead man's family. As solicitor to the bereaved, Lloyd George advised that the burial should go ahead in defiance of the Rector. The result was the prosecution of the family, who were successfully defended by Lloyd George. As a result of the publicity surrounding the case, he became a household name in Wales, and his claims to a parliamentary seat were greatly enhanced.

In January 1889, hard upon the heels of Llanfrothen, came the elections to the new county councils. Significantly, Lloyd George declined the modest role of a candidate, preferring instead to campaign on behalf of his fellow Liberals – a presumption about his own reputation which was evidently accepted. The shrewdness of his tactics was underlined by the action of the Liberals, who won a majority in Caernarfonshire, in promptly making him an alderman at the age of 26. In this way he had become, by 1889, a political leader of some standing, in spite of his youth, and was in demand at meetings from Cardiff to Liverpool.

This political advance coincided with a new phase in his personal life, for in January 1888 he had married Margaret Owen whom he had been courting since 1884. The only child of a prosperous Calvinistic Methodist farmer near Criccieth, 'Maggie' had enjoyed the advantage of lavish affection and a good education. Richard Owen and his wife were initially unenthusiastic at the prospect of marrying their daughter to an impecunious young solicitor with a reputation for extreme ideas and mild philandering. But Margaret was accustomed to getting her way, and once she had succumbed to her suitor's mixture of boldness and charm they would not deny her.

The relationship of Lloyd George and his wife is not easy to portray fairly. The English traditionally regard him as sexually demanding and congenitally unfaithful. The Welsh tend to present him as a good husband and father. Yet both views are rather inaccurate. On the positive side the relationship was deeply rooted; husband and wife were finally parted only by Margaret's death in 1944. Nor was their marriage sustained simply by convenience; the real affection would not have been so clear but for the survival of 2,000 letters by Lloyd George to his wife. Of course the formidable number of letters is itself a sign of long periods spent apart, yet in such a notoriously poor correspondent as Lloyd George it testifies to an enduring and sincere love.

On the other hand, the substance of his letters also underlines the fact that he and Margaret were not an ideal couple. The reason has little to do with Lloyd George's supposed sexual appetite. Before their marriage he made it crystal clear that his political career must be the priority for *both* of them:

> My supreme idea is to get on. To this I shall sacrifice everything – except I trust honesty. I am prepared to thrust even love itself under the wheels of my Juggernaut, if it obstructs the way. . . . Do you not really desire my success?[4]

The candid answer to this would have been 'no', for Margaret simply did not share his priorities. Though superficially a quiet, unassuming wife, she was in some ways too like her husband; secure and self-aware with a strong, stubborn character, Margaret felt reluctant to sink her own identity in his. Her interests and priorities centred around her home, her family, her garden, and north Wales; she refused to subordinate everything to the demands of the great political game he wished to play. London, in particular, repelled her where it fascinated him. Consequently, the praise and encouragement which Lloyd George craved for his every political triumph, and the comfort for his setbacks, was invariably denied to him by his wife.

One may wonder why Margaret married him at all. Her comment much later in life that his political career was 'unexpected' appears scarcely credible in the light of his frank declarations. But the explanation may be that she did not take his exuberant talk very seriously. Similarly, though aware of his reputation for chasing the girls, she doubtless believed that once married to her he would settle down to the life of a country solicitor and family man. Indeed in the second year of their marriage he became the father of Richard (1889) – in subsequent years of Mair (1890), Olwen (1892), Gwilym (1894), and Megan (1902). But Margaret's hopes were not realised. For marriage was followed all too closely by the chance of a by-election in 1890 which catapulted the young husband to Westminster.

.   .   .

ELECTION TO PARLIAMENT

Liberal dominance in the Welsh constituencies during the 1880s was by no means an unmixed blessing for Lloyd George, for most of the incumbent Members were prosperous entrepreneurs or even landed gentlemen. Not until 1887 when Liberal federations were created for north and south Wales did rank-and-file radicals pose a challenge to the traditional pattern of representation. In these circumstances Margaret's scepticism about Lloyd George's chances seems well founded, for he lacked both the social standing and the wealth required to cultivate a constituency, to finance election campaigns, and to support himself once elected. Safe Liberal seats were as yet beyond his grasp, as he found when he showed an interest in Merioneth in 1886 and in South Caernarfonshire in 1887. A marginal constituency was the best he could expect. Fortunately one was to hand in the shape of the Caernarfon District of Boroughs comprising Caernarfon, Bangor, Conwy, Nefyn, Pwllheli, and Criccieth.

In spite of the new householder and lodger franchises in the 1867 Reform Act the electorate of the Caernarfon Boroughs stood at only 4,500, not much more than half of the adult male population. It included the business and professional middle class, some farmers and gentry, and a few craftsmen and self-employed working men.[5] As a result, the constituency had favoured squires and landowners as its MPs, whether Liberal or Conservative. Though a Liberal won narrowly in 1885 he had been a reassuring establishment figure. Not surprisingly, local Liberals looked askance at the abrasive and impecunious Lloyd George whose Chamberlainite radicalism and assaults upon the bench of magistrates were not best calculated to attract the votes of the respectable citizens who had given Caernarfon back to the Conservatives in 1886. Like small towns everywhere, the boroughs were full of public houses which put Lloyd George, as a known temperance advocate, on the defensive. Nor was a reputation for Welsh nationalism a great asset here. For the three larger boroughs constituted outposts of English culture and Anglicanism; since the arrival of the railway their economy had become dependent on tourism. For such a seat Lloyd George was not a natural candidate, and he was adopted only with considerable misgivings by the Liberals.

Consequently, the death of the sitting Member, Edmund Swetenham, in March 1890, presented Lloyd George with a difficult campaign, despite the national revival of Liberal fortunes. Against him the Tories ran a typical candidate in Ellis Nanney, a popular local squire, though a lacklustre politician. His position was underpinned by a network of Primrose

League habitations and Tory working-men's clubs. Lloyd George's chief asset lay in his oratory and his capacity to inspire enthusiasm, which may explain the increase of 400 in the turnout at the by-election. But while arousing the radicals, he also took care to trim to the orthodox Gladstonian line by accepting Home Rule as the priority. On land reform, land taxation, and Welsh Home Rule he became noticeably vague and reticent, so much so that his opponents, and even some supporters, berated him for opportunism and insincerity. However, several prominent Welsh MPs such as S. T. Evans and William Abraham, as well as the anti-tithe campaigner Thomas Gee, came to speak on his behalf. In the event he scraped home by only 18 votes after a recount, thus beginning a 55-year association with the Caernarfon Boroughs.

The new Member selected a suitable opportunity to address the House of Commons when he rose on 13 June 1890 to attack Lord Salisbury's government over its proposal to allocate £350,000 as compensation to those who had been deprived of licences to sell alcohol. In his letter to Margaret, Lloyd George claimed he had 'scored a success and a great one. . . . I have been overwhelmed with congratulations.' It is possible that, being unused to the effusive language of parliamentarians, he took the kind words of Gladstone and John Morley at face value. In *Hansard*'s pages his maiden speech is an amusing but lightweight affair of seventeen minutes. His jokes at the expense of Lord Randolph Churchill, whom he accused of 'mushroom teetotalism', showed an unusual assurance, but his points were very routine if concisely handled.

This speech initiated fifteen years of parliamentary graft on the opposition benches. During the 1890s Lloyd George intervened regularly on issues of local interest such as employment at the Nefyn stone quarries, the lack of harbour facilities in Cardigan Bay, the discriminatory freight charges imposed by the London and North West Railway Company, and the 1897 strike by workers at Lord Penrhyn's slate quarries. In addition, he tackled a variety of general Welsh questions including a Local Veto Bill and a Tithe Rent Charge Bill, an Elementary Education Bill, an Agricultural Land Rating Bill and the Bill to disestablish the Welsh Church in 1894. His prolonged filibuster on the Clergy Discipline Bill in 1892 was an acknowledged triumph in guerrilla warfare undertaken out of pure partisan mischievousness. During his parliamentary apprenticeship Lloyd George eschewed the laborious set-piece oration; his merit as a Commons performer lay in his concise, conversational style, his ability to come quickly to the point, and his sheer relentlessness in seizing opportunities to intervene.

This concentration on constituency and Welsh matters in Parliament belies the fact that Lloyd George was never a particularly assiduous constituency member. His fundamental antipathy to dealing with correspondence and his highly unsystematic working habits lay at the root of the problem. Deprived of a secretary, he habitually failed to open his letters, let alone answer them. Victorian MPs were certainly expected to minister to their constituents' needs, for Members' postbags brought requests for charity and for patronage, especially in connection with official employment. Lloyd George's unwillingness and inability to cultivate the Boroughs in this sense was obviously hazardous. Against this neglect, however, he could rely upon the fact that he was known to be constantly championing Wales in Parliament. Moreover, his own absence from the constituency was partly obscured by the presence of his brother, uncle, and wife. In the event, he managed to hold the seat by slender margins in 1892, 1895, and 1900, though not until the Liberal landslide of 1906 did he win comfortably.

The importance of his family in his political career was acknowledged by Lloyd George himself, especially in later life, when he paid lavish tribute to Uncle Lloyd's role not merely as an inspiration but as a source of detailed advice; at his most hyperbolic he credited his uncle with authorship of the People's Budget. However, natural instinct led him to chart his own course from an early stage, even in the face of disapproval from his elders, and as he moved beyond the family sphere into national political life he left his uncle in the role of an admiring observer. When Lloyd George sought advice it was usually over which of two speaking engagements he should honour. In such cases Uncle Lloyd, whose world increasingly revolved around the newspaper reports of his nephew's speeches, invariably urged him to stay in England and speak there – which was exactly the advice Lloyd George wanted! If he disagreed with the family's views he simply brushed them aside, and, as William observed, on substantive issues he avoided seeking their opinion.

However, there can be no doubt about the depth of his

gratitude to his uncle, which he conspicuously demonstrated by adopting his name. Jealous colleagues frequently referred to him as 'George', and even *Hansard*'s entries fluctuated between George and Lloyd George in the 1890s. Yet one of Lloyd George's most attractive qualities was an absence of snobbery. As a boy he had been known in Llanystumdwy as 'Davy Lloyd', whereas William was apparently discouraged from using the name. Thus the adoption of an unhyphenated 'Lloyd George' represented a mutual compliment between uncle and nephew, a mark of pride and satisfaction for the one and of profound gratitude for the other.

As he began to make his mark as a politician during the 1890s Lloyd George suffered only two serious anxieties: money and marriage. Inevitably he found London life much more congenial than Criccieth; equally inevitably Margaret did not. Thus, when he took his seat in the House and when he delivered his maiden speech, she was absent. Indeed during 1890 Margaret hardly visited London at all; and in 1891 she spent only a few months there. Throughout 1892 she remained at Criccieth. For his part Lloyd George showed himself loath to take what was admittedly a nine-hour train journey to Criccieth at weekends. Even the long summer and autumn recess found him speaking around the country and indulging in holidays abroad in the company of political acquaintances. By 1894 he had begun to spend Christmas away from his family. Equally stubborn, neither husband nor wife showed much inclination to compromise. He constantly complained of the loneliness and discomfort of his bachelor life, though Margaret, who received his laundry through the post, doubtless thought he exaggerated his plight with such pleas as: 'I haven't changed my drawers for a whole fortnight .... Please send me a pair per parcels post.' Deprived of his wife's company for lengthy periods, Lloyd George was almost bound to succumb to temptation. His friendship with a certain Catherine Edwards the wife of Dr David Edwards of Cemmaes in Montgomeryshire, became public in 1896 when she confessed to adultery and attributed the paternity of her child to Lloyd George. Fortunately for him, when Dr Edwards sued for divorce, she named a different co-respondent, and he opted not to appear in court. This case, which could so easily have wrecked Lloyd George's career, lay behind an unusually blunt exchange between him and Margaret in 1897:

Be candid with yourself – drop that infernal Methodism which is the curse of your better nature and reflect whether you have not rather neglected your husband. I have more than once gone without breakfast. I have scores of times come home in the dead of night to a cold, dark and comfortless flat without a soul to greet me. I am not the nature either physically or morally that I ought to have been left like this .... You have been a good mother. You have not – and I say this now not in anger – not always been a good wife .... My soul as well as my body has been committed to your charge and in many respects I am as helpless as a child.[6]

This underlines the point that Lloyd George's marital problem did not lie primarily in his sexual appetite. It was not so much a wife and mistress that he needed as a single wife-and-mother figure. It is this latter element that was supplied by the ladies with whom he established prolonged relationships. Mrs Timothy Davies, the wife of a Welsh MP, ran a comfortable and welcoming home in Putney where she gladly mothered the new Member. In the Edwardian period a similar role was filled by Julia Henry, the wife of another Liberal MP, Sir Charles Henry, whose hospitality was on a more lavish scale.

It may be surmised that Margaret, though naturally upset by his friendships with married women, to some extent accepted the force of his argument that he had been neglected. Yet she was slow to resolve the problem. Not until 1899 did she agree to move into a house near Wandsworth Common with the family. However, by this time, separation had become a habit for them both. During the Edwardian period they effectively resolved the problem by establishing their own headquarters, she at Brynawelon, a substantial house with a large garden on a hill above Criccieth, and he at houses in Brighton and at Walton Heath in Surrey provided by Lord Rendel and Lord Riddell respectively.

The maintenance of a house in Wales, accommodation in London, and the support of a rapidly growing family inevitably placed a strain on Lloyd George's limited finances. Until he became a Cabinet minister in 1905 he enjoyed no salary for his political work. He managed to earn a little money by writing for the *Star* and the *Manchester Guardian*, and in 1897 he set up a solicitor's practice for expatriate Welshmen in

London. On the whole, however, he drew on the profits of 'Lloyd George and George' which William assiduously built up; at least his name helped to stimulate the firm's business. Though never extravagant in his tastes, Lloyd George was obviously no puritan. His exotic foreign holidays were often financed by political friends, but one finds him, or rather William, paying for a recuperative holiday at Biarritz in 1905 like any upper-class politician. Feeling a little guilty, he kept this trip a secret from Uncle Lloyd. With his limited means and his desire for comfort, Lloyd George remained anxious to obtain some financial windfall which would give him the freedom to pursue his career in the style to which his colleagues were accustomed. This explains his ventures in speculative businesses. The first of these involved the Welsh Patagonian Gold Fields Syndicate, established in 1892 by one David Richards a mining engineer from Harlech. In return for the use of Lloyd George's name and his active help in persuading others to invest in the company, Richards gave him 500 shares and the legal fees for setting up the syndicate. Although it rapidly became clear that Patagonian gold was a mirage, Lloyd George maintained his involvement until 1896, by which time he possessed 1,000 shares and William 600. He had been naïve in accepting Richards's unsubstantiated claims and a little unscrupulous in urging others to risk their money.

Unfortunately, like most people, Lloyd George failed to learn from experience and continued to jump at speculative ventures in order to make himself rich quickly. This was the road that was to lead him to the Marconi Scandal in 1912. On the other hand, his behaviour cannot be represented as particularly unusual or reprehensible. Men blessed with infinitely more wealth and standing habitually lent their names to dubious business propositions. That Lloyd George dwelt upon this inequity is underlined by various interventions in Parliament during 1896. In that year he first drew attention to Joseph Chamberlain's connection with the firm of Kynoch and Company, well endowed with government contracts; he moved that the vote of Sir William Houldsworth on the London and North West Railway Company Bill be disallowed as he had a direct pecuniary interest as shareholder and director; and he attacked Henry Chaplin over the personal financial gain which his Agricultural Land Rating Bill would bring him. He clearly felt that while others did not scruple to advantage themselves, it would have been quixotic to deny himself some legitimate gain from his public reputation.

During this period Lloyd George's political role was played out within the framework of Welsh radical politics. Yet although the Welsh MPs appeared to be a coherent group who appointed their own whip, they never attained the status of a political party. Under the leadership of Stuart Rendel they relied more upon quietly influencing the Liberal leaders than upon mobilising rank-and-file pressure, in spite of the temptation to ape the Irish Nationalists. Gladstone himself shrewdly appreciated the difference between the two. While the Welsh undoubtedly represented a cultural nationalism, they lacked the Irish determination to achieve political separation. Welsh grievances could, therefore, be satisfied piecemeal without the necessity for Home Rule. Welsh radicals felt themselves part of a wider British Liberalism, expected solutions within the British system, and wanted recognition of their place in it.

In spite of his spirited championship of Welsh Home Rule, Lloyd George himself was no exception to this philosophy. He displayed some inclination to attempt to outflank the Welsh Members in the manner of a Parnell by his bold speech on Home Rule to the South Wales Liberal Federation in February 1890. It was simply inconsistent, he argued, to support Irish Home Rule but not Welsh, for the essential arguments were equally applicable in each case. This helped him to make his mark, but it led the staid Welsh politicians to regard him as a stirrer and an opportunist. As an MP he found himself championing Welsh causes as a freelance, not as part of a concerted strategy; and in the House close collaboration was limited to friends such as Herbert Lewis, Sam Evans, and Frank Edwards.

When Gladstone returned to office in 1892 with a small majority it seemed only natural to Lloyd George that Wales should make full use of its bargaining position, and not be reduced to automatic obedience simply because Tom Ellis, MP for Merioneth, had become a Liberal whip. Consequently he adopted a critical line over the Bill to disestablish the Church in Wales brought in by H. H. Asquith; and in 1894 he renounced the Liberal whip when Rosebery indicated that the measure would no longer enjoy priority. It was at this time that a nationalist organisation, the Cymru Fydd, was expanding rapidly and succeeded in winning the North Wales Liberal

Federation to Home Rule. Although Lloyd George played a prominent part in this movement, he largely lacked an appreciation of the literary and cultural foundations which lay at the base of Cymru Fydd's nationalism. By 1895 the next step in its strategy was to merge the South Wales Liberal Federation with that of the North and thereby turn Liberalism into a single crusade for Welsh self-government. This was the situation by June 1895 when the rebel Members reduced the Government's majority on the Disestablishment Bill to seven. Shortly afterwards the Government suffered a defeat on a different question, resigned and lost office in the subsequent general election. Lloyd George's critics attacked him for disloyalty, though it is unlikely that this damaged him in Caernarfon. The demise of the Rosebery Government was no great loss since it had achieved little for Wales. By playing up the Home Rule and disestablishment issues Lloyd George at least avoided the demoralisation suffered by many candidates in the 1895 election. Early in the next year he took the Cymru Fydd fight to the South Wales Liberal Federation at Newport, only to find himself outvoted by nearly two to one and even shouted down at one point. This effectively put an end to Welsh Home Rule within Liberalism and it led Lloyd George himself to abandon the issue. He still had the option of bidding for the leadership of the Welsh MPs; but when invited to stand for the chairmanship in 1898 he firmly declined to do so. It was no longer a prize worth winning. His ambitions could be more surely realised within the broader framework of British Liberalism.

. . .

NOTES AND REFERENCES

1. George W 1955 *My Brother and I.* Faber & Faber, p. 33
2. D Lloyd George to Margaret Owen, 28/8/86, quoted in Morgan K O (ed.) 1973 *Lloyd George: family letters 1885-1936.* University of Wales Press, p. 16
3. Quoted in George W R P 1976 *The Making of Lloyd George.* Faber & Faber, p. 115
4. D Lloyd George to Margaret Owen, not dated, 1885, quoted in Morgan K O (ed.) 1973, p. 14
5. Price, R Emyr 1975 Lloyd George and the by-election in the Caernarfon Boroughs 1890, *Caernarfon Historical Society Transactions*, 36: 140-2
6. D Lloyd George to Margaret, 21/8/97, quoted in Morgan K O (ed.) 1973, p. 112

Chapter 2

IN THE FOOTSTEPS OF
CHAMBERLAIN
1899 – 1908

By 1898 Lloyd George had evolved into a skilled back-bench partisan; but he was untested by major political controversies and remained largely unknown outside Wales. Between 1899 and 1908, however, he demonstrated his political genius by his capacity for turning highly unpromising situations to his advantage. The South African War, the 1902 Education Act, and his presidency of the Board of Trade provided three major opportunities. Of these, his role during the conflict with the Boers first elevated Lloyd George to the front rank of politicians, where he was to remain for the next forty years.

. . .

THE SOUTH AFRICAN WAR

The problems of southern Africa – which do not appear to have engaged Lloyd George's interest before 1899 – originated in the rivalry between the British settlements in Cape Colony and Natal and the Boer territories of the Transvaal and Orange Free State. It was a long-standing objective of British imperialists to incorporate all of these colonies into a single South African federation. To such visions the Boer settlers represented an irritating obstacle. Back in 1881 they had inflicted a defeat on the British at the Battle of Majuba Hill, to which Gladstone had responded by conceding effective self-government to the Transvaal. Majuba Hill consequently became an emotional political symbol for Conservatives, some of whom sought to erase the humiliation by military action. However, under Lord Salisbury even Conservative governments grew wary of costly imperial engagements. Although South Africa had some strategic importance astride the secondary route to India, it was scarcely plausible to argue that the Boers threatened this British interest. As so often, local initiative rather than national policy set the pace. The dramatic discoveries of gold on the Witwatersrand and diamond fields at Kimberley stimulated immigration into the area. As a result, the Boer population was exceeded by the non-Boers by the 1890s. However, the denial of political rights to these settlers by the Transvaal Government offered a new lever to British expansionists. The arrival of Joseph Chamberlain at the Colonial Office in 1895 provided the imperialists with a sympathetic audience for their grievances in London. Chamberlain realised that if he attempted to extract social reforms from Salisbury he would be working against the grain of his administration, whereas a bold imperial strategy would be more congenial. Although Chamberlain's attitude to the Empire did not make a war inevitable, it made one much more likely. This was rapidly underlined by the Jameson Raid in December 1895, a foolish attempt to invade the Transvaal from Cape Colony with a view to provoking a rising by the non-Boers and overthrowing President Kruger's government. Though Chamberlain had not initiated the raid, the Boers understandably suspected that some further coup would be attempted with the connivance or assistance of the British authorities. As a result, Chamberlain felt obliged to leave the initiative in the hands of Sir Alfred Milner, the British High Commissioner, who conducted negotiations with Kruger to obtain voting rights for the non-Boers. Kruger made so many concessions that eventually Milner contrived to break off the talks for fear of reaching a settlement. Interpreting this action as a sign of Britain's intention to resort to force, the Boers decided to act quickly and issued an ultimatum in October 1898. 'This [ultimatum]', wrote Chamberlain, 'relieves us of the necessity of explaining to the people of Britain why we are at war.'

This confession epitomises the irresponsible manner in which Chamberlain approached what he anticipated would be a minor war. It coloured Lloyd George's initial reaction when he heard of the breakdown while on a visit to Canada. For him the war was simply unnecessary: 'I shall protest with all the vehemence at my command against the outrage which is perpetrated in the name of freedom.'

Why did Lloyd George adopt and persist in this opinion? The emotion generated by the war led to accusations that he was a 'Pro-Boer' and a virtual traitor to his country, an absurd calumny which has, however, been repeated uncritically by some historians. On the other hand, it seems, at first sight, scarcely credible to describe him as essentially an imperialist, which other writers have done. Certain things, are, however, clear enough. In the first place, Lloyd George's opposition to the Boer War did not arise from pacifism. He had, after all, joined the Volunteers as a youth; he realistically appreciated the necessity for armed force, and was always prepared to accept that war could be morally justified, especially if conducted against an opponent such as the Turks. However, the State should never go to war 'lightly or wantonly', which he believed Chamberlain had done. Nor was Lloyd George a 'Little Englander' in the sense that he wanted to dismember the British Empire, or even halt its expansion. This was not as obvious as it should have been because his own interventions on imperial matters in the 1890s had been few and far between. Yet, at this time, many of his Liberal colleagues took a highly critical view of the scramble for Africa. During 1893–94, for example, a controversy broke out over the attempt by Lord Rosebery, then Liberal Foreign Secretary, to impose a British protectorate over Uganda. In March 1893 Henry Labouchere introduced a motion in the Commons opposing the armed mission which had been sent to Uganda on the grounds that it was a step towards annexation. Significantly, Lloyd George, despite his rebellious behaviour in this period, failed to join the 46 supporters of this motion. The fact is that he generally supported Rosebery's conduct of foreign and imperial affairs, which stood squarely in the Chamberlainite tradition.

As for South Africa itself, he believed British rule there to be desirable, but he argued that it was totally unnecessary to wage war in order to extend British control. This was, in fact, recognised at the time even by newspapers unsympathetic to him:

> Mr Lloyd George is one of the school of Lord Rosebery on all other topics except the South African one. Even on this subject he is at one with the objects of the Government, believing that the peace and prosperity of South Africa depend upon British rule being supreme in that part of the world. This object he believes would have been attained by pacific methods. The fact that the Government are

attaining it by more forcible methods has impelled him for the time being to go into the camp of the enemy.[1]

Consequently his strategy in Parliament was to ridicule Chamberlain's claim that Britain was fighting for the democratic rights of the settlers in the Transvaal; Kruger had already offered them the franchise based on a seven-year residence qualification, so it was only a matter of time before the injustice was remedied. He also pointed out how favourably conditions in the Transvaal compared with those in Britain: wages were four times as high, and the men enjoyed a legally binding eight-hour day. Thus the notion of the Boer states as some intolerable tyranny from which the settlers yearned to be released was a mere fiction. As for the Boers themselves, Lloyd George clearly felt some sympathy for them as fellow Europeans in a hostile climate; if his picture of them as a small, virtuous, pastoral people rather like the Welsh was a little romantic, he undoubtedly resented an attempt by Britain to bully them. On the other hand, he claimed that most of the settlers were German Jews. They showed no inclination to fight for themselves, but relied upon the British troops who received a miserable 1s. 3d. a day for their suffering. This was partly a shrewd attempt to capitalise upon anti-Semitism by portraying the conflict as a war fought for the benefit of Jewish financiers; but it also reflected a genuine prejudice on Lloyd George's part.

His anti-war stance also included a domestic dimension. He appreciated that the conflict both distracted attention from domestic questions and diverted financial resources from social reform. As a member of the recently appointed Parliamentary Select Committee enquiring into old-age pensions he felt strongly about this: 'There was not a lyddite shell which burst on the African hills that did not carry away an Old Age Pension.' Ironically Chamberlain himself had tried to outflank the Liberals by promising pensions, and Lloyd George naturally lambasted him for his failure to fulfil the pledge. Yet, partisanship apart, Lloyd George appreciated his sincerity as a reformer, regretting all the more that the radical hero of his youth had become a tool of Toryism.

The Liberal Party as a whole proved less adept than Lloyd George at marshalling its case on the Boer War. Since Gladstone's retirement in 1894 the leadership had been a void filled most inadequately by Rosebery, Harcourt, and, in 1899, by Sir Henry Campbell-Bannerman. Under him the party became bitterly divided, for a time, between the 'Liberal Imperialists' such as Asquith, Sir Edward Grey, and Richard Haldane, and the so-called Pro-Boers, notably John Morley, Henry Labouchere, and James Bryce. When Campbell-Bannerman attempted to chart a middle course on the war he only found his party splitting three ways.

In associating himself with the radical left of the party Lloyd George exposed himself to considerable danger, both political and personal. After a speech at Bangor in April 1900 he was hit on the head in the mêlée, while even in Criccieth he was burnt in effigy. After a series of rowdy meetings from Cornwall to Scotland, he faced a difficult struggle to hold his seat in the general election in September; his opponent, Colonel Platt, alleged that he had been 'on the enemy's side throughout the war, and has insulted the Generals and Soldiers of the Queen'. In the event, he won by 296 votes, a surprisingly comfortable margin for the Caernarfon Boroughs. His constituents did not necessarily agree with him over the war, but they respected his courage in sticking to an unpopular line.

However, the worst had now passed. After the election, the endless ramifications of the South African War thoroughly destabilised the Government. When the new Parliament met in December Lloyd George promptly reopened the question of the business interests of the Chamberlain family and the profit they had made from government war contracts. He accused Chamberlain not of corruption but of impropriety and negligence in failing to prevent 'any suspicion of influence or favouritism in the allocation of such contracts'. It soon emerged that a whole network of firms with Chamberlain connections had been involved in supplying the war effort; Chamberlain, his brother, Arthur, and his son, Austen, were either shareholders or chairmen of Kynoch's, Hoskins and Sons, and Tubes Ltd; and the latter firm had been in desperate financial straits until rescued by Admiralty contracts. Chamberlain gave no precise replies to charges that Kynoch's had been treated preferentially by the War Office; confining himself to generalisations, he merely asserted that his family's interests were quite separate from his own, and that they were unknown to him. This was unconvincing, but the government simply relied upon its huge majority to defeat Lloyd George's motion by two to one. Yet the affair dented their patriotic posturing, and allowed Lloyd George to demonstrate his effectiveness as an opposition leader even from the back benches.

However, the argument rapidly shifted away from the responsibility for the war to the conduct of operations which were not concluded until 1902. Lords Roberts and Kitchener, the British commanders, finding themselves unable to quell Boer resistance by defeating them in battle, attempted to deprive them of their bases. This involved burning farms, herding civilians into concentration camps, and partitioning the veld with barbed wire and blockhouses. As a result of the disease and poor hygiene in the camps 20,000 people died between January 1901 and February 1902. Kitchener's willingness to offer the Boers an amnesty in 1901 was vetoed by the British Government, thus obliging the generals to persist with what Campbell-Bannerman castigated as 'methods of barbarism'. With this one utterance the Liberal leader began to restore his own authority and to consolidate his fractured party. Initially, however, Campbell-Bannerman's new stance pushed the Liberal Imperialists into a more pronounced detachment from the party. More than the war divided them from their colleagues. In domestic matters they despaired of the negative Gladstonianism represented by the 'faddist' policies of the National Liberal Federation, and looked for a more positive policy of social reform and national efficiency.

An appreciation of this schism is essential to our understanding of Lloyd George's behaviour in the aftermath of the war. In view of his record during 1899 and 1900 it would have been natural for him to have cemented an alliance with Campbell-Bannerman after the 'methods of barbarism' speech. On the contrary, he adopted a highly ambiguous stance. While paying tribute to his leader for his staunch adherence to principle, Lloyd George also went out of his way to heap praise on Rosebery, who re-emerged in 1901 to challenge Campbell-Bannerman. Rosebery's initiative culminated in a famous speech at Chesterfield in December 1901 in which, like the other Liberal Imperialists, he went beyond the question of war and imperial expansion to domestic politics. Mocking the 'fly-blown phylacteries' of Campbell-Bannerman and the Gladstonians, he challenged them to rid Liberalism of the albatross of Irish Home Rule. In this situation Lloyd George made clear publicly and privately his view that Rosebery was indispensable to the party. Herein lies the real significance of his notorious public meeting at Birmingham in December 1901 just after the Chesterfield speech. Lloyd George's appearance in the Chamberlainite citadel provoked a mob of 30,000 people to storm the hall, thereby forcing him to escape disguised as a policeman for fear of his life. Yet in the excitement of the Birmingham meeting it was, and still is, often forgotten that he had not come to rehearse the arguments over the war. Under the chairmanship of a Liberal Imperialist, he intended to deliver a speech pointedly praising Rosebery. Moreover he continued privately to urge Rosebery to sustain his Chesterfield initiative by fighting a campaign in the country to win the party over to his views. As late as 1905 he was still persisting in this.[2]

Such behaviour cannot be explained simply as opportunism on Lloyd George's part; for it reflected an underlying conviction that Rosebery was a more exciting leader and far more in tune with social problems than the staid Campbell-Bannerman. At this distance it is easy to forget that many other radicals shared his view; this is why Rosebery had been chosen by radicals as the first chairman of the London County Council in 1889. In this respect Lloyd George displayed a consistency of approach which is often overlooked. For what attracted him in Rosebery was very much what had appealed in the philosophy of his original hero, Chamberlain: a certain mixture of a constructive, interventionist domestic policy with a bold, patriotic approach to foreign and imperial affairs. Despite the exigencies of politics this formula began to show through persistently in his own career. For Lloyd George the future of Liberalism lay here: with the Gladstonians it had only a glorious past.

Of course self-interest also played a part in his strategy. By 1903 he was 40 years old; a career on the back benches had long since lost its charm. But in 1901 few could feel confident of Campbell-Bannerman's ability to lead the Liberals to victory; nor could he be relied upon to welcome Lloyd George into his Cabinet. During 1901–02 it seemed possible that from the disarray of both Government and Opposition, Rosebery might emerge as the alternative Prime Minister of a ministry of national efficiency, drawing support from both parties. If Lloyd George were to be able to take advantage of this possibility he had to avoid close attachment to the orthodox party leadership.

Ultimately this convoluted strategy proved unnecessary, for

Rosebery lacked the will to sustain his challenge, and as the party closed ranks he rapidly faded. The summer of 1902 brought peace to South Africa on terms which even Lloyd George agreed were generous towards the defeated Boers. Though forced to accept British sovereignty, they continued to enjoy self-government as before the war. Britain had won no more than a nominal victory as the long-term evolution of South Africa was to prove. Having urged the inevitability of conciliation, Lloyd George appeared to have been vindicated. As the fever of wartime subsided, he stood out in the eyes of Liberal and Labour politicians as a man of judgement, principle, and courage. He had attained the stature of a national figure at last.

. . .

THE EDUCATION CONTROVERSY

No sooner did the war pass than he faced a new dilemma in the shape of A. J. Balfour's Education Bill of 1902. This long-overdue measure was designed to rationalise and extend educational provisions up to the age of 14 by bringing both voluntary and board schools under the aegis of the county councils. Though widely welcomed by educationists, the Bill led to a resurgence of complaints by Nonconformists that Anglican and Catholic schools would be maintained out of the rates. However, Balfour's Bill was not simply a dole for the voluntary schools. Those that received public funds were to be obliged to meet certain standards, to be subject to a board of six managers including two from the education authority, and to concede control of all secular education and the appointment and dismissal of teachers. Thus it was a genuine compromise which gave the Nonconformists a good deal of what they wanted. This, however, failed to avert a crusade against the Bill, spearheaded by the famous Baptist minister, Dr John Clifford, which made a powerful contribution to the Liberal revival of the early Edwardian period.

Lloyd George's reaction to the education controversy reflected more sharply than anything else his peculiarly equivocal relationship with radical Nonconformity: public involvement and intellectual detachment. Significantly, his initial response showed his appreciation of a sweeping and constructive reform:

Llanystumdwy School will now be under the County Council and a very great improvement it is. Up to the present I rather like the Bill. It is quite as much as one would expect from a Tory Government.[3]

Indeed, at this stage the only flaw which he could identify was the failure to make the takeover by county councils compulsory, though this was rectified before the Bill became law. He thought the measure especially attractive for Wales because the county councils, largely under Liberal control, would be quicker than the English to grasp the opportunity to improve educational services. There could be no more striking evidence that he simply did not approach such matters from the viewpoint of a Welsh radical Nonconformist.

However, as soon as hostility to the Bill manifested itself, he adopted a more critical stance, though he made it clear that he did not object to the new system as such and would accept the abolition of the school boards. It would have been extremely difficult for him to have gone any further in supporting the Government's policy. By 1902 Lloyd George had barely emerged from a prolonged association with an unpopular cause in the course of which he had received support from many people who did not altogether agree with his views. To refuse to adopt the Nonconformist line on education would have been to desert his own best allies. This, significantly, was the argument employed by Lloyd George himself with the Irish Members who, though they liked the Bill, owed a debt to British Nonconformists for years of support for Home Rule. With characteristic boldness he proceeded to put himself at the head of the protest in Wales. Although Nonconformists took up a strategy of passive resistance to Balfour's Bill, the Free Churches Council was divided over whether to defy the law by withholding rates. As a result of its indecision only 7,324 people had received summonses for failure to pay rates by January 1904, and the campaign in England turned out to be a damp squib. Lloyd George, however, shrewdly separated the campaign in Wales from that in England. As a majority in Wales, the Nonconformists could use their power through the county councils to challenge the Government by more subtle methods. It would be foolish simply to cut off rate aid to voluntary schools; but under the new legislation county councils were entitled to have them inspected to determine whether they reached the prescribed standard before assisting them. Moreover, in Lloyd George's view, they should insist on the abandonment of all religious tests for teachers, and on the acceptance of public control by the trustees. Though this interpretation of the Act was not really correct, he had calculated shrewdly in making it; for this approach allowed the rebels the satisfaction of doing something concrete to register their protest, while making it relatively difficult for the Government to intervene against them. As such it was a classic example of Lloyd Georgian politics.

For the Government it was politically much more embarrassing to act against a phalanx of county councils than against individual passive resisters; and the trouble of compelling elected local authorities to stick to the letter of the law was scarcely worth while. In any case the process took some time and Lloyd George hoped that meanwhile a way would be found out of the dilemma. At a conference between Welsh county councils and representatives of the voluntary schools in March 1903 he and the Bishop of St Asaph tried hard to reach a compromise; enforcement of the Act in Wales was meanwhile postponed until February 1904. A fresh round of local elections in that year reinforced the rebels' position by producing majorities for full public control of maintained schools and abolition of religious tests for teachers in every Welsh county except the relatively Anglicised Brecon and Radnor. Eventually the Government did proceed to enact a Default Bill in August 1904 to allow it to deduct from county council grants the money they had failed to spend on education. By the end of 1905 five authorities had been penalised by this means.

In this way Lloyd George pulled off a remarkable triumph. He had contrived to maintain himself as the unofficial leader of Welsh radicalism, at a time when a Nonconformist revival was sweeping the country, in spite of his own reservations about the Nonconformist attitude on education. The morale of the movement in Wales had been sustained by contrast with the rather ignominious collapse of passive resistance in England.

None the less, by 1904 he was undoubtedly anxious for an opportunity to drop the education question without loss of face, for it tended to deflect him from the much less complicated cause of free trade, around which Liberals were now rallying. As so often in Lloyd George's career this arose from a Chamberlainite initiative. Although pressure for protective tariffs had been building up since the 1880s, it did not become a major issue until May 1903 when Chamberlain launched his crusade in a speech to his Birmingham constituents. As always, he offered not just a policy to protect industry, but a broad vision of reconstruction. He envisaged a preferential tariff as a step towards a common economic policy for the Empire. By safeguarding the domestic market he would secure the employment of industrial workers; and the additional revenue yielded by tariffs would finance social reforms without the need for penal taxation. In 1903 he calculated that an initiative of this sort was required to pull the Conservatives out of the doldrums: he would rally the party in the country by a bold campaign and rapidly isolate the Conservative free traders. To a considerable extent he succeeded. However, tariff reform had an even more stimulating effect upon the Liberals in that it completed the process of reunion and gave them a popular cry in the country. Lloyd George's appreciation of the constructive scope of Chamberlain's policy made him all the more concerned to 'Go for Joe' in the two years which culminated in the Liberal landslide of January 1906. He reminded his audiences that Chamberlain had promised them old-age pensions before. He attacked the protectionists for proposing 'stomach taxes', and in the Commons he drew a formal admission from Chamberlain:

> if you are to give a preference to the colonies ... you must put a tax on food. I make the hon. gentlemen opposite a present of that.

. . .

PRESIDENT OF THE BOARD OF TRADE

This heady period reached a climax on 4 December 1905 when Balfour suddenly announced the resignation of his government. Despite some complicated manœuvring by Asquith, Grey, and Haldane, Campbell-Bannerman quickly established a Liberal administration. The new Prime Minister was under no illusions about Lloyd George's view of him; and his elevation to the Cabinet, though not unexpected, was by no means automatic. 'I suppose we ought to include him', Campbell-Bannerman grudgingly concluded. His appointment had the virtue of flattering Wales, while also maintaining the balance within the Cabinet, which was tipping heavily towards the Liberal Imperialists who held the Exchequer, Foreign Office, and War Office. Lloyd George was apparently considered for the Home Office where he would have been obliged to handle Welsh disestablishment, but had to make do with the Board of Trade, a post much lower in status, and which carried a salary of only £2,000 instead of the more usual £5,000. Lloyd George's oratorical skills seemed a useful asset in the continuing debate with the Opposition over tariff reform; but whether a man with his reputation was likely to prove a diligent administrator when faced with the largely humdrum work of the Board of Trade remained, for the time being, uncertain.

However, at the age of 42 he found himself, at last, being sworn in as a Privy Counsellor, and embarking on what turned out to be seventeen years' continuous membership of the Cabinet. 'Am so proud of this', wrote his uncle, 'after all his self-spent life of efforts of all kinds on [Wales's] behalf.' But before enjoying the fruits of office the Liberals had to win the general election, which was held in January 1906. By now this seemed to present no problem, for the targets offered by the collapsing administration were too large to miss. The staple topic remained the defence of free trade and cheap food. But Lloyd George could not resist taking up the emotive subject of 'Chinese Slavery', which was the Liberal description of Milner's new policy of importing Chinese indentured labourers to work in the South African mines; he mischievously suggested that the next step might be to employ Chinamen in the Welsh quarries at a shilling a day. As a public speaker Lloyd George was in a different class from most of his Cabinet colleagues. In contrast to the massive, polished periods of Asquith or the grandiloquence of the young Churchill, his speeches were informal and homely, with short, digestible sentences and pithy asides, freely punctuated with biblical allusions and pictures painted from nature in which mountains, trees, and storms figured prominently. Above all, he wielded the essential weapons of the stump orator – humour and wit. Addressing some Welsh farmers on one occasion, he had remarked:

'We will have Home Rule for Ireland and for England and for Scotland and for Wales.'
'And for hell,' interposed a deep, half-drunken voice.
'Quite right. I like to hear a man stand up for his own country.'[4]

When in more serious vein, his oratory showed the style of the lay preacher, carrying his audience along by means of short, rhythmic pairs of sentences. A typical example of this is provided by the following passage from a speech at Bangor in 1905:

> You have unemployment in this country. But so they have in every country. Take a highly Protectionist country like France; unemployment is greater there than here. It is almost impossible to prevent unemployment. Business is as difficult to understand and appreciate in its fluctuations as the weather. All you know is that it is like the tide; one moment it surges up and seems as if it would cover the land with wealth and prosperity; the next moment it recedes, leaving a high and vast muddy bank. You can hardly tell why.[5]

By the time he uttered these words Lloyd George was in an understandably buoyant mood. His elevation to the Cabinet had been taken as an honour to Wales which his constituency was not likely to spurn. 'It has been said that I am the first Welshman to be a member of the cabinet since the days of Archbishop William', he merrily told an audience in Caernarfon, 'I follow the footsteps of an Archbishop, and I am therefore, in the apostolic succession to that extent (laughter and cheers).' With the double advantage of enhanced personal standing and the tide to Liberalism, he enjoyed a comfortable run for the first time, being returned by 3,221 votes to 1,997 for his opponent.

Along with 400 other Liberals Lloyd George embarked joyfully upon the work of the new Parliament. But the anti-climax came all too soon. Bills on subjects dear to the Government's supporters such as land reform and education perished at the hands of the House of Lords, while Home Rule and disestablishment were conspicuously neglected. To enjoy a huge majority but still lack the power to enact legislation was inevitably demoralising. Yet, where other ministers became bogged down, the President of the Board of Trade skimmed across the legislative quagmires with apparent ease.

Lloyd George's two years at the Board of Trade have understandably been overshadowed by his chancellorship and his premiership, but they are of great significance none the less. He found himself presiding over a staff of 750, with a budget of

£270,000 and responsibility for industrial relations, commerce, industry, and transport. In common with most ministers in both parties Lloyd George entered his office largely innocent of practical business; but this proved to be immaterial because of his readiness to use the informed advice available to him. Political advice came from his Under-Secretary, Hudson Kearley, one of the entrepreneurial successes of the time who had established the International Stores. Practical and confident but without arrogance, Kearley proved to be a perfect junior partner. In addition Lloyd George had the benefit of Hubert Llewellyn Smith as his Permanent Secretary. Like a number of civil servants at the Board of Trade, he was intellectually distinguished and highly qualified; his experience of social work in London's East End as a young man had left him sympathetic to labour and social reform. He was thus particularly well suited to a reforming minister like Lloyd George. The concatenation of able and ambitious politicians and administrators helps to explain why the Board of Trade rather than the dull and hidebound Local Government Board became the focus of social reform in the Edwardian period.

Instead of contenting himself with a ritual defence of free trade, Lloyd George used his two years as President to win his spurs as a legislator, beginning promptly with a Merchant Shipping Bill in 1906. Since 1894 three committees had reported in favour of tightening up the regulations imposed upon shipowners. The new Bill raised the standards of conditions in which merchant sailors worked, particularly their food, medical treatment, accommodation, and repatriation. In addition, it extended British safety regulations affecting life-saving equipment, the load-line and seaworthiness to all foreign ships using British ports. This proved reassuring to British owners fearful of being undercut by competitors who were free to take greater risks with their vessels and men. Conscious of the danger of antagonising the shipowners, Lloyd George went out of his way to involve them in discussions from an early stage. This was evidently genuine consultation, for he allowed them to see early proposals so that they might make detailed objections without feeling that the minister's mind was already made up. His readiness to make minor amendments ensured an easy passage for the Merchant Shipping Bill when it reached the House of Commons.

The year 1906 brought other practical and uncontroversial

measures from the Board including a Census of Production Bill which required companies to submit the information necessary to enable the Board to produce comprehensive statistics for the output of domestic industry. Again Lloyd George made a point of consulting interested MPs and industrialists so as to arrive at an agreed measure. He continued this bipartisan approach in his second year in office. March 1907 brought the Patents and Designs Bill which was intended to deter foreign companies from taking unfair advantage of British patent law. Some took out patents merely to check competition; others put British patentees to considerable expense by challenging their patents in the courts, or resisted new British applications by taking out very wide patents themselves. The new legislation allowed foreign patent holders only twelve months in which to begin working their patents in Britain, which stimulated several companies to establish new factories. In future all claims involving patents were to be heard by a Chancery judge who specialised in this type of work in order to render abuse more difficult. Meanwhile Lloyd George was constructing his Bill to establish the Port of London Authority. This too reflected a long-standing need to incorporate the three private dock companies into a single body enjoying the powers wielded by Trinity House, the Thames Conservancy, and the Watermen's Company in the Port of London. This involved the, by now, usual talks with the interested parties as well as a personal visit by the minister to some of the European ports. Introduced in April 1908, this Bill was Lloyd George's last achievement before promotion carried him on to greater heights.

The immediate significance of Lloyd George's work at the Board of Trade is obvious. It helped to compensate for the disappointments of the Government's first two years; only the Home Office under Herbert Gladstone and Herbert Samuel generated more legislation. His achievements took the wind out of Conservative sails in that he demonstrated that a free trader need not be inhibited about standing up for British interests. For Lloyd George personally the record provided emphatic proof that he was no mere stump orator but a skilful legislator and handler of men. In a Cabinet dominated by legal and academic intellect his realism shone out like a beacon.

However, it is less clear whether his work in this period has any deeper ideological significance. At the time a number of

Conservative Members went out of their way to compliment him on his Bills on *protectionist* grounds. This was doubtless partly genuine, but partly mischievous on their part; and historians must be wary of assuming that Lloyd George was fundamentally a protectionist himself. This surprisingly durable myth was still lively in the 1920s. Strictly speaking the inspiration behind his legislation was administrative not political; William Beveridge, who joined the Board in 1908, claimed that Lloyd George had simply taken up a string of ready-made measures. Although this is an exaggeration, it seems clear that the officials perceived an opportunity to catch up on accumulated business now that they had an alert minister with a penchant for finding practical solutions. But whatever may be said of Lloyd George, the civil servants were largely free traders, and the imputation of protectionist motives seems misplaced. He himself consistently defended free trade – indeed he could do no less – though he refused to invest it with a *moral* justification: 'some of you chaps have got free trade consciences,' he told Charles Masterman, 'now I have not!' For him free trade was to be justified pragmatically in terms of the advantages it secured for Britain, namely, cheap imports for consumers, low costs for industry, and, through the maximisation of world trade, huge invisible earnings from shipping, insurance, and foreign investments. Yet he remained sufficiently open-minded to appreciate that when other states infringed free trade to the detriment of British interests, some intervention was necessary.

It is also unwise to interpret his fruitful co-operation with businessmen at the Board of Trade as a sign of lack of sympathy with labour. While undoubtedly appreciative of the self-made entrepreneur, Lloyd George had grown up in a society in which the manual worker could still aspire to become a small employer himself; there was no deep or fixed distinction between the two. Of course, his experience of an organised working class, with the values of class solidarity rather than individual enterprise, was limited. But the notorious dispute in 1897 between Lord Penrhyn and the north Wales quarrymen made him more conscious of the wider industrial scene. Penrhyn's crassitude in refusing to negotiate with the men – not untypical of Edwardian employers – strengthened Lloyd George's feelings for the workers. Moreover, he thought of the working class politically in terms of the Lib–Lab tradition;

labour, like Nonconformity, was a regiment in the army of Liberalism. One effect of the Boer War was to bring Liberal and Labour politicians closer together, and by 1906 Lloyd George had become a welcome speaker on the platforms of Labour Representation Committee candidates. His record in office shows no lack of sympathy towards the unions; indeed, the Merchant Shipping Act was, in substance, a measure of social reform for the seamen. His stance was also defined sharply as a result of the conflict between the Amalgamated Society of Railway Servants (ASRS) and the railway companies in 1907. To him the central problem lay in the employers' refusal to recognise the union. As a result, the men eventually held a ballot and announced a strike in October. Lloyd George told his brother: 'Conciliation at first but, failing that, the steam roller. The Companies must give way on that point I am definite.'[6] Accordingly he summoned twenty-nine company chairmen and managers to meet him at the Board where he persuaded them to accept negotiations conducted by six of their representatives. While bringing the employers round he also invited Richard Bell and the executive committee of the ASRS for separate talks. He managed to keep the two sides in play until the owners had agreed to accept a permanent conciliation scheme backed up by independent arbitration if necessary, and the workers had agreed to withdraw the threat to strike. In retrospect, such an outcome may appear merely a matter of common sense so that one is reluctant to ascribe credit to its authors. But in industrial disputes where pride is at stake the common-sense solution invariably proves to be elusive; the railway dispute had dragged on for months until Lloyd George's intervention and, in view of the recalcitrance of the owners, it would have produced a major strike but for his efforts.

If there is a thread running through Lloyd George's work during 1906–08 it is his readiness to invoke the power of the state to serve the vital interests of the community at large. This is reflected both in his approach to labour relations and in his legislative attempts to promote the greater efficiency of British industry. But his methods were as striking as his objectives. For he repeatedly revealed a penchant for drawing the interested parties – businessmen, trade-unionists, experts – into consultation. This had the effect of minimising the formal role of politicians in the process, for Parliament invariably found itself presented with an agreed measure. Such a procedure was no doubt intuitive rather than deliberate on Lloyd George's part. Life, not ideology, had taught him the importance of treading a careful path between conflicting pressures, and how to get his way by a mixture of charm and boldness. However, the aim and the method provided a perfect illustration of 'national efficiency' in operation. Enthusiasts for national efficiency deplored the effect of amateur party politicians while they sought to utilise the relevant skill and knowledge of the expert and the businessman. Lloyd George's serendipity lay in his arrival at the ministry where these assets could most readily be exploited. His bipartisan approach reminded some political opponents of his Roseberyite past; and although their admiration for him ebbed and flowed according to his own partisan role in the subsequent years, the seeds of co-operation across party lines had been sown.

This vision of Lloyd George as a bipartisan figure was, however, rapidly extinguished. In April 1908 Campbell-Bannerman resigned for reasons of ill health, and as expected, Asquith succeeded him, thereby vacating the Treasury. John Morley, typically bitter and disappointed, claimed that Lloyd George had put a pistol at Asquith's head in order to get the Treasury for himself. This is highly unlikely. For one thing, Lloyd George could not afford to risk resignation for financial reasons. Moreover, Asquith was shrewd enough to appreciate the political advantages of appointing him Chancellor of the Exchequer. He would reassure the radicals among whom Asquith had never been popular. Asquith might well have promoted Reginald McKenna who had been Financial Secretary to the Treasury; but he knew that McKenna, though highly competent, was too conservative on taxation to fit the bill. For the Treasury was essentially a political job in which Lloyd George's ignorance of finance would be immaterial. The appointment proved to be the most important single decision of Asquith's career. As Chancellor himself he had prepared certain radical financial innovations and major social reforms; this work must be carried on, but with flair and style if the full political advantages were to be realised. The mercurial Lloyd George would provide these qualities and make an excellent foil to the Prime Minister's own *gravitas*. Together they were a formidable partnership. For Lloyd George the promotion brought the immediate and tangible pleasures of a rise in salary to £5,000 and the occupancy of Number 11 Downing Street for nine momentous years.

. . .

NOTES AND REFERENCES

1. *Western Mail* 6/4 1900, quoted in Du Parcq H 1913 *Life of David Lloyd George* vol II. Caxton Publishing Company, p. 213
2. Du Parcq H 1913, pp. 301–3;   see also Marquess of Crewe 1931 *Lord Rosebery*, vol II. John Murray, pp. 589, 591
3. D Lloyd George to Margaret 24/3/02, quoted in Morgan K O (ed.) 1973 *Lloyd George: family letters 1885–1936*. University of Wales Press, pp. 131–2
4. Gardiner A G 1914 *Prophets, Priests and Kings*. J M Dent, p. 134
5. Dated 29/12/05. Lloyd George Papers, House of Lords Record Office, B/4/1/3
6. D Lloyd George to William George 21/10/07, quoted in George W 1955 *My Brother and I*. Faber & Faber, p. 212

Chapter 3

THE NEW LIBERALISM
1908 – 1914

The year 1908 found Lloyd George at the height of his powers, poised on the edge of a vital formative stage in twentieth-century British history. For, during his chancellorship, he largely established the framework of the modern taxation system, and laid the basis of the social reforms which, after 1945, came to be known as the 'Welfare State'. His key role in these developments made him the outstanding constructive statesman of the present century; more immediately, it put him in the eye of the political storm.

Somewhat to Lloyd George's relief, Asquith introduced the 1908 budget in which he had already made provision for a scheme of old-age pensions financed by the State. It fell to the new Chancellor, however, to handle the separate legislation for pensions later in the summer, as a result of which he won undeserved credit and the gratitude of a generation of pensioners who, saved from the indignity of the Poor Law, sometimes spoke of themselves as being 'on the Lloyd George' when they drew their pensions at the post office. While avoiding exaggeration of Lloyd George's contribution to social reform, one must equally guard against the tendency of some contemporaries to disparage his role; Keir Hardie, for example, claimed that he had 'no settled opinions' on social and labour questions in 1908, a point echoed by some historians who consider that his ideas on these subjects had been retarded by his immersion in Welsh politics. Yet we have already seen that there is reason to be sceptical about the depth of his involvement in traditional, sectarian politics. In fact he served his political apprenticeship in the decade in which conventional assumptions about both the extent and the causes of urban poverty were being comprehensively challenged.

39

Based in London, he had a lively awareness of Charles Booth's investigations in the East End. Given his natural impatience with traditional Liberalism and his instinctive sympathy for the underdog, Lloyd George was receptive to the new ideas. On pensions, his record seems clear. At the 1895 election he advocated a pensions scheme, costing £5 million, to be paid for by death duties, a tax on ground rents, royalties, and tithe. When, in 1899, he served on the Parliamentary Select Committee enquiring into old-age pensions he advocated a non-contributory scheme, so that those most in need would benefit, and, according to J. L. Garvin, he persuaded some Tory members to support a state scheme, despite the cost. 'Never mind', he told Margaret, 'it goes all to the poor who really need it.' In the light of this evidence, to speak of his 'conversion to social reform during his visit to Germany in the summer of 1908'[1] is surely a misrepresentation. That visit was undertaken at a time when he was devising a detailed strategy for reform and typically wanted to learn about the operation of existing schemes; it was more a *consequence* than a cause of his commitment to social reform.

This is not to imply that Lloyd George was greatly in advance of radical opinion in the 1900s. In 1906 a large majority of Liberal and Labour candidates, as well as some Conservatives, pledged themselves to pensions. The proposal for a 5s. weekly pension to single persons aged 70 whose income fell below £26 only satisfied a long-established case. In the Commons, Lloyd George agreed to pay the full rate to couples rather than the 7s. 6d. originally proposed. He also accepted that instead of the abrupt cut-off at £26 there should be a sliding scale of pensions payable from £31 10s 0d. and reaching the full payment at £21 income. If such concessions made the scheme more costly than Asquith had anticipated it mattered little to Lloyd George:

> These problems of the sick, of the infirm, of the men who cannot find means of earning a livelihood ... are problems with which it is the business of the State to deal, they are problems which the State has neglected too long.[2]

What had exercised the more thoughtful Liberals over the previous twenty years was not simply the humanitarian case for state intervention but the economic implications. A phalanx of intellectuals including J. A. Hobson, L. T. Hobhouse, Herbert

Samuel, L. C. Money, and Charles Masterman, had challenged the traditional Gladstonian view of taxation as a necessary evil designed simply to enable the State to provide a few basic services. Their arguments gradually encouraged Liberals to adopt new principles: that taxation ought to reflect capacity to pay; that indirect taxation was iniquitous; that 'unearned' income should be taxed more heavily than earned; and that a limited redistribution of income was actually in the interests of the wealthy, both because of the necessity of a healthy, efficient workforce, and because of the stimulating effects upon the domestic market of an increase in the purchasing power of the poor.

Now although Lloyd George was by no means a student of the new texts on Liberalism, he had the advantage of starting off relatively unencumbered by the traditional dogma. He does seem to have read *Progress and Poverty*, the famous book by the American land reformer, Henry George. While his emphasis on land taxation might appear old-fashioned to the modern ear, land was, in fact, a central part of the 'New Liberalism' of the 1900s; for the rapidly rising value of urban land provided a major example of the unearned income which radicals wanted to appropriate for the good of the community. Yet Lloyd George showed no *intellectual* interest in economic ideas or in Liberalism. Colleagues liked to describe him as ignorant and unwilling to read; but by this they really meant that he was not bookish and lacked the apparatus of a classical education typical of Victorian politicians. The Latin tags and French phrases that tripped so lightly off Asquith's tongue were never to be heard from Lloyd George. F. S. Oliver once penned a satirical sketch of a discussion between Asquith, Lloyd George, and Lord Kitchener:

> The P.M. explained the situation to him by the maxim 'vox populi vox dei', to which, as the Goat took it to be Greek for 'wait and see', he was unable to find any answer.'[3]

Yet many colleagues acknowledged that Lloyd George had a more relevant talent than the capacity to accumulate information: a natural skill in using facts to generate solutions. The Edwardian journalist, A. G. Gardiner, put it into words as best he could:

He picks up a subject as he runs, through the living voice, never through books. He does not learn: he absorbs, and by a sort of instantaneous chemistry his mind condenses the gases to the concrete.[4]

In this light one may understand the distinction between Lloyd George and the more cerebral 'New Liberals'; he had nothing to unlearn. Of course, the typical Liberal had moved a long way from that point in the mid-1870s when Gladstone had seriously contemplated abolishing the income tax. As all governments retreated, albeit reluctantly, from retrenchment during the 1880s, the income tax rose to 8d. in the pound. In 1894 Sir William Harcourt raised it to 9d., but also extended the exemption from tax from incomes up to £150 to those of £160, as well as introducing his famous scheme for graduated death duties. This budget prefigured Lloyd George's own measures in relieving the tax burden on modest incomes and concentrating upon the really wealthy. By 1902 the war in South Africa had driven income tax up to 1s. 3d., but although Liberals attacked the Government for its profligacy, they were more disposed to regard tax revenues as an opportunity than as a moral failing. 'I am not sure that we have exhausted the resources of civilisation in respect to the income tax', as Richard Haldare delphically put it in 1902.

. . .

THE 'PEOPLE'S BUDGET'

By 1908 these ideas about taxation and state welfare had acquired an immediacy and centrality that they had lacked in the 1880s. In its attempts to escape from the high taxation of the Boer War the Balfour Government had become engulfed in Chamberlain's tariff reform campaign. Tariffs represented a direct challenge to Liberal finance because of the claim that revenue from tariffs would permit the State to pay for social reforms without punitive taxation. By sticking to free trade and traditional taxation the Liberals would neither achieve significant social reform nor defend the jobs of British workers. During 1906–08 it was not clear whether the Liberals had found the answer to this. In a period of recession and high unemployment the free traders were vulnerable to Chamberlain's case, and the breakthrough of thirty Labour MPs into

Parliament in 1906 underlined the existence of an alternative force if Liberalism should fail. This convergence of all three parties on social and economic questions in the Edwardian period explains why the whole basis of British politics shifted at this point.

In fact, however, Asquith had quietly charted the new course not simply by the state pensions scheme, but by financial innovation. He prepared the ground by introducing compulsory returns of all categories of income, by instituting inquiries into the feasibility of graduated taxation and income differentiation, and by overcoming Treasury opposition to a supertax. In 1907 he reduced the tax on earned incomes below £2,000 to 9d. while leaving it at 1s. for the rest. Lloyd George therefore took over at a critical moment when the financial groundwork had been done and the political situation required an initiative to stem the drift of both working- and middle-class support from the Liberals. In spite of its huge majority in the Commons, the Government had failed to overawe the peers who mutilated Bills dealing with traditional Liberal issues like education, licensing, and land. The peers took confidence in the belief that these issues would not provide sufficiently popular causes for the Liberals to challenge the House of Lords at an election. With his natural contempt for power derived from birth alone, Lloyd George launched spirited attacks on the Upper Chamber, claiming that it acted as the watchdog of the Constitution only when Liberal governments were in office. But, beyond a vague belief that a Second Chamber could be dispensed with altogether, he did not yet know what to do about the peers. As Chancellor in 1908 he did, however, consciously decide to use his first budget as a Trojan Horse to smuggle through reforms for licensing and land which would have been rejected as ordinary legislation. This would undoubtedly help to restore morale among Liberals, but he sensed that his budget must do more; it must 'stop the electoral rot' by restoring to them the initiative in social reform.

In this aim Lloyd George enjoyed two important allies: Asquith, who had already shown his appreciation of the sea-change in British politics and was to provide essential support in Cabinet, and Winston Churchill, the new President of the Board of Trade. In spite of his sterling service to Liberalism since leaving the Tories in 1904, Churchill was regarded as a man on the make. 'He is full of the poor whom he has just discovered', commented Charles Masterman when Churchill began to champion social reform in 1908. This, however, did not bother Lloyd George, and the two men, sharing a detachment from party, formed a natural political partnership as well as becoming good friends. After Lloyd George's visit to Germany he and Churchill devoted the summer and autumn of 1908 to devising a comprehensive social strategy for the Cabinet in which a radical budget would play a central part. The programme was to begin with the Board of Trade's scheme for Labour Exchanges, followed by the 1909 budget which would generate the resources both to stimulate industrial development and enact social reforms. The third stage in 1910 would comprise a scheme for 'invalidity' insurance devised by Lloyd George, and finally unemployment insurance prepared by Churchill. Though it took rather longer than anticipated, this proved to be the basic policy followed by the Cabinet. As Churchill observed with satisfaction, the type of legislation they envisaged was 'just the kind the House of Lords will not dare to oppose'. The need to commit the government to this strategy as a matter of urgency helps to explain why, by October 1908, Lloyd George was trumpeting his intention to tackle the problems of the aged, the infirm, and the unemployed as in this speech at Swansea:

> I have one word for Liberals . . . . If at the end of an average term of office it were found that the present Parliament had done nothing to cope seriously with the social condition of the people, to remove the national degradation of the slums and widespread poverty and destitution in a land glittering with wealth . . . then a real cry will arise in this land for a new party, and many of us here in this room will join in that cry.

In addition to this broad political calculation, there was an immediate reason to produce a drastic budget in 1909, namely the prospect of a substantial deficit for 1909–10. Indeed Lloyd George initially hoped to reduce expenditure on the armed forces to mitigate this problem. But Haldane had already trimmed £2 million from the army estimates, while at the Admiralty Reginald McKenna demanded funds to build six new Dreadnoughts. In the face of a widespread, but baseless, fear that Germany was outbuilding Britain, the Cabinet eventually agreed to eight new ships, which meant that the

Chancellor had to find an extra £3 million for the navy. In addition, it transpired that whereas Asquith had estimated that 572,000 old people would be eligible for pensions, some 668,000 had qualified. As a result, pensions cost £2.5 million more than originally budgeted for. Still worse, the trade depression was reducing the Government's usual revenue. Hence Lloyd George's notorious remark: 'I have got to rob somebody's hen roost next year.' Characteristically, he made a virtue of necessity, telling a sceptical Cabinet in 1909 that he faced a deficit of £16-17 million, the result of a £6 million fall in revenue and additional expenditure of £10 million. This made it virtually impossible to resist radical innovations in state taxation.

In putting together his detailed proposals, Lloyd George experienced severe obstruction from his officials, notably Sir George Murray the Permanent Secretary at the Treasury, who saw his role as essentially negative: to limit expenditure. But Murray objected not just to the substance but to the methods employed by Lloyd George. As he had shown at the Board of Trade, Lloyd George actually liked to receive clear advice and could be persuaded to take it, but Murray never adapted to his new master, and as a result, Lloyd George relied upon Sir Robert Chalmers, Chairman of the Inland Revenue, who was a radical more in the mould of Llewellyn Smith. Similarly, he found it difficult to work with his Financial Secretary, Sir Charles Hobhouse, who regarded him as ignorant, idle, and unsystematic in his approach to work. There was some truth in this. It was his unsystematic habit of jumping from one subject to another that first led his officials to dub him 'The Goat'. But even Hobhouse conceded that Lloyd George was not idle so much as addicted to discussing business in unorthodox circumstances such as on the golf-course, to which he frequently retreated. 'Lloyd George will look at no papers and do no office work ... [he] has an extraordinary power of picking up the essential details of a question by conversation.'[5] No doubt Asquith had put Hobhouse at the Treasury as a safe pair of hands to tackle routine business and, as was evidently the practice, to report to him behind the Chancellor's back. Lloyd George, meanwhile, was to handle the politics of the Treasury with the assistance of his unofficial advisers, Masterman and Rufus Isaacs.

By March 1909 Lloyd George was ready to put to the Cabinet

his proposals for meeting the anticipated deficit by raising £13.5 million in extra revenue, and by diverting £3 million from the Sinking Fund. He proposed to increase income tax by 2d., to 1s. 2d., on unearned incomes over £700 and on earned incomes above £2,000, which would yield an extra £2.75 million. Additional death duties would generate £4.8 million, and stamp duty £1.25 million of revenue. There would also be additional duties of £1.8 million on spirits and £2.0 million on tobacco. The more novel measures included a supertax on incomes over £5,000, payable at 6d. in the pound on the income above £3,000. This would yield £1.2 million. Then there were the controversial land taxes. The Chancellor wished to levy a 20 per cent tax on the unearned increment of land, payable when it changed hands, and to impose a 1d. in the pound tax on the capital value of all land worth over £50 an acre. These two were estimated to yield £0.5 million in the first year. Then came a proposal calculated to win approval from old-fashioned radicals, a £2.25 million rise in the cost of liquor licences paid by publicans and brewers. Finally, alighting on a conspicuous form of wealth, he imposed a 3d. levy on a gallon of petrol and introduced licences for motor-cars.

The Cabinet debated these proposals in no fewer than fourteen meetings during March and April. The critics were Lewis Harcourt, Walter Runciman, Reginald McKenna, and John Burns, while the budget's best supporters were Haldane, Churchill, Lord Carrington, and Asquith. The former group felt, rightly, that Lloyd George was deliberately exaggerating the size of his deficit; indeed it eventually turned out that he had underestimated revenue from existing taxes by £1 million. On the other hand, the suspiciously low estimates for the new supertax and land taxes were justified in view of the difficulties likely to be encountered in collecting them in the first year. The Chancellor's plan for a 1d. tax on land was abruptly dropped, but replaced by a ½d. in the pound levy on the value of undeveloped land, excluding agricultural land, and a 10 per cent reversion duty on the benefits gained by a lessor on the termination of a lease. Finally the income-tax changes were modified with a view to minimising the number of victims. The tax on earned income up to £2,000 was held at 9d., and put at 1s. on the £2,000–£3,000 range. For those with incomes below £500 a tax relief of £10 for every child under 16 years was introduced. Thus the Cabinet's intervention did not detract from the overall sweep and radicalism of the budget, rather it reflected the desire to spare the middle classes on modest salaries from extra burdens. Indeed, since income-tax payers above the £3,000 mark numbered only 25,000, and supertax payers above £3,000 only 10,000, it is quite clear that the Chancellor's aim was very precise.

Politically the budget was calculated to appeal to traditional Liberals, as well as to New Liberals, by its use of the land and drink issues to attack the powers of the House of Lords. For, although the higher liquor licences were expected to raise revenue, they would also put a number of urban public houses out of business. The £0.5 million to be collected from new land taxes was a purely nominal figure whose purpose was really to legitimise the inclusion of land reform in the budget. Hardly any revenue would actually be collected in the first year, but the taxes required a complete valuation of land which would facilitate the effective taxation of landed wealth in several years' time.

This completed the momentous 'People's Budget' as it was soon to be called. It changed the whole basis of British public finance from the Victorian pattern to the system that has lasted throughout the twentieth century. It shifted the chief source of revenue from indirect to direct taxation; it established the principle that taxation ought to be related to capacity to pay and it inaugurated a limited redistribution of income for the benefit of the poor through social welfare schemes.

Meanwhile there were some formidable obstacles to be overcome. Lloyd George presented his budget on 29 April in an unhappy speech lasting four and a half hours. Such a large and detailed brief could not be safely committed to memory, as was his habit, but, unaccustomed to reading speeches, he made a rather flat job of it, stumbling over his lines, which allowed his opponents to say that he did not understand a word of it. For once, however, substance mattered more than style. He had seized the initiative in raising money to 'wage implacable warfare against poverty and squalidness'. While his own party was exhilarated, the initial reaction of the Opposition proved rather subdued; Austen Chamberlain acknowledged the necessity to tackle social problems with bold financial innovations. Soon, however, they grasped the underlying political significance of the budget as a challenge to the protectionist strategy currently dominant in the Conservative ranks. Lloyd George's formula of free trade and cheap food, combined with the revenue to pay for both social reforms and new Dreadnoughts, checkmated the Chamberlainites. Only a major recession would have restored the case for the tariff and this failed to materialise. This explains why the protectionists provided the staunchest resistance to the budget. On 3 May, Viscount Ridley, chairman of the Tariff Reform League, asserted that, contrary to the prevailing constitutional convention, the House of Lords had the right to reject and amend a budget.

It must be emphasised that this was no part of Lloyd George's original plan. He had not devoted months of labour to the measure in order to have it thrown out by the peers. Quite the opposite. He had told his brother he was 'thinking out some exquisite plans for outwitting the Lords on licensing', one of several indications that he assumed they would have no option but to swallow what they would have rejected in ordinary legislation. This is what Asquith meant when he referred to the budget as a 'partial solvent' of the constitutional dilemma. However, once Conservatives themselves began to speak bravely of rejecting the budget Lloyd George rapidly concluded that there might be even *more* advantage in encouraging them down this path. By May they had begun to characterise his proposals as revolution and socialism, and a new organisation, the Budget Protest League, sprang up to co-ordinate the multitude of pressure groups purporting to defend property from the threat of appropriation. For some time, however, Lloyd George remained embroiled in the committee stage of his legislation, and evidently believed that after letting off steam the Tories would swallow the budget. But the evidence of Liberal enthusiasm and the Government's success in defending four seats in by-elections in July underlined the potential advantage to be extracted from the issue. At a meeting at Limehouse in London's East End on 30 July he deliberately stoked up the controversy by training his guns on wealthy landowners who, he said, were refusing to do their duty by contributing a fair share to the costs of national defence and social welfare; their selfishness, he suggested, would lead society to 'reconsider the conditions' under which land was held. Such language had not been heard from a leading politician since 1885 when Joseph Chamberlain had attacked those 'who toil not, neither do they spin'. Superficially, Lloyd

George appeared to be following his hero in setting class against class, and, as Asquith reported, the King was 'in a great state of agitation and annoyance in consequence of your Limehouse speech'.

However, Lloyd George refused to be deflected from his strategy. By raising the stakes he would ensure that the Liberal Party would be wedded to radicalism, and that the Tories would be drawn into a trap. To retreat now on the budget would be a demoralising anticlimax for them, but to reject it would enable the Liberals to fight a general election with every prospect of winning a mandate to clip the wings of the House of Lords. Either way the Tories would lose badly. By August Balfour had decided for rejection, partly because the alternative would have disrupted the unity of his party, and because an election, though he did not expect to win it, would at least reverse much of the Liberal landslide of 1906. Thus by the autumn Lloyd George had begun to look with some pleasure towards extending the budget controversy into a campaign to curtail the powers of the hereditary peerage. Speaking at Newcastle upon Tyne on 9 October he was more extreme, as well as more entertaining, than at Limehouse:

There has been a great slump in dukes . . . . They have been making speeches lately. One especially expensive duke made a speech, and all the Tory press said, 'Well now, really, is that the sort of thing we are spending £250,000 a year on?' Because a fully-equipped duke costs as much to keep as two Dreadnoughts – and they are just as great a terror – and they last longer . . . . Let them realise what they are doing. They are forcing a revolution, and they will get it . . . . The question will be asked whether five hundred men, ordinary men chosen accidentally from among the unemployed, should override the judgement – the deliberate judgement – of millions of people who are engaged in the industry which makes the wealth of the country. That is one question. Another will be: who ordained that a few should have the land of Britain as a perquisite? Who made ten thousand people the owners of the soil, and the rest of us trespassers in the land of our birth? Who is it who is responsible for the scheme of things whereby one man is engaged through life in grinding labour to win a bare and precarious subsistence for himself, and when, at the end of his days, he claims at the hands of the community he served a poor pension of eight pence a day, he can only get it through a revolution, and another man who does not toil receives every hour of the day, every hour of the night, whilst he slumbers, more than his poor neighbour receives in a whole year of toil? ... The answers are charged with peril for the order of things the peers represent.

Not surprisingly in the face of such insults and threats, the peers threw out the budget at the end of November by 350 votes to 75. 'At last, with all their cunning, their greed has overborne their craft. We have got them at last', declared an exuberant Lloyd George at the National Liberal Club. The House of Commons condemned their action as 'a breach of the Constitution', and proceeded to a dissolution of Parliament. As Lloyd George, Asquith, and Churchill stormed the country, the Conservatives were completely outclassed in the early weeks of the campaign. Liberal morale, boosted by the improvement in trade and the enthusiastic co-operation of the Labour Party, seemed very high. Indeed a key part of Lloyd George's triumph lay in outflanking Labour. This did not, in fact, involve preaching socialism or a class war, except in a very limited sense. In attacking parasitic landowners Lloyd George sought to make common cause between all who created wealth, both entrepreneurs and working men; private wealth would not be confiscated, it would simply contribute a fair share to national needs; only the selfish clique entrenched in the House of Lords refused to do their duty. He loved to contrast their behaviour with that of the Liberal candidates, sometimes quite wealthy men, on whose platforms he spoke:

You will find these rich men in the House of Commons sitting up night after night, risking health, some of them most advanced in years, and what for? To pass a measure which taxes them to the extent of hundreds, maybe thousands, of pounds a year. All honour to them.

In the event, the result of the election proved to be slightly disappointing for the Liberals since they lost their huge majority of 1906. With 275 MPs and the backing of 40 Labour and 82 Irish Members they enjoyed a comfortable lead over the 273 Conservatives. But some asked why they had not done better. The campaign had lasted eight weeks with an interruption for Christmas; the Liberals had reached a peak too soon and inevitably lost momentum in the New Year as the Opposition made more play with Home Rule, German naval scares, and tariffs. Some felt that the violent rhetoric of Lloyd George and Churchill had succeeded only too well in arousing the working class, as demonstrated by the Liberals' success in the North, Wales, Scotland, and London, but at the cost of frightening middle-class voters especially in the South and the rural and suburban areas. In fact, the majority of middle-class taxpayers were no worse off as a result of the budget; as Sir Edward Grey noted, a man with under £2,000 income paid less than under the previous Government. But many on modest incomes clearly chose to associate themselves with the wealthy, perhaps persuaded that the budget represented only the start of an attack upon property.

. . .

LLOYD GEORGE AND COALITION

More serious was the discovery that the election had settled the budget, but no more. On 2 December Asquith had declared in a speech at the Albert Hall that he would not hold office again without 'safeguards' to ensure the passage of legislation. This was taken to mean that after the January election he would introduce a Bill to modify the powers of the Upper House which would, if necessary, be passed by the votes of 500 new Liberal peers created by the King. However, the King made it clear through his secretary, Lord Knollys, that he would not do this until the Government had won a second general election. Nor was the Cabinet agreed upon how to restrict the powers of the peers, some favouring a suspensory veto, some joint sittings of the two Houses, with Lloyd George an isolated advocate of abolition of the Upper Chamber. On 26 February the notably vague King's speech exposed the embarrassing fact that the Cabinet had not yet decided what to do. Given this failure of leadership by Asquith, Lloyd George's mind began to cast around for alternative ways of achieving radical goals. To Herbert Lewis he spoke of an alliance of radical Liberals, Labour, and the Irish, while to Masterman he talked of a government of progressive businessmen. These idle specula-tions were a sign of his impatience with the strait-jacket of conventional parties by 1910.

Eventually the Cabinet produced its proposals for reform of the Lords: they were to lose all control over anything designated by the Speaker as a money Bill; other legislation could be delayed for two years, but if passed in three sessions by the Commons, it would go on to receive the royal assent; and the length of Parliament's life would be shortened from seven to five years. However, before the argument over these proposals had proceeded very far, one of the central figures in the constitutional crisis, King Edward, died. At this point the Liberal Chief Whip, Alexander Murray, seized the initiative by urging that the politicians should avoid putting pressure on the new, inexperienced King, George V, by finding a compromise solution themselves. Thus by June 1910 a five-month truce had begun, during which period a constitutional conference was held. At twenty-one meetings Asquith, Lloyd George, Crewe, and Augustine Birrell argued with the Tory representatives, Balfour, Austen Chamberlain, Lansdowne, and Cawdor, over the handling of ordinary, financial, and constitutional legislation on which the two Houses of Parliament disagreed. Perhaps the reason the constitutional conference lasted so long was that Asquith wanted to prove to George V that, a serious attempt at compromise having been made, he had no option but to accept the advice of his elected government and create peers.

Characteristically, Lloyd George grew bored with the interminable arguments, and by August he had produced an extraordinary plan for bypassing the constitutional imbroglio. This took the form of a memorandum, dated 17 August, proposing a coalition government. He communicated this first to Churchill, then to Murray, and subsequently to Asquith and several other leading Liberals. Among Conservatives the first to be told was F. E. Smith, followed by Balfour, who consulted Chamberlain, Lansdowne, Cawdor, Bonar Law, and J. L. Garvin, editor of the *Observer*. Thus, while the formal negotiations continued, Lloyd George engaged in informal discussions both with Liberals and with Conservatives. This tactic of keeping the two sides apart until they were ready to accept a compromise had been used successfully at the Board of Trade, but it was wholly unrealistic in the circumstances of 1910. It involved an element of deception. To Balfour, Lloyd George spoke of tariff reform, naval expansion, and compulsory military service, in return for the acceptance of a plan for devolution which would give Home Rule to Ireland, Scotland, and Wales. Yet his original memorandum, which was seen only by Liberals, made only the briefest of references to naval and military matters and mentioned vaguely an inquiry into tariffs. It dwelt largely on the national insurance scheme, as well as widows' pensions, educational and agricultural reform, and the reduction of licensed premises. This explains why Asquith was so relaxed about Lloyd George's machinations: he did not believe there was the slightest chance of the Tories agreeing to join a coalition on such terms.

Meanwhile, Balfour and Bonar Law were enchanted by Lloyd George and intrigued by his proposal, not because they contemplated accepting it, but for what it suggested to them about the author. Others, notably F. E. Smith, whose contempt for his own party made him instinctively a coalitionist, were more positive. But no one could fail to be astonished by Lloyd George's audacity. 'What will his people say of him?' wondered Chamberlain. Here was the rub. Was it credible that he would jeopardise his position as the outstanding radical leader in British politics? Since 1906 Liberals like McKenna and Runciman had encouraged the Conservatives to believe that Lloyd George wore his Liberal principles very lightly. This proved appealing to a certain school of radical Tories, such as J. L. Garvin, Lord Milner, L. S. Amery, and F. S. Oliver, who looked to a rearrangement of party politicians around a programme of state social reform, Home-Rule-All-Round, and imperial development. In their eyes Lloyd George might credibly evolve into the second Joseph Chamberlain.

However, historians have probably devoted too much attention to this strange episode. There was no plan for a government of national efficiency, and the most that one can say is that his initiative kept Lloyd George's lines of communication to the Tories open in spite of their public disagreements. The episode shows us two things about him. First, he was surprisingly naïve. His manœuvres made no real progress, and had they done so, they would have had a most demoralising impact upon the Liberal Party, given the passions that had been stoked up in the controversies of 1909-10. The mere knowledge that an attempt at coalition had been made proved damaging to Lloyd George's reputation in later years. Second, the coalition scheme was the most emphatic proof of his constructive approach to government. He constantly sought immediate solutions to immediate problems, and it is abundantly clear what, in August 1910, the problem was. Emerging from some frustrating negotiations with the insurance companies, who were thwarting his plans for widows' and orphans' benefits, he looked for a new political framework under whose aegis he might find compromise; hence the prominence of widows' pensions in his memorandum.

However, in November Balfour called off the game and spurned his offer; the constitutional conference had also collapsed by this time. Having wasted the best part of a year, the Liberals proceeded to fight another election in December, but armed with a promise from a reluctant King that he would create the necessary peers if the Lords refused to pass the Parliament Bill. The campaign was focused largely on the peers whom Lloyd George mocked as descendants of 'French filibusters' and 'the ennobled indiscretions of kings'. Since the result was a repeat of the January election, the Commons soon passed the Parliament Bill which reached the Lords in May. The revelation that 500 peers would be created, if necessary, led to a bitter scrimmage within the Tory ranks between the hedgers, who were for swallowing the Bill and preserving their majority, and the ditchers who wished to hold out. Eventually the Bill squeaked through by 131 votes to 113.

. . .

NATIONAL INSURANCE

As the constitutional controversy reached its conclusion in 1911, Lloyd George immersed himself in the next stage of his strategy: the plan for health and unemployment insurance. The unemployment scheme, prepared by Churchill, eventually became part two of the National Insurance Bill which Lloyd George introduced. Unemployment was so large and potentially expensive to handle that the Government tackled it piecemeal rather than adopting the ideas of Sidney and Beatrice Webb, which involved setting up a Ministry for Labour and full acceptance by national government of responsibility for the unemployed. Nor could they risk the implications of the Labour Party's Right To Work Bill which Keir Hardie used effectively as a stick with which to beat John Burns who, as President of the Local Government Board, was most directly responsible for the unemployed. Lloyd George and Churchill simply bypassed the Webbs, Hardie, and Burns with a three-part programme which began with the Labour Exchanges, 430 of which had been set up by 1913. Then, in the 1909 budget, came the Development Commission which was envisaged as a vehicle for schemes of state investment which would generate employment. Meanwhile, the old Poor Law system was to remain as a safety net, though some workers were to be saved from the Guardians by means of a compulsory scheme of unemployment benefits to which they, their employers and the State would make contributions. Though the initial scheme covered only 2.5 million skilled men, it was regarded as an experiment which would be extended later, which it was.

Health proved to be a more treacherous area. Here Lloyd George faced a great patchwork of provisions for the nation's sick, including the voluntary hospitals, Poor Law infirmaries, the system of panel doctors provided by friendly societies and some trade unions, and the policies of commercial insurance companies. Of course, many sick people, especially women, received little or no treatment of a professional kind, and preferred to rely on patent pills and home-made medicines. One drastic answer to all this, advocated by the Webbs, was to ignore existing ill-health and to concentrate the State's resources on preventing poor health in the next generation. But as a practical politician who wanted to see results for his money, Lloyd George proposed, instead, a scheme of insurance – a familiar concept – which would replace people's income when they fell ill. Yet this apparently simple remedy led him into a minefield of vested interests. In order to conciliate and outmanœuvre them he drew upon all his reserves of charm and skill. Many hours were spent receiving delegations of doctors, taking breakfasts with the Secretary of the Ancient Order of Foresters, and talking endlessly with journalists, as well as fending off the Webbs.

Essentially the vested interests feared the competition of a state scheme. By 1900 many friendly societies already faced the prospect of bankruptcy, though the state pensions scheme had helped by effectively relieving the demands upon them. Lloyd George went further by allowing them to become approved societies to whom state benefits might be paid. The insurance companies, who sent 70,000 collectors into millions of homes every week, were regarded as a serious political threat if antagonised. Lloyd George conciliated them by making it clear that there would be no funeral benefit in his scheme, by abandoning his original proposal to give pensions for widows and orphans, and by permitting the companies also to become approved societies under the scheme.

His chief assistants in this work were three civil servants, W. J. Braithwaite, J. S. Bradbury, and R. G. Hawtrey, as well as the Liberal ministers, Charles Masterman, Rufus Isaacs, and William Wedgwood Benn. His methods were typically irregular and involved endless discussions in bizarre settings. In December 1910 he dispatched Braithwaite to Germany to investigate the Bismarckian system of insurance. In January he arranged to meet Braithwaite in Nice. There, with an entourage including Masterman, Isaacs, and Bradbury, Lloyd George settled down in a corner of the pier, bought a round of drinks for his colleagues, and urged: 'Now then, tell us all about it.' He certainly allowed himself to be advised by Braithwaite on both minor and major matters. For example, the term 'health insurance' which he suggested, seemed more attractive than 'invalidity benefits', and indeed the word 'insurance' was itself calculated to give the impression that the scheme was voluntary rather than compulsory. Braithwaite struggled for a long time to persuade Lloyd George against the dividing-out principle, which was leading the friendly societies into difficulties, and in favour of the normal insurance company practice of building up a reserve fund. The scheme presented to the Cabinet in April involved compulsory insurance for workers over 16, earning under £160 per annum, financed by contributions of 4d. by a man, or 3d. by a woman, 3d. by the employer and 2d. by the State. This would bring sick pay of 10s. weekly for 13 weeks (7s. 6d. for a woman), and 5s. for a further 13 weeks, followed by a 5s. disability benefit. The worker would also enjoy free treatment from a doctor, including treatment in a sanatorium for tuberculosis; and the wife of an insured man would be entitled to a 30s. maternity benefit. This was expected to cost the Government £20 million by comparison with £4.5 million for the unemployment scheme.

In May 1911 the British Medical Association (BMA) mobilised some of its members and threatened to boycott the new system. Lloyd George, however, was able to outmanœuvre them when he discovered that the income of doctors in the country ranged from 2s. 6d. to 6s. per patient per year, with the average about 4s. He offered more than this, and as many younger and provincial doctors realised how lucrative panel practice could be, resistance collapsed and the rich doctors of the BMA were left high and dry. Faced with some criticism from Labour over the compulsory contributions, Lloyd George decided to allow trade unions to become approved societies under the state scheme, which stimulated a sharp rise in membership for some unions. In Parliament Ramsay MacDonald welcomed the Bill in spite of some carping from his socialist wing. In order to make sure of Labour's backing, the Government gave a firm promise to introduce the payment of salaries to MPs at this stage. The provisions were made more attractive by an extension of the full-rate sick benefit from 13 to 26 weeks, and by the exemption of workers on a daily wage-rate of under 21s. from contributions. The contributions began in July 1912 and the first benefits were paid in January 1913. 'Confound Lloyd George. He has strengthened the Government again', commented Austen Chamberlain. Although for some months the Conservatives made what capital they could out of the novelty of the national insurance stamps, they were eventually reduced to claiming that they would make it an even better scheme.

. . .

FRANCES STEVENSON

In 1912 Lloyd George reached his forty-ninth birthday. He was now at the height of his achievements in politics; but from this point his career was threatened from several directions. In the first place 1912 formed a turning-point in his life because it marked the beginning of his relationship with Frances Stevenson. A characteristically emancipated Edwardian girl, Frances had been educated at Clapham High School where she had been a classmate of Lloyd George's daughter, Mair. From there she went to Royal Holloway College to study classics and subsequently found employment as a teacher. In June 1911 the Welsh housekeeper at her school took her to hear Lloyd George speak at a Welsh Baptist chapel near Oxford Circus. In July she paid her first visit to the Chancellor at 11 Downing Street, in response to a request which had come via her headmistress for someone to give private lessons to Megan in the summer. Already fascinated by his power on the platform, Frances found Lloyd George's kindness to her disarming; he revealed 'a magnetism which made my heart leap and swept aside my judgement'.[6] In due course she began to work for him over the land campaign; he invited her to attend evening debates in the Commons, to come to his room for a chat afterwards, and sometimes to dine. They began to write to each other daily. Since teaching bored her, the invitation to become his secretary at the end of 1912 seemed very attractive. But Lloyd George never deceived her about their relationship. He presented her with a copy of Kitty O'Shea's biography of Parnell, the Irish leader whose career had been ruined by a divorce scandal. He would not marry Frances unless and until he was free to do so. Although admitting that the role of mistress was 'in direct conflict with my essentially Victorian upbringing', she decided in January 1913 to devote herself to Lloyd George.

Biographers of Lloyd George, such as Peter Rowland, have sometimes adopted an attitude of starched disapproval towards this relationship; and even the perceptive John Grigg writes of it as the mere infatuation of a middle-aged man for a young woman. This does less than justice to either party. Lloyd George's personal life was dominated by two enduring relationships with Margaret and Frances. To obtain physical satisfaction on a casual basis was the easiest thing in the world for an Edwardian politician; but to establish a permanent relationship with a woman not one's wife, even though masked as a personal secretaryship, was far more risky. That it lasted for thirty years and culminated in marriage points to only one interpretation: Lloyd George was greatly in need of a stable, loving relationship with one woman. Margaret did not provide it because she was absent, neglected his home comforts, and could not share fully in his political career. Frances filled the gap, but the relationship was much closer to that of husband and wife than to that of philanderer and mistress. She gave Lloyd George the praise and support he needed, shared his worries and burdens. She was also a very competent shorthand typist who brought order to his chaotic correspondence and paperwork, as well as being a fluent speaker of French, which he was not. Yet Frances also emerges as an intelligent person capable of forming her own opinions in spite of her admiration for Lloyd George. At critical points in his career she was prepared to tell him if she thought he was doing the wrong thing. Ultimately the relationship hinged upon her own fascination with the world of high politics and, no doubt, the flattering attentions of a leading player of the game. The real passion they shared was simply politics. In return for this excitement Frances had to suffer the unremitting condemnation of her family and the lack of any public acknowledgement of the important role she played. But at least, as secretary, she had no need to resort to surreptitious meetings, and her free access to Lloyd George was facilitated by J. T. Davies, the other personal secretary, as well as by Sarah Jones, the family's Welsh housekeeper, who considered that Lloyd George was badly neglected by Margaret. As long as they kept out of the divorce courts, his career was safe. Margaret evidently acquiesced, though she could hardly approve, partly because she already had the life she wanted, and because one stable, relatively domestic relationship was preferable to the alternatives.

. . .

THE MARCONI SCANDAL

During 1912 Lloyd George felt the need for Frances's support most acutely, for he faced a major threat to his career in the shape of the Marconi Scandal. Despite his £5,000 salary, he continued to yearn for the wealth that would render him truly independent in politics, and, no doubt, make threats of resignation more credible. His friends perceived all too clearly the temptations to which he was exposed; 'hold fast to your integrity', George Cadbury warned him in March 1912, doubtless because of the rumours about his speculation in shares. Yet it was shortly after this that Lloyd George gratefully accepted an offer from the Attorney-General, Rufus Isaacs, to buy 1,000 shares in the American Marconi Company at £2 each. The Chief Whip, Alexander Murray, also bought 1,000. Soon the shares were selling for £4 on the open market. Isaacs had acquired some 10,000 shares because his brother, Godfrey, was a director of the company. However, he also held a directorship in the English Marconi Company which had recently won a contract from the British Government to construct a chain of wireless stations throughout the Empire. Apart from Godfrey Isaacs, the two companies had no link except in that the English company had a holding in the American; however, the decision to extend the capital of the American company by $6 million suggested that it expected to benefit indirectly from the success of the English company.

The three ministers' speculations received publicity in several minor weekly journals, *Outlook, Eye Witness*, edited by Cecil Chesterton, and the *National Review*, edited by Leo Maxse. While Maxse's motive was party political, Chesterton's was anti-Semitism; he eagerly linked the Isaacs brothers to Herbert Samuel who, as Postmaster-General, had been responsible for the wireless contract. Samuel, who was totally innocent, explained his decision in Parliament; but in order to appease the Opposition, Asquith felt obliged to appoint a Select Committee in August 1912. In the debate on this proposal Rufus Isaacs denied, rather disingenuously, that he or his colleagues had had any dealings with 'that company'. Since Lloyd George did not speak, he was implicated in this foolish deception. Inevitably it emerged that *two* Marconi companies existed, and that the ministers had been involved with the American one. To make matters worse, Murray had purchased 3,000 shares with Liberal Party funds, but could not give evidence to the committee because he had gone off to Bogotá in Colombia. However, the party political ramifications made it all the more necessary for Asquith to support Lloyd George and refuse to accept his resignation. After a two-day debate on the Select Committee's Report, in which the Opposition did no more than charge the ministers with 'want of frankness', the Government enjoyed a majority of 78. Lloyd George himself appeared genuinely to feel that he had done nothing wrong; 'I am not in a white sheet. It does not suit me', he told Riddell defiantly. He gave no consideration to the view that a Chancellor of the Exchequer ought to be above any suspicion of having used knowledge acquired as a minister to make money. Since the American company did not hold shares in the English, he could certainly be acquitted of any charge of actual corruption. But even friends like C. P. Scott believed that he had come much too close, and that he should have made an unreserved apology: 'If you had thought more about it you wouldn't have done it', he commented frankly.[7]

To Scott, Cadbury, and other Liberals Lloyd George's folly over Marconi consisted ultimately in the squandering of his influence to the detriment of the radical causes they all sought to promote. There is some reason for thinking that for some time he felt constrained by the realisation that his career had been saved from disaster only by Asquith's firmness. 'I think the idol's wings are a bit clipped', the Prime Minister observed with smug satisfaction. Whether this was true is difficult to prove, but Asquith may well have had in mind such issues as women's suffrage which was troubling the Cabinet during 1911-13. He had long adopted a highly illiberal attitude on the women's question. This had not mattered much, in a party political sense, before 1900; but by the Edwardian period the argument about the merits of the case was largely over. What increasingly occupied politicians' thoughts was not whether, but on what *terms* women should be enfranchised. In this situation Asquith's remoteness was proving a liability to the Liberal Party in that he was alienating Liberal activists, especially women. For this reason suffragist ministers, such as Sir Edward Grey and Lloyd George, tried hard to use their influence to persuade Asquith to offer concessions over suffrage legislation.

. . .

WOMEN'S SUFFRAGE

As early as 1879 Lloyd George had heard Miss Lydia Becker speak at Porthmadog on 'Women's Rights', but had not been impressed: 'very few real arguments . . . she was rather sarcastic', he noted. But like many men, he came to support the enfranchisement of women in spite of its advocates. According to Frances Stevenson's account, 'Ibsen's *Doll's House* was the work that converted him to women's suffrage, and presented the woman's point of view to him.'[8] He voted in support of women's suffrage Bills in 1908, 1911, 1912, and 1913, but against in 1910. Since 1905 he had been forced to take account of the militant campaigns of the Women's Social and Political Union, whose strategy involved securing the defeat of government candidates in by-elections until such time as they agreed to introduce a government Bill for women's suffrage. As a frequent speaker Lloyd George had to endure many attempts to disrupt his meetings; at Kennington, in July 1912, he was even assaulted by a (male) suffragette and fell to the ground in the mêlée. In the following February a bomb exploded at a house which was being built for him by Lord Riddell at Walton Heath, an exploit for which Mrs Pankhurst claimed responsibility. 'They are mad,' Lloyd George exclaimed at one stage, 'Christabel Pankhurst has lost all sense of proportion and of reality.'

Yet this was less an expression of personal irritation than one of frustration at the political damage that the militants were doing to a good cause; their activities merely complicated the already difficult task of bringing an anti-suffragist prime minister round to a constructive view of the issue. In February 1910 an all-party Conciliation Committee had been formed to promote a Bill designed to enfranchise single women occupiers and householders who were thought to number about one million. When this Bill secured a majority in the Commons in May 1911, the Cabinet held a heated discussion on whether to grant the time for it to proceed. While Grey, Haldane, Runciman, Birrell, and others argued in favour of a free vote in the House, Lloyd George resisted the suggestion. His objection was essentially party political; the Bill, he claimed, would, 'on balance add hundreds of thousands of votes throughout the country to the strength of the Tory Party'. This view was, in fact, strongly endorsed by the party organisation. For Lloyd George, then, the terms of any women's Bill must be fairly democratic, by which he meant a proposal that would 'put the workingmen's wives on the register as well as spinsters and widows'. Given a measure of this kind, he claimed that 'even the Prime Minister was prepared for it'.[9]

While arguing with Cabinet colleagues during the summer of 1911, Lloyd George was simultaneously negotiating with the constitutional suffragists through C. P. Scott and H. N. Brailsford, proposing a franchise for householders which would allow a husband and wife to qualify for the same property. The deal he offered involved the introduction of a government Bill to extend male suffrage but which would be open to amendment to include women. For a time it seemed that this strategy might succeed. Under pressure from his suffragist colleagues, Asquith had eventually agreed to allow a free vote in Parliament on whether to grant time for the Conciliation Bill; but by the end of 1911 he had been persuaded to abandon this risky course in favour of the introduction of a government measure to create adult male suffrage and abolish plural voting. Just as Lloyd George had suggested to Scott and Brailsford, the Commons was to be left free to add a women's clause to this Bill if it wished. Although this initiative successfully scuttled the Conciliation Bill, it soon came to grief because in 1913 the Speaker ruled that the addition of a women's clause would change the nature of the original Bill. The fiasco over the withdrawal of the government Bill

undermined Lloyd George's credibility among the constitutional suffragists: 'I am becoming rather discredited as a
false prophet because I have so often predicted better things of
Mr Lloyd George than he has performed', commented
Catherine Marshall.[10]

What emerges from all this is that Asquith had, reluctantly,
made some concessions to suffragist pressure within his
government; and his conciliatory response to a deputation in
1914 under Sylvia Pankhurst corroborates Lloyd George's view
that he had been convinced of the necessity to give
representation to *working-class* women. Yet the pressure was
too little and too late to resolve the problem by 1914. Not that
too much emphasis should be given to Lloyd George's
weakness, for it is always extremely difficult to force a prime
minister to reverse his position when dug in as firmly as
Asquith was. His face had to be saved; and it is partly for this
reason, as well as because it reflected his own preference, that
Lloyd George used what influence he had in favour of an adult
suffrage solution rather than a measure limited to women.
However, it is a mistake to underestimate his determination.
During 1914 he continued to try to shift the Liberal Party
towards the suffrage by monitoring the views of Liberal
politicians on the issue, and intervening to persuade anti-
suffragist candidates to change their policy. After Asquith's
meeting with Sylvia Pankhurst in June he continued talks with
her and with George Lansbury, apparently with a view to
finding a solution which they and the constitutional suffragists
could unite around; this was done with the approval of the
Prime Minister, as was Lloyd George's intervention with the
Home Secretary, McKenna, designed to persuade him not to
rearrest Sylvia Pankhurst under the 'Cat and Mouse' Act.[11]
Thus by 1914 the essential legislative solution, that was to be
enacted in 1917, had emerged, and in this Lloyd George had
played a significant part; what had not quite been achieved was
the sensitive business of saving the Prime Minister's face.

. . .

THE LAND CAMPAIGN

These frustrating experiences over women's suffrage and over
the Bills for Irish Home Rule and Welsh disestablishment
between 1912 and 1914, encouraged Lloyd George to look for

fresh ways of restoring the initiative and *élan* to Asquith's slightly battered administration. This explains why, from 1912, his mind ran increasingly on a new land campaign. In characteristic fashion he proceeded by setting up a Land Committee under Arthur Acland and C. R. Buxton, which was unofficial, but enjoyed Asquith's general approval; several noted reformers such as Seebohm Rowntree and C. P. Scott participated in its work, while the radical industrialists, Sir William Lever, Joseph Rowntree, Joseph Fels, and Baron Maurice de Forest, financed its inquiries. By stages the committee gathered evidence, then issued a Rural Report in October 1913, followed by an Urban Report in April 1914. Lloyd George launched a campaign in its support with a major speech at Bedford in the autumn of 1913, and hoped his efforts would culminate in legislation during 1914 and 1915. It proved to be an ambitious project which generated a wealth of information and a number of important objectives. One target, soon identified, was the introduction of minimum wages for agricultural labourers – not such a novel step for a government which had already established minimum wages for coal-miners and for the 'sweated trades' under the Trade Boards Act. Then a system of land courts was to be created to fix fair rents for the benefit of tenant farmers under pressure from higher wage-rates. A new ministry of lands and forests would also be set up, empowered to acquire land and build cottages to remedy the appalling conditions of rural housing. Finally the proposals had an urban dimension. This included tackling the long-standing grievances of urban leaseholders, often small businessmen, who found that landlords raised their charges dramatically when leases came up for renewal. They were promised compensation. Then there was the question of local finance and rising land values, a subject regularly raised by Charles Trevelyan and a group of ardent land reformers. By the end of 1913 Lloyd George had committed himself to the idea of the rating of site values as a way of allowing local authorities to tap rising land prices to relieve the burden on rates levied on buildings.

Some historians have been inclined to write off the land campaign as 'arcadian fantasy' by Lloyd George, or as a flop politically, or as a sign that the reforms of New Liberalism had ground to a halt by 1914. These are easy claims to make since the land question was suddenly suspended on the outbreak of war in August 1914 while debate was still going on and before anything had been achieved. Yet it must be remembered that *all* Lloyd George's great constructive reforms present the same slightly chaotic impression at the half-way stage! As with national insurance or the budget, he was unlikely to get everything he wanted from the land campaign, but to suggest that nothing of advantage was likely to come of it would be rash speculation. Nor would many contemporaries have agreed with historians who see land as anachronistic. For Lloyd George was acting against a background of widespread agreement about the need to keep men on the land, improve the housing stock, and assist local councils trapped by urban land prices and limited finance. The Labour Party regarded the land as an absolutely central question. And the Conservatives, readily conceding that the Liberals had an excellent case, noted the success of candidates who espoused land reform at by-elections, such as E. G. Hemmerde at North West Norfolk and R. L. Outhwaite in urban Hanley. Indeed their chief concern was to avoid provoking Lloyd George into a repeat of the controversies of 1909-10, so much so that one MP, Leslie Scott, offered to help in passing the legislation if Lloyd George would refrain from 'Limehousing' the landlords! Remarkably, the only sustained attack consisted in the jokes about Lloyd George's remarks at Bedford on the effects of field sports upon agriculture, in which he painted a familiar picture of farmers' mangel-wurzels being devoured by voracious pheasants. Critics seized on this as proof of his ignorance of the eating habits of game birds, and, by implication, of farming generally. Thereafter the cartoonists delightedly portrayed him as an impish figure trailing a line of pheasants and mangels behind him. In fact he was better informed than his critics; during the hard winter months, then as now, pheasants habitually descended upon turnips and other standing crops. But he was evidently sensitive on the point, and in his papers is preserved a photograph, carefully cut from the *Daily Chronicle*, of pheasants at London Zoo being fed upon mangels! This apart, the Conservatives' best tactics lay in trying to play down the whole question, as Lloyd George himself perceived: 'The Tory press have evidently received instructions from headquarters to talk Ulster to the exclusion of land', he noted in October 1913, 'if they succeed we are "beat".'[12] In the event his final reforming blow before the war came in the shape of another budget which raised an additional £9.8

million revenue. This involved a further increase in death duties and the supertax, as well as raising income tax to 1s. 4d. on unearned incomes. In this way he was able to offer Exchequer subsidies to local authorities to reduce rates by 9d. in the pound, a move well calculated to bring relief to lower-middle-class voters alienated from the Liberals in 1910. Thus Lloyd George appeared to be on course for another victory at the election which was expected in 1915, with his radical social and financial strategy intact as the last days of peace ran out in the summer of 1914.

. . .

NOTES AND REFERENCES

1.   Morgan K O (ed.) 1973 *Lloyd George: family letters 1885–1936*. University of Wales Press, p. 8;   D Lloyd George to Margaret 26/7/99, quoted in Morgan K O (ed.) 1973 p. 118
2.   Deb H C 15/6/08 c.564–86
3.   Austen Chamberlain Papers, Birmingham University, AC/14/6/56
4.   Gardiner A G 1914 *Prophets, Priests and Kings*. J. M. Dent, p. 135
5.   Sir Charles Hobhouse's Diary 10/7/08, 5/8/08, quoted in David E I (ed.) 1977 *Inside Asquith's Cabinet*. John Murray, pp. 72–3
6.   Lloyd George F 1967 *The Years That Are Past*. Hutchinson, p. 42
7.   C P Scott to Lloyd George 7/6/13, quoted in Wilson T (ed.) 1970 *The Political Diaries of C P Scott 1911–28*. Collins, p. 71
8.   Taylor A J P (ed.) 1971 *Lloyd George: a diary by Frances Stevenson*. Hutchinson, p. 43
9.   D Lloyd George to the Master of Elibank 5/9/11, Elibank Papers, National Library of Scotland, Box 5
10.   C Marshall to F D Acland 4/11/13, Marshall Papers, Cumbria Record Office
11.   D Lloyd George to R McKenna 6/7/14 Lloyd George Papers, House of Lords Record Office C/5/12/9. See the discussion in Holton S S 1986 *Feminism and Democracy*. Cambridge University Press, pp. 124–5
12.   D Lloyd George to P Illingworth 24/10/13, Lloyd George Papers, House of Lords Record Office C/5/4/7.

Chapter 4

WAR AND PEACE
1908 – 1916

When composing his *War Memoirs* in the 1930s Lloyd George went out of his way to establish his lack of responsibility for the policies which had led Britain into the First World War in August 1914:

> During the eight years that preceded the war, the Cabinet devoted a ridiculously small percentage of its time to a consideration of foreign affairs .... Of course, certain aspects of foreign policy were familiar to those Ministers who attended the Committee of Imperial Defence, but ... There was a reticence and a secrecy which practically ruled out three-fourths of the Cabinet from the chance of making any genuine contribution to the momentous questions then fermenting on the continent of Europe ... nothing was said about our military commitments .... Apart from the Prime Minister and the Foreign Secretary, there were only two or three men ... who were expected to make any contribution on the infrequent occasions when the Continental situation was brought to our awed attention.

While this conveys a plausible general impression of the atmosphere in Cabinet, it is a gross and palpable distortion for what it implies about the writer's own role in the formulation of policy. One must remember that in the inter-war period, when Lloyd George's reputation as a great war minister was no longer the asset it had been, he was anxious not to let the supporters of Asquith – his bitter enemies since 1918 – escape their share of blame for the descent into Armageddon.

However, any suggestion that Lloyd George was in ignorance of or excluded from the decision-making bodies is largely false, especially from 1908 onwards. The direct and familiar way in which he dealt with Grey, Churchill, Haldane, or McKenna makes the claim that he was in awe of the mandarins of foreign affairs absurd. His role in the protracted debate over defence and foreign policy after 1906 does appear ambiguous at first sight in that he threw his weight first to one side then to the other. This reflected the fact that he remained genuinely torn right up to the declaration of war, hating the idea of war yet seeing quite clearly the necessity for it in certain circumstances. However, his behaviour is more consistent if one keeps in mind the fact that his 'anti-war' interventions invariably took the form of criticism of the naval and military estimates, whereas on specific questions of strategy and foreign relations he tended to follow the views of Grey, at least privately. The Boer War had placed Lloyd George in a false position by leaving him with a reputation as a radical opponent of war. During the eight years up to 1914 he steadily divested himself of this encumbrance though the transition was obscured by public statements and press interviews in which he spoke of improving relations with Germany through a cessation of the naval race.

Lloyd George approached international affairs from a positive, Roseberyite view of the British Empire, though he felt that this required the aggressive use of military force only in exceptional circumstances. Beyond this, he had not thought very much about the problems of defence which absorbed British governments during the 1890s and in the aftermath of the Boer War. Squeezed between the rival systems of the Triple Alliance and the Dual Alliance, and increasingly unable to maintain sufficient naval strength to match her liabilities in all parts of the globe, Britain had been driven in 1902 to an alliance with Japan. This novel commitment, coming on top of her growing concern with the expansion of the German navy, led to the signing of an *entente* with France in 1904. However, when the Liberals returned to office in December 1905 Britain still had no alliance with the French, and the military weaknesses exposed by the conflict with the Boers had not been corrected. The launching of the first Dreadnought in 1906 gave another twist to the situation by creating a fear that Germany might build similar ships more quickly. Under Richard Haldane the British army was drastically reorganised into a Field Force of professionals capable of rapid mobilisation, and a Home Force or Territorial Army of partly trained men. The underlying question was to what use would the Field Force be put? Under the aegis of the Committee of Imperial Defence, British strategists identified the central problem facing the country: in a continental war France would be quickly defeated by a German sweep through the Low Countries to Paris, which would leave the British Isles highly vulnerable. If Britain's own security was tied up with the survival of France as a Great Power, it followed that the proper application of the Field Force was on the left wing of the French armies where it might check the German drive for Paris. By 1909 the Committee of Imperial Defence had largely agreed upon this approach, though this was resisted by the Royal Navy until 1911 out of pique at being turned into a mere conveyance for the army.

Initially Sir Edward Grey, as Foreign Secretary, took the lead in this development of policy. Always highly suspicious of Germany as an expansive power, Grey took office at a time when she was putting pressure on the French in Morocco. This led him to endorse the joint naval staff talks with the French which began the gradual process of turning the nebulous *entente* into a military alliance, though never formally so. The same fear of Germany encouraged Grey to settle differences with Russia in 1907 and to conciliate King Leopold of Belgium in his African ambitions because of the need to co-operate with the Belgians in Europe. These were aspects of a policy which many Liberals found novel and distasteful; for it aligned Britain with repressive regimes like Tsarist Russia, involved abetting Belgian exploitation of the Congo, and meant pandering to French desires for a war of revenge against the Germans who should have been natural friends of Britain. Lloyd George, while at the Board of Trade, was too absorbed with administration to play a significant role in these matters. During 1908, however, he became a much more central figure. For as Chancellor of the Exchequer he was elevated to membership of the Committee of Imperial Defence. Though he apparently attended only two of fifteen meetings of the committee in the next three years, he sat on a subcommittee considering the question of an invasion threat to the British Isles. More immediately he had to face up to the financial costs of the naval competition with the Germans.

Consequently 1908 found Lloyd George facing both ways in foreign affairs. Addressing a peace conference in July, he disparaged Dreadnoughts and sympathised with the Germans' fear of encirclement; yet, according to a fellow member of the Committee of Imperial Defence, Lord Esher, he had already warned the German Ambassador that if necessary he would borrow £100 million in order to maintain British naval superiority.[1] When visiting Germany in August to study the social security system he spoke of the need to improve relations between the two countries. Though irritated with him for speaking without prior consultation, Grey found the substance of his remarks unobjectionable; indeed it is significant how *relaxed* the Foreign Office was in 1908 about his views, despite his public stance. Before his visit to Paris in April a Foreign Office official, Walter Tyrrell, gave the following appreciation of him to the British Ambassador there:

> Lloyd George belongs to that section of the cabinet which is described as Germanophil whose love for the Fatherland, however, has decreased in proportion to the length of time he has been in office. A pleasant stay in Paris may contribute to complete his conversion.[2]

This steady shift in Lloyd George's position was obscured by his intermittent pursuit of reductions in the naval estimates, a noisy but almost wholly ineffective effort, from 1908 to 1914. On becoming Chancellor he faced a demand for naval estimates in the following year of £38 million, an increase of £3 million to pay for six new Dreadnoughts. The Cabinet eventually reached its famous 'compromise' of building four immediately and four 'contingently'! Hence the cynical but telling tribute by Esher: 'Lloyd George, in his heart, does not care a bit for economy. . . . He is plucky and an Imperialist at heart, if he is anything.'[3] Perhaps Lloyd George humoured Esher, but the fact is that in 1909 and on every subsequent occasion he always found the money for extra ships.

The years from 1909 to 1911 were the crucial period in which the subcommittees of the Committee of Imperial Defence hammered out a continental strategy for the deployment of the British Expeditionary Force (BEF). Though primarily occupied with domestic matters, Lloyd George clearly felt acutely the inconsistency between his public reputation and his private position. In conversations with colleagues he showed himself perfectly familiar with the military arguments on which the new strategy was based, yet complained that he was being kept in ignorance. This may account for the establishment of a new Cabinet Committee on Foreign Affairs in January 1911 comprising Asquith, Grey, Lloyd George, Morley, Crewe, and Runciman, which pursued the mirage of an Anglo-German naval agreement. This served the purpose of underlining the Government's wish to improve relations with Germany. The lengths to which Lloyd George himself was prepared to go to maintain his fading credentials as an opponent of war are apparent from his dealings with C. P. Scott at this time. As an ally of Lloyd George during the Boer War and editor of the *Manchester Guardian* Scott was seen as a barometer of provincial radical opinion; by keeping in touch with him Lloyd George hoped to retain his support in the country. By the spring of 1911 it was apparent that as a result of the naval scares of 1908 Britain had exaggerated the German shipbuilding programme. Thus in Cabinet the economists had a strong case for reducing expenditure. Lloyd George gave Scott to understand that as a result of his own threat of resignation made to Asquith, the First Lord of the Admiralty, Reginald McKenna, had backed down over the naval estimates. In fact, however, the current estimates were *increased* by £4 million with a promise of unspecified reductions over the two following years. Subsequently McKenna argued that the cuts were contingent upon German willingness to slow down the rate of building and on the agreement of the army to share some of the loss. Of course neither condition was met. Lloyd George accepted a bargain of this sort more than once, and it is difficult to avoid the conclusion that its chief virtue was to save his own face. As for his trumpeted resignation it is one of many reported over the years by Scott and by Frances Stevenson, but in the absence of corroboration it should be discounted. Lloyd George knew that he simply could not afford the luxury of resignation, and his deep commitment to the National Insurance Bill at this time makes it particularly improbable.

Later in 1911 Lloyd George's adherence to Grey's view of foreign policy became public for the first time. The occasion was the second Moroccan crisis precipitated by Germany's vehement objection to French expansion in North Africa and the dispatch of the German gunboat, *Panther*, at the beginning of July. This was a good issue for Lloyd George to choose in that Germany, by her demands for a base on the Moroccan coast and for territorial compensation in the French Congo, seemed to have revealed herself as a belligerent power. Grey was particularly incensed that Germany appeared determined to impose a settlement by excluding Britain altogether. In order to demonstrate the strength of Britain's feeling both to Germany and to France, for whom a further humiliation might destroy the value of the *entente*, Grey considered sending a British warship to the scene. This, however, was resisted in Cabinet by Morley, Harcourt, McKenna, and Loreburn, though not by Lloyd George. But an equally dramatic warning was issued in the form of a speech by him at the Mansion House on 21 July:

> If a situation were to be forced upon us, in which peace could only be preserved by ... allowing Britain to be treated as if she were of no account in the Cabinet of nations, then I say emphatically that peace at that price would be a humiliation intolerable for a great country like ours to endure.

Though the speech had been approved in advance by Grey, it was Lloyd George's own initiative. Coming from a politician with his reputation it was the best possible warning to the Germans and reassurance of support for the French. 'The impression I got', noted C. P. Scott, 'was that he is not immune from the microbe of Germanophobia.'[4] For his part Lloyd George condemned the German Chancellor privately as a 'coarse bully', and insisted in his protracted arguments with Scott over the merits of British intervention that the danger now existed that France might be eliminated as a Great Power; he therefore felt it necessary, as he put it to Arthur Murray MP, to engage in 'an endeavour to inculcate a little common-sense and patriotism into the head of Scott'.

In retrospect, the Moroccan crisis of 1911 brought war appreciably nearer in that it led all parties to think very carefully about the circumstances in which they would fight. It also led Grey and Lloyd George into a particularly cordial and mutually appreciative phase in their relationship; 'as sound as a bell', was now the Foreign Office view of the radical Chancellor. However, other Liberals felt appalled by what seemed dangerous brinkmanship by the Foreign Secretary, and their misgivings came to a head in November when the Cabinet in effect rebuked Grey for unconstitutional behaviour in having sanctioned staff talks with the French without obtaining Cabinet approval. The situation was defused by the appointment of another Cabinet committee including Lloyd George and further attempts to seek a naval agreement with Germany. Though Lloyd George stepped back from foreign affairs for a time it is significant that he played virtually the same role during the Balkan War in 1913. Faced with the danger of Austria being drawn into the war, Lloyd George again took the opportunity of the Mansion House speech to warn the Central Powers against provoking Russia.

By the autumn of 1913 the perennial controversy over the naval estimates was reaching new heights as a result of Churchill's promotion as First Lord. An uninhibited big-navy man, Churchill proposed estimates of £50 million for 1914-15 and the laying down of four new battleships. Lloyd George responded publicly with an interview in the *Daily Chronicle* on 1 January 1914 in which he claimed there had been an improvement in Anglo-German relations and alluded rather crudely to the resignation of Churchill's father, Lord Randolph, over his opposition to high levels of military expenditure. This may well have been Lloyd George's way of reminding ordinary Liberals that he himself was still far from being a warmonger. He well knew how unpopular Churchill had become in Liberal circles both for his belligerence and because he seemed to be reverting to support for Ulster Unionist claims at a time when the Home Rule crisis was reaching a climax. In spite of his earlier collaboration with Churchill, he now regarded him as a rival who had been over-promoted by Asquith, and may well have wanted to encourage him towards a hasty resignation.

None the less, in Cabinet the real resistance to the naval estimates was conducted by McKenna and Sir John Simon whose case for economy was all the stronger in view of Britain's comfortable 43-26 lead in Dreadnought-standard ships over Germany. Yet Churchill got his four new ships and escaped with a contingent promise of cuts in 1915-16. Once again Lloyd George endeavoured to reassure Scott that his heart was in the right place by claiming to have put his resignation on the table. On hearing of this claim McKenna 'only dissolved in Homeric laughter'.[5] The fact is that by 1914 Lloyd George had ceased to be a reliable ally of the critics of defence and foreign policy even on the military estimates; and as a result it was clear well before the crisis of August 1914 that the anti-war section of the Cabinet would decisively lack the leadership and force that he might have given it.

. . .

THE ENTRY INTO WAR

By the summer of 1914 Lloyd George's optimistic suggestions in January about improvements in Great-Power relations appeared to have some justification; the only conflict that seemed imminent was a civil war in Ireland. Most politicians naturally concentrated their attention on the clashes between British troops and civilians in Dublin on 26 June. The assassination two days later of Franz Ferdinand, heir to the throne of Austria, at Sarajevo did not immediately dominate their thoughts. However, Grey soon learned that the Austrians intended to hold Serbia responsible for the assassination and to humiliate her, which would virtually oblige the German government to support Austria against Russian retaliation. Grey's hopes of being able to restrain Russia in co-operation with the French were shattered by the Austrian ultimatum to Serbia, as a result of which the Foreign Secretary warned the Cabinet on 24 July of the prospect that the four continental Great Powers would be drawn into a war. The pronouncement in *The Times* on 27 July that France and Russia could rely on British support brought C. P. Scott to the Treasury, thoroughly alarmed, for a difficult interview with Lloyd George. The Chancellor went out of his way to reassure him, saying 'there could be no question of our taking part in any war in the first instance. Knew of no minister who would be in favour of it.' Clearly it was essential to avoid provoking Scott and the *Manchester Guardian* into public criticism of the Government at an early stage; but as the conversation proceeded Lloyd George attempted to educate Scott into the reality of the situation as he saw it:

> he admitted that a difficult situation would arise if the German fleet were attacking French towns on the other side of the Channel and the French sowed the Channel with mines .... As to the prospect of war he was very gloomy. He thought Austria *wanted* war ... Germany did not want war, but would be bound to support Austria.[6]

He went on to explain how Germany would mobilise troops within a week, strike quickly at France, and then have time to turn against the slow-moving Russian forces in the East. Considering that this was on 27 July, before the Austrians had even attacked Serbia, it shows a remarkably firm grasp of the essential problem and of the likely sequence of events. Equally significant in this conversation is the way in which Belgium was referred to. Lloyd George merely mentioned a German invasion of Belgian territory, but gave no indication that this would justify Britain's participation; for him the argument rested upon the balance of force in Europe and on the vulnerability of the Dual Alliance.

The next day the picture Lloyd George had sketched began to materialise with alarming speed. Austria launched her attack on Serbia, the Russians began to mobilise on 31 July, and on 1 August Germany declared war on Russia. From 30 July the Cabinet met daily with at least half its members opposed initially to British involvement in war, though not in *all* circumstances. In the absence of a full or formal record of meetings it is difficult to be certain of the role played by Lloyd George, though the diaries of Scott, Frances Stevenson, Lord Riddell, and Sir Charles Hobhouse, himself a member of the Cabinet, throw some light on it. Hobhouse asserted that Lloyd George, having begun in a very anti-German mood, toned down his views. This is corroborated by Frances Stevenson to whom Lloyd George emphasised how he was being pressed by colleagues to support Britain's entry into war. She evidently felt he required little persuasion:

> My own opinion is that L.G.'s mind was really made up from the first, that he knew we would have to go in, and that the invasion of Belgium was, to be cynical, a heaven-sent excuse for supporting a declaration of war.[7]

During the crucial days between Friday 31 July and Sunday 2 August Lloyd George played an important intermediate role between the group consisting of Grey, Asquith, Churchill, Haldane, and Hobhouse, that was most solid for backing the French, and the group that seemed firmly for neutrality comprising Morley, Harcourt, Simon, and Burns. He favoured a public announcement by Britain that she would defend France's northern coast and preserve Belgium's neutrality; or, to put it another way, he was prepared to commit himself to resignation from the Government and to opposition to war if the Germans gave an undertaking to abstain from attacks on the French coast and to respect Belgian neutrality. This, as he knew, was highly improbable; but in his views one can discern the bridges by which the Cabinet shifted from ambivalence to intervention in the war comparatively painlessly. On 2 August the Cabinet resolved to authorise Grey to give the French an undertaking to defend their northern coast – a recognition of the obligation arising out of the mutual rearrangement of Anglo-French naval forces in the North Sea and the Mediterranean. At this point only four ministers were expected to resign, and Lloyd George now threw his weight behind Asquith's efforts to persuade them to withhold their resignations until Grey had addressed the House of Commons on Monday 3 August. In the event Grey was well received because the House accepted that, notwithstanding his suspicion of Germany, he had laboured to maintain peace between the Great Powers, as he had successfully done during the Balkan War of 1913. Only two ministers, Burns and Morley, persisted in their resignations. As a result the Government was able to issue its ultimatum to Germany on 4 August virtually united. That evening Lloyd George sat in the Cabinet room with Asquith and several other colleagues waiting disconsolately for the last minutes of peace to run out, and listening to the cheers of the crowds in Whitehall as Big Ben tolled the passing of Edwardian England. However much he was convinced intellectually of the need to join the war, Lloyd George remained as appalled at the prospect as was Grey; that they, along with their colleagues had hesitated and struggled for peace was no more and no less than men of humanity and intelligence would do in such circumstances. Unlike the situation in 1899, war would not be arrived at lightly or wantonly. Lloyd George in particular agonised because he expected the military balance, now so unfavourable to the Dual Alliance, to tip against Germany in a fairly short time, thereby relieving Britain of the necessity to intervene. Thus he argued with Riddell: 'How would you feel if you saw Germany overrun and annihilated by Russia? . . . in 1916 Russia will have a larger army than Germany, France and Austria put together.'[8]

One final qualification must be made in depicting Lloyd George's support for British entry into war in 1914. He seems to have shared with most of his colleagues an expectation that the conflict would be a limited one for Britain. Writing to Margaret on 11 August he said:

We are keeping the sea for France, that ought to suffice her for the moment especially as we are sending 100,000 men to help her to bear the brunt of the attack. That is all that counts for Russia will come in soon.[9]

Clearly he envisaged that Britain's contribution would be primarily naval and industrial not military, in spite of the dispatch of the BEF on 6 August. Though he rapidly adapted to the idea of a major land war, he was initially preoccupied with the need to support Britain's allies with the products of British industry. This seemed at first threatened by the prospect of disruption in industry, rising unemployment, and a general strike. However, the anti-war meetings rapidly collapsed and the trade-union leaders showed themselves highly patriotic. As men rushed to volunteer for the armed forces it soon transpired that the problem would be not a shortage of employment but a shortage of manpower. Rising prices – the consequence of Britain's heavy dependence upon imports of basic food items – posed an immediate problem which the Government countered by buying food abroad for release on to the domestic market.

On the whole, however, such matters fell more within the sphere of the Board of Trade than the Treasury and, as Chancellor, Lloyd George suddenly found himself occupying a relatively peripheral position. His most important contribution was to help ride out the financial crisis caused by the declaration of war. As early as 1 August the bank rate had been raised to 10 per cent, the banks were beginning to panic, and the Stock Exchange ceasing to function. Lloyd George, who had not hitherto taken much interest in this side of his work, took advice from his Under-Secretary, Sir John Bradbury, Rufus Isaacs, Sir George Paish, and the Governor of the Bank of England, Sir Walter Cunliffe. The bank holiday on 3 August was extended for three days while various measures were taken to restore the credit system and bolster confidence, such as the issuing of £1 and 10s. notes – 'Bradburys' – by the Treasury. By 7 August when the banks reopened bank rate had been cut to 5 per cent; confidence returned and Lloyd George was pleasantly surprised to find that he had won golden opinions in the most unlikely quarters of the financial world. After initially obtaining a vote of credit for £100 million from the House of Commons he drew up a war budget in November which set out the chief ways by which the cost of the war would be paid for. Increased income tax, supertax (up to 2s. 8d. in the £), and duties on tea and beer were to yield a modest £65 million in a full year. By contrast some £350 million was to be raised by a war loan bearing interest of 3½ per cent which was below the commercial rate. The over-subscription of this loan encouraged all wartime chancellors to follow Lloyd George in an excessive reliance upon borrowing.

But having accomplished these things, what was there for a chancellor to do in wartime? The vast schemes of constructive reform must be laid aside; the party truce ruled out public politicking. Inevitably Lloyd George's mind turned to the great issues affecting the war – recruitment, munitions, and strategy. All of these brought him into conflict with the new Secretary of State for War, Lord Kitchener. Politically the choice of Kitchener was brilliant, for the Conservatives and the press could not attack him as they would have done a Liberal minister. But Kitchener was no administrator. Though he made a great poster he could not and would not communicate with his colleagues. His stubbornness and vanity led him to discard the existing Territorial Army system in order to fashion the volunteers into the new 'Kitchener' armies. Almost at once, Lloyd George began to row with him over his petty refusal to allow Nonconformist chaplains at the front, to create a purely Welsh regiment, and to permit the men to speak Welsh on parade and in billets. However, it is significant that on each point Kitchener backed down. Indeed during the early years of war the civilians by no means abdicated control to the soldiers. Through Asquith's War Council the politicians imposed major decisions, including the replacement of the Commander-in-Chief in France, the launching of the campaigns at Salonika and in the Dardanelles, and the removal of powers from the Secretary of State for War himself.

However, Lloyd George, whatever his criticisms of Kitchener, fully accepted his view that the war would last for at least three years and the corollary that Britain must raise a large army to see it through. The initial success of the voluntary recruiting system rendered this fundamental shift of British strategic thinking relatively uncontroversial. Even so, Lloyd George did not publicly commit himself to the idea of a 'big' war until 19 September when he delivered his famous Queen's Hall speech in London. By this time the initial euphoria over the war had subsided as a result of the sobering news of the Russian defeat at Tannenberg and the retreat of the Allied forces to within a few miles of Paris. Though usually nervous and irritable before a major speech, Lloyd George was excessively so on this occasion; doubtless he had sensed that in taking a deliberate stance on the war he had reached a turning-point in his political career. It was at the Queen's Hall that he elaborated on his view of the war as a noble fight on behalf of the small nations, Belgium and Serbia, and characterised the enemy in the shape of the Prussian *Junker* as 'the road-hog of Europe'. And his moving peroration on the theme of sacrifice was widely applauded by press and politicians alike:

> I envy you young people your opportunity. ... For most generations sacrifice comes in drab and weariness of spirit. It comes to you today, and comes today to us all, in the form of the glow and thrill of a great movement for liberty, that impels millions throughout Europe to the same noble end. ... The people will gain more by this struggle in all lands than they comprehend at the present moment. It is true they will be free of the greatest menace to their freedom. That is not all. There is something infinitely greater and more enduring which is emerging already out of this great conflict – a new patriotism, richer, nobler and more exalted than the old. ... We have been living in a sheltered valley for generations. We have been too comfortable and too indulgent, many, perhaps, too selfish, and the stern hand of Fate has scourged us to an elevation where we can see the great everlasting things that matter for a nation – the great peaks we had forgotten, of Honour, Duty, Patriotism, and, clad in glittering white, the great pinnacle of Sacrifice pointing like a rugged finger to Heaven.

This was a prime ministerial speech, though not consciously so; it revealed in Lloyd George a capacity for leadership and popular inspiration which Asquith and the rest of his colleagues patently lacked. But in substance it was not a particularly *liberal* speech. For although he made a point of saying both publicly and in private correspondence that the war was being waged not against the German people but against a military caste, by his repeated use of words like 'barbarism' in referring to Prussian *Junkers* and his emphasis on atrocities committed by them, he contributed powerfully to the caricature of the Germans as a subhuman enemy. By his eloquence Lloyd

George had earned more praise in Conservative circles, already impressed by his unexpectedly adept handling of the financial crisis; and he had launched himself upon a swelling tide of chauvinism which was to carry him shortly on to alien shores.

Meanwhile the war had passed through its first decisive phase. After their retreat during the Battle of Mons the Allies had staged a counter-attack on the Marne during September, pushing the German armies back again. Although Antwerp fell in October, the German attempt to roll up the Allied flank along the coast was decisively checked by the First Battle of Ypres and both sides settled into a line of trenches from the Channel to the Swiss frontier. The Schlieffen Plan had been checked, but no one knew what to do next. Lacking any experience or knowledge of military matters, and deprived of direct responsibility for them, Lloyd George began to cast about for a constructive role. He was quick to see that the huge numbers of men pouring into recruiting offices would soon create problems of supply which the War Office was ill-equipped to handle. Asquith shared his concern to the extent of appointing a Cabinet committee – the Shells Committee – to investigate the supply of munitions, despite Kitchener's opposition. Membership of this committee gave Lloyd George his first toe-hold in the military sphere. No sooner had it been set up than he, characteristically, made plans to visit France to enquire into French methods of supply. Arriving at Dieppe on 17 October he proceeded to interview arms manufacturers, generals, and politicians on the process by which industry had been turned over from the production of consumer goods to the weapons of war. He soon noted how the indiscriminate call-up of men to the forces had restricted munitions production. Above all, the visit brought Lloyd George into close physical proximity to the war for the first time – within 1,500 yards of the enemy line to be exact. He felt a little of the danger and came away with a vivid impression of trench warfare: 'It is stalemate', he wrote to Margaret. From this point onwards he felt confident about dabbling in military matters, sensing that neither Kitchener nor any of the other professionals really knew how to cope with the problems of trench warfare. Nor would he allow himself to be eclipsed by Churchill who enjoyed the advantage of military experience and control of the Admiralty, but had already blundered by rushing off to preside over the defence of Antwerp.

. . .

MUNITIONS AND STRATEGY

Exhilarated by his brush with the enemy and emboldened by his talks with the French, Lloyd George plunged into the question of armaments supply which was traditionally the responsibility of the Master-General of the Ordnance, subject to the Secretary of State for War. The existing Master-General, Sir Stanley von Donop, relied upon the Royal Arsenals and a handful of private firms such as Vickers-Armstrong, Cammell Laird, and the Coventry Ordnance Works who could comfortably meet the army's requirements. It soon emerged that the rate of consumption of shells and ammunition was far greater than the army had anticipated, and that trench warfare called for less shrapnel and more heavy explosives. But the reluctance of Sir John French, the Commander-in-Chief, to raise his demands for shells – at least until searching for an excuse for his setbacks – meant that von Donop himself was slow to persuade his suppliers to expand their output. Labour was one part of the problem. Many skilled engineers had volunteered and it was not always easy to fill their places with unskilled men. This problem, as Kitchener readily accepted, lay within Lloyd George's natural sphere. Conferring with trade-union leaders, a very patriotic group of men, the Chancellor obtained what was called the 'Treasury Agreement' on 17 March 1915. Though not legally binding the agreement committed the unions to giving up strike action, accepting compulsory arbitration, and allowing the dilution of labour, that is, the employment of unskilled men and women in work hitherto designated as skilled.

Yet the caution and conservatism of the War Office remained a formidable obstacle. Lloyd George, having abandoned the usual Treasury practice of careful control of military spending, found to his surprise that von Donop failed to take advantage and showed himself reluctant to broaden the range of companies to whom contracts were given, arguing that only a few could meet the army's high standards. In a country which was particularly well endowed with engineering plant, this seemed to Lloyd George sheer defeatism. Kitchener, though not himself as narrow-minded as his staff, lacked the administrative skills to get to grips with the problem and see that his instructions were implemented. As a result, the Shells

Committee began to usurp his power by increasing the orders for field guns and bringing forward delivery dates. By May it had introduced no fewer than 2,500 new firms to the War Office list of suppliers; and from March, when Lloyd George introduced the Defence of the Realm Act, the Government had the power to commandeer factories and workshops for war production. In response to these leaps forward Kitchener sulked and stopped attending meetings of the Shells Committee, thereby delaying the implementation of its plans. Though unwilling to antagonise him, Asquith imposed a new 'Treasury Committee' with powers to place contracts independently of the War Office, which served to bring the clash between Kitchener and Lloyd George to a head. In April the Prime Minister resolved the dispute by giving the committee, under Lloyd George's chairmanship, full authority to organise the supply of munitions. Though still handicapped by the tendency of the War Office to withhold information, the committee provided Lloyd George with invaluable experience which he used subsequently as Minister of Munitions.

Kitchener's prickly reaction also derives from his simultaneous but unsuccessful attempt to stop both Lloyd George and Churchill trenching upon military strategy. By the beginning of 1915 it was clear that in the spring Britain would be able to deploy at least half a million fresh troops. In a memorandum of 31 December Lloyd George had urged Asquith to summon the War Council to consider where the new force might most effectively be employed: 'if this superb army is thrown away upon futile enterprises such as those we have witnessed during the last few weeks, the country will be uncontrollably indignant at the lack of prevision and intelligence shown in our plans'.[10] His assumption that further frontal assaults in France and Belgium were calculated to win only insignificant pockets of land at exorbitant cost was fully shared by Churchill and Sir Maurice Hankey, the secretary of the Committee of Imperial Defence. They argued that Britain should capitalise upon the flexibility which her sea power gave her by striking where the enemy was vulnerable and by keeping her allies well supplied with armaments. Churchill became closely associated with the scheme for attacking Turkey by means of a naval assault at the Dardanelles which was expected to lead to the collapse of the Turkish Government, the mobilisation of the Balkan states, and closer co-operation with

Russia. Lloyd George also felt the attraction of this, partly because it offered the prospects of a dramatic victory and partly because of his natural aversion for the Turks. But the defeat of Turkey would not in itself do much to weaken Germany, and he was inclined to give priority to knocking out Austria. To this end he advocated landing an Allied force at Salonika or on the coast of Dalmatia which would serve to rally Serbians, Romanians, and Greeks against their common enemy. The attack would oblige Austria to withdraw troops from the North-east which would thus be more open to a Russian advance, while Italy would be strongly tempted to join the Allies with a view to sharing the spoils at Austria's expense. In this way, the most vulnerable flank of the Central Powers would be rolled up and Germany isolated.

Asquith's response was to allow these ideas to be discussed by the War Council, a body comprising the leading Liberal ministers and A. J. Balfour, as well as the naval and military authorities. The professionals argued with justice that the Germans remained dangerously close to Paris, so that any neglect of the Western Front could quickly result in an Allied defeat. Similarly, the admirals feared that any diversion of ships from the North Sea risked the defeat of Jellicoe which would open Britain to a German invasion. However, the amateur strategists got their way to a considerable extent, perhaps because the professionals had nothing very convincing or positive to offer; the effect of their arguments was not to stop the new initiatives so much as to deprive them of resources and to delay their implementation. Initially the War Council expected the Dardanelles campaign to be a naval one, and it agreed that if the situation on the Western Front had not changed by the spring it would be feasible to open up a new theatre of war as Lloyd George urged. During 1915, as it emerged that Serbia was in dire straits, both Asquith and Kitchener warmed to the idea of a landing at Salonika to keep her in the war. Kitchener, however, prevaricated over the dispatch of troops, and the decision to fight in the Balkans involved a resolve by the War Council to overrule Sir John French's objections. Unfortunately, troops were diverted to the Dardanelles to 'pull the chestnuts out of the fire for the Navy' as Lloyd George put it; and by the autumn of 1915, when the Salonika campaign eventually got under way, the Germans were ready to launch a massive attack on Serbia. Thus, for a variety of reasons, the initiative came too late and Lloyd George was left with the feeling that on strategy, as with munitions, he had diagnosed the problem correctly but been frustrated by lack of power.

In the midst of these debates over strategy the political composition of the Government had changed in ways which did appear to strengthen Lloyd George's influence. In August 1914 little serious consideration had been given to forming a national government with the other parties; indeed, the very thought of a coalition with the Tories had helped to keep the Cabinet fairly united. However, as Opposition figures such as Balfour and F. E. Smith were given an official role, in addition to Kitchener who was a known Unionist, the idea of all-party co-operation gained currency. Lloyd George himself made use of the advice of Austen Chamberlain and Lord St Aldwyn in Treasury committees. To him this was no more than an extension of the methods he had often used since coming to office in 1905, and there is no evidence that he was actively working for a formal coalition in 1915. Events, however, conspired to create the opportunity for one. The key lay in the dilemma facing the Conservative Party, several of whose leaders, including Lord Curzon and Walter Long, severely criticised Bonar Law for sticking to the party truce and failing to attack the Government. The emergence of several back-bench committees created an increasingly dangerous situation for Law within his own party.

In the middle of May the conjunction of two controversies, over the resignation of Fisher as First Sea Lord and the well-publicised complaint of Sir John French that his recent offensive had failed for lack of shells, placed Law under intolerable pressure. If he were to avoid launching an attack on the Government over Fisher and munitions as his back-benchers demanded, the only alternative was to smother their rebellion by entering a coalition government. However, Law, whose relations with Asquith had always been distant, could have no idea how responsive the Prime Minister would be to such an idea. Therefore his first action when he learnt of Fisher's resignation on 17 May was to visit Lloyd George at the Treasury where he felt sure of a friendly reception. The two men agreed that coalition was the best way out of the political dilemma and they proceeded at once to 11 Downing Street. Lloyd George then went, alone, to see the Prime Minister next door. Asquith had already thought out the options. Though he felt he could have defied the Conservative attack with his Liberal–Labour–Irish majority, he clearly contemplated a coalition as a more lasting solution. He therefore readily agreed to Lloyd George's suggestion that Bonar Law be summoned, and the three men settled the matter in 'less than a quarter of an hour' in Lloyd George's words. In his *War Memoirs* he made no attempt to deny his role as a go-between in the formation of the coalition, but equally he wanted it to be clear that he had not conspired for one or put pressure on Asquith. It seems to be true that though always favourably disposed to the idea, he simply took the opportunity when it came suddenly in May 1915. When Fisher resigned he reported at once to Frances Stevenson, but his *first* thought was evidently that Churchill would have to resign too![11] It was this rather than the possibility of a coalition that initially occupied his mind. Frances Stevenson's account also provides further explanation about the ability of Asquith, Bonar Law, and Lloyd George to reach agreement so quickly. It seems to have been understood that the creation of a coalition government would remove the need for Kitchener whom the politicians blamed for incompetence and for misleading them. Lloyd George, who had recently been struggling with Kitchener over his new munitions committee, felt particularly strongly on this. Subsequently Asquith changed his mind about Kitchener, seeing him as a valuable prop to his own position as Premier; and a violent attack upon the War Minister by Northcliffe in the *Daily Mail* on 21 May provoked a wave of sympathy which made it dangerous to attempt to sack him.

Thus the coalition proceeded with Kitchener still in place. Lloyd George was particularly torn over his role in the Government. It was essential that a new ministry should be created to keep Kitchener out of the munitions question; but Lloyd George could not decide whether to take the new post, remain at the Treasury, or to combine the two. Bonar Law, quite reasonably, claimed one of the major posts, but Lloyd George, not unpleased at seeing Churchill demoted to the Duchy of Lancaster, evidently had no wish to raise up another rival to himself as the second in rank in the Cabinet. He therefore co-operated with Asquith in confining Law to a relatively minor post at the Colonial Office, while he took over Munitions. His hesitation may have been partly due to personal circumstances as the Prime Minister's wife shrewdly saw: 'I *implore* you to make H. stand *firm* over Chan[cellor] of

Exch[equer]. You will then keep your house.'[12] In the event, though McKenna became Chancellor, Lloyd George did remain as the resident of Number 11 Downing Street on the basis that Munitions would only be a temporary job.

Though Lloyd George cannot be said to have engineered the coalition of 1915, it undoubtedly created the conditions in which his succession to the premiership became possible. Both Churchill and Asquith, who were seen as primarily responsible, bore the brunt of the criticism among Liberals. The coalition soon proved to be instrumental in disintegrating the Liberal Party itself, and also in breaking up its alliance with the Irish and with Labour. In addition, dissatisfaction remained acute within the Conservative ranks, where most leading figures regarded Bonar Law as no more than a stop-gap leader who was not fit to be pushed into the premiership should the opportunity arise. This all made for an unusually fluid situation in the parties, from which Lloyd George, with his versatility and instinct for bipartisanship, stood to profit. The coalition quickly gave him allies in Cabinet when he chose to take up issues which, hitherto, had only isolated him from his colleagues.

In view of his experience in dealing with businessmen and trade unions at the Board of Trade, Lloyd George was a natural candidate for the Ministry of Munitions. As a result of his involvement with the two Cabinet committees, he had already made a constructive impact on the munitions question, and had a good grasp of the problems on entering office. Yet he had taken a terrible risk; for he was exposed to the complaints of every failed general. French, for example, had assured Kitchener that he was amply supplied with munitions, only to instigate subsequently a press campaign attributing his failure at Festubert to a lack of explosives. In the mood of wartime the public instinctively sympathised with a general, however third-rate, rather than a politician. Perhaps partly for this reason Lloyd George contemplated only a three-month stint at Munitions, setting the system up, before returning to the safer waters of the Treasury or going on to the War Office itself.

Yet he spent just over a year in his new office. In some ways it was his happiest post of all, partly because it was a new ministry free of tradition, and also because he had a very well-defined problem to tackle. In this period his working day began at seven; at eight he breakfasted with visitors and colleagues, and from nine he worked in the ministry where he remained until eight in the evening. In retrospect Lloyd George exaggerated the size of the problem and the scale of his achievement somewhat; he liked to say that he had had to struggle as hard to get a carpet and some furniture for his new ministry as to obtain £50 million for extra munitions. It was undoubtedly necessary to assert himself. 'Delighted to hear you are coming to help me', wrote Kitchener, affecting to believe that the new ministry would be no more than a subdepartment of the War Office! Lloyd George immediately refused to have his assistants thrust upon him. He borrowed Llewelyn Smith from the Board of Trade, and appointed Dr Christopher Addison as his Parliamentary Secretary. And he began to absorb able men from the War Office; notably Lord Moulton of the explosives department. He also recruited a galaxy of businessmen including Eric Geddes, a dynamic Scots entrepreneur and manager of the North East Railway Company who had experience in the United States and India; for Lloyd George, Geddes proved to be the ideal type of administrator.

With his new team, Lloyd George proceeded to divide the country into ten areas each with a board of management; he himself held regular talks with the nine leading private manufacturers about ways of increasing output. By the end of 1915 some sixty national shell and explosives factories had been established with state finance, while others had been privately built with the assistance of government grants. The War Office continued to obstruct and to dispute orders. It was not until August that the Ministry of Munitions took over the four Royal Ordnance Factories and, with the Prime Minister's support, suspended the Royal Ordnance Board. Though the costs were high, Lloyd George achieved a huge increase in production. The monthly output of shells which had been 70,000 in May 1915, rose to over one million by July 1916 when he left his office; machine-gun production which averaged 6,000 during 1915, reached over 33,000 during 1916, and 80,000 during 1918. It was the most conspicuous single triumph by any politician throughout the war.

Although his year at Munitions greatly advanced Lloyd George's reputation as a war minister, in the long run it disrupted the entire course of his political career; for, by leading him into the problems of labour supply, alcoholic drink, and military conscription it drew him further away from his radical and Labour constituency towards the right. Increasing the supply of armaments inevitably meant squeezing the maximum out of the workforce and limiting the right of the men to change jobs. Under the new Munitions of War Act the voluntary provisions in the Treasury Agreement over the prohibition of strikes and compulsory arbitration were given statutory force, and workers involved in government contracts could not be employed elsewhere without obtaining a leaving certificate. When he addressed the Trades Union Congress (TUC) at Bristol in September 1915 Lloyd George found the union leaders co-operative as usual, but conscious that in the factories their authority had been undermined by shop stewards who capitalised on the grievances of artisans, resentful of the introduction of unskilled labour. Back in March a register had been opened for women willing to undertake industrial work, and in July Lloyd George had taken up Mrs Pankhurst's suggestion of holding a huge procession of women culminating in a deputation to the Government to press their services on the State. A year later there were 340,000 women working in munitions factories in jobs formerly held by men. It was in order to confront the hostility to dilution of skilled labour that Lloyd George made a notorious visit to Glasgow, a centre both of militancy and of engineering, at Christmas 1915. A local socialist newspaper commented:

> The best paid munitions worker in Britain, Mr Lloyd George (almost £100 a week), visited the Clyde last week in search of adventure. He got it.

Though accustomed to rough receptions from election crowds Lloyd George had not expected to be severely heckled and shouted down in Glasgow, and it is probably no accident that the strikers there were tackled with some firmness; David Kirkwood and nine other leaders were deported and the socialist press suppressed. Kirkwood himself felt that Lloyd George had succeeded in capturing the union leaders; his Glasgow meeting had been packed by the militants and largely boycotted by the union establishment. However, such experiences helped to drive a wedge between Lloyd George and the labour movement which, after the war, could never be completely removed.

His responsibility for munitions also stimulated his interest in curbing the consumption of alcohol. As early as February 1915 he had begun to denounce workers for losing time and efficiency through over-indulgence. 'We are fighting Germany, Austria and Drink', he declared melodramatically, 'and so far as I can see, the greatest of these deadly foes is Drink.' It was characteristic of Lloyd George that, once seized with the urgency of a specific problem, he was apt to be carried away by his own exuberance. He proposed to achieve prohibition by means of complete state purchase of the country's breweries and public houses, a scheme costing £250 million, which his startled colleagues turned down emphatically. To Asquith it underlined that he was 'totally devoid of either perspective or judgement'. Yet it seemed incumbent upon the Government to take some action. Thus they set up the Central Liquor Board to control the sale and transport of alcohol, shortened licensing hours, diluted the strength of the beer, and instituted a state take-over of the trade in certain key munitions areas. Shifting rapidly from the extremes of state control to traditional voluntaryism, Lloyd George succeeded in inveigling the King into setting an example for the country by announcing his pledge to abstain entirely from alcoholic drink until the end of the war. The politicians, usually keen to demonstrate their patriotism, signally failed to take the pledge; and even Lloyd George, though only a moderate drinker, found teetotalism a bridge too far. The effect of his crusade, therefore, was to leave 'His Majesty and his Household high and dry' for over three years. The fact is that Lloyd George's campaign against drink went right against the grain, especially in wartime. Although there had been a modest decline in consumption since the mid-1870s, it was still widely believed that a manual worker must imbibe alcohol at intervals throughout the day in order to maintain his strength; and periods in which money wages rose, such as the First World War, invariably stimulated consumption. Official statistics do show that total consumption fell during the war, and that convictions for drunkenness dropped by three-quarters. However, the absence of a large proportion of the nation's heavy drinkers is doubtless the chief explanation.

.   .   .

MILITARY CONSCRIPTION

The ultimate solution to the shortage of munitions seemed to lie in the manpower available. Lloyd George had noticed early in the war how many skilled men had been carried off to the army through the voluntary system of recruiting. And although the authorities had tried to protect the labour force by issuing special badges to those engaged in essential war work, this did not stop them enlisting. Lloyd George repeatedly pressed Kitchener for the return of key workers, and by October 1915 some 45,000 men who had not yet gone abroad were released. But this was not enough, and as the flow of volunteers dwindled during the autumn, the army became less co-operative. As a result Lloyd George had taken to advocating conscription by August 1915. This was a highly illiberal attitude. The Edwardians had taken great pride in repudiating 'Prussian' methods of raising an army, and even the Conservatives had avoided the idea of compulsory service in peacetime. In August 1914 Churchill had been alone in Cabinet in advocating compulsion. However, the coalition altered the balance of opinion at a time when pressure for more men was mounting. In September Lloyd George risked making his views public in the preface to a volume of war speeches, *Through Terror to Triumph*, and in October he began to meet privately with Churchill, Curzon, and Long in order to put pressure upon Asquith to adopt conscription. Asquith at first resisted by warning Kitchener that one of the objects of the conspirators was to oust him as an obstacle to conscription. However, Kitchener had additional reasons for retreating from his original support for voluntaryism; for the War Office was demanding more men than were now coming forward. Eventually Kitchener was persuaded to adopt the figure of 35,000 recruits a week which compared with the 55,000 who were recruited during the whole of December. Consequently, by the end of the year the opposition to conscription was reduced to a hard core of Liberals in the Cabinet, and Asquith capitulated for fear of breaking up his government. Single men were conscripted in January 1916 and married men in June.

For many on the Left this seemed morally outrageous. It marked the eclipse of their original hopes that the war could be run by Liberal means. Moreover, Lloyd George increasingly emerged as the catalyst in the flight from Liberal methods. Just before the outbreak of war C. P. Scott had sent him an ominous telegram from Manchester:

Feeling of intense exasperation among leading Liberals

here at prospect of Government embarking on war. No
man who is responsible can lead us again.

Though the threat was brushed aside easily enough in 1914, a
year later it was apparently a statement of the obvious. During
1915, and periodically throughout the war, Scott held
discussions with Lloyd George on issues like conscription,
hoping to persuade him to hold on to his radicalism and resist
the pressure to adopt illiberal policies: he always failed.
Conscription underlines more sharply than anything else how
Lloyd George's ability to get his way over specific issues tended
to weaken his wider political position. In fact, by 1916, success
had left him surprisingly isolated. His association with the
Tories over conscription attracted condemnation in the Liberal
press and was taken to presage some further conspiracy; leaks
about his 1910 scheme for a national government seemed to
prove the point. In government he had lost previous
collaborators like Churchill, Masterman, and Isaacs, and after
May 1915 he rapidly drifted apart from Asquith with whom
relations had been close. This was partly because at Munitions
he saw much less of the Prime Minister, and because the new
Chancellor, McKenna, a bitter enemy of Lloyd George, did his
best to turn Asquith against him. Not surprisingly, he relied
more than ever upon Frances Stevenson for unqualified
support and advice. Whenever they were apart, however briefly,
daily letters of love flew between them:

> I miss you so much although you have only been gone just
> a few hours . . . . I love you so dearly, my heart throbs with
> tenderness for you. You are all in all to me and I could not
> now even exist without you.

Of course, Lloyd George worked with several Conservatives,
but while willing to co-operate on specific issues they would
not as yet give him wider support. Though recognising his
talents as a war minister, they remained deeply distrustful of
him. Thus, however frequently Lloyd George spoke of
resignation, he knew it was an indulgence he simply could not
afford; a hasty resignation in 1915 or 1916 would probably have
cast him into political oblivion. Against this background, any
assumptions about the inevitability of his rise to the
premiership are grossly misconceived.

Far from plotting to seize the premiership, he characteristically concentrated his efforts on identifying the bottlenecks in the war effort, which suited Asquith perfectly. Only when his constructive drive was frustrated did he become a live threat to his leader. Indeed Asquith managed his new Cabinet in a highly skilful if essentially negative way. He played on Conservative rivalries by keeping Bonar Law in a minor office, yet created ill will between him and Lloyd George by offering the Tory leader his old job as Deputy Leader of the House. Meanwhile, Asquith had kept his allies like Grey and Kitchener in place, while elevating supporters like McKenna and Balfour. The more quarrelsome the Cabinet became, the more essential Asquith appeared to be as the calm centre of the storm.

As munitions gradually ceased to be a problem, Asquith continually found new jobs for Lloyd George to tackle. In April 1916 he attempted to send him on a visit to Russia, but, suspecting a ploy to get him out of the way, he declined to go. In May, however, he allowed himself to be persuaded to take on the intractable problem of Ireland, albeit temporarily. The Easter Rising and its bloody suppression was creating widespread support for Sinn Fein. Lloyd George's task was to find some settlement to check Nationalist disaffection before it seriously threatened the war effort. To general surprise, he managed to persuade Redmond and Carson to accept an immediate grant of Home Rule to the twenty-six Nationalist counties and the exclusion of the six Ulster counties. However, this was not intended as a final solution, and agreement seems to have been based upon contradictory impressions: the Nationalists expected Ulster to join the rest of Ireland after the war, while the Unionists believed it had been permanently excluded. In the event, several die-hard Tory ministers including Long and Lansdowne, refused to accept the compromise and after five weeks the Cabinet abandoned the plan. Since Lloyd George had apparently promised Redmond that he would resign if the Cabinet failed to back the deal, he was, again, dangerously exposed by the enterprise.

Then, on 6 June, a fresh crisis arose. He telephoned Frances Stevenson who was holidaying in Cornwall, asking her to return immediately to be with him, for HMS *Hampshire* had gone down off the Orkneys on its way to Russia with Kitchener on board. In choosing a new Secretary of State Asquith's first instinct was to continue his complicated game of elevating a

Conservative such as Austen Chamberlain over the head of Bonar Law. But rather than suffer this new humiliation Law insisted on appointing Lloyd George. In fact, the War Office was a gilded cage, as Lloyd George well knew, for Kitchener had been reduced to the role of recruitment officer and departmental administrator. Not only had he lost Munitions, but the appointment of Sir William Robertson as Chief of the Imperial General Staff (CIGS) in October 1915 had also robbed him of military strategy; Robertson enjoyed the sole right to advise the Cabinet on all questions of strategy. Thus Lloyd George told C. P. Scott he would not accept the War Office 'except on condition that it carried the full ordinary powers of the Secretary of State'.[13] He drafted two letters of refusal but failed to send them. After seven days of prevarication he accepted the post without any restoration of powers. Moreover, he was forced to take as his Under-Secretary a Tory, Lord Derby – a guarantee to the army that there would be no changes at the War Office. This capitulation underlines the weakness of his position in 1916. During his brief, unhappy reign as Secretary of State Lloyd George made no real challenge to military policy, as he had done so freely in 1914 and 1915, and found himself committed to the costly Somme campaign which dragged on from July to October. 'I am the butcher's boy who leads the animals to slaughter', he lamented. His most constructive achievement was to persuade Sir Douglas Haig to employ Eric Geddes to sort out his transport problems in France. But when he attempted the old trick of dispatching Robertson to Russia he got nowhere; Robertson threatened to resign, and Asquith backed him up. On 4 September Lloyd George paid a visit to the Western Front, which Haig dismissed contemptuously as a huge joy-ride involving 'breakfasts with newspapermen, and posings for the cinema shows'.[14] And when he questioned General Foch about the relative merits of the French and British generals he sowed the seeds of future clashes with Haig.

Yet in public Lloyd George gave the impression of someone united with the commanders in his determination to win the war. When the American President Woodrow Wilson increased the pressure for a negotiated peace he riposted with a famous interview with an American journalist in which he insisted: 'We must fight to a finish, to a knock-out blow.' Thus, by the autumn of 1916, as the Somme campaign petered out hopelessly, Lloyd George had nothing to look forward to except another year of the war of attrition for which he was responsible but over which he exercised no control.

. . .

THE FALL OF ASQUITH

This time, however, Asquith had been too clever. In boxing Lloyd George in at the War Office he drove him at last towards resignation by depriving him of the constructive outlet he needed. Since the Allies were patently not winning the war, his mind turned to new ways of organising the war machine at home with a view to bypassing the obstructionism of the War Office and the generals. Returning from a conference at Chantilly in November he discussed with Hankey the idea of a small executive Cabinet capable of imposing key decisions upon the departments, a proposal which Carson had advocated in 1915. The nearest Asquith had come to this was the War Council, subsequently renamed the Dardanelles Committee, and then the War Committee. Each body had grown larger and larger, and proceedings had become as slack and verbose as those of the Cabinet itself. The delay in appointing controllers to handle the mounting crises over food and merchant shipping led Lloyd George to push hard for a new executive body to introduce some efficiency into the war machine.

At first the only politician keen to co-operate with him was Carson who had resigned from the Government in 1915. Carson's value lay in his capacity to frighten Bonar Law by organising a revolt among discontented back-bench Tories. To avert a party split Law was prepared to bring Carson back into office and thus to join the discussions about a new War Cabinet. However, though unhappy about the conduct of the war, Law was loath to conspire against Asquith and he therefore informed him about the discussions. By 25 November the three had drawn up a document specifying a four-man body, free of departmental duties which would meet daily and enjoy executive powers. Though Asquith might be the nominal President of such a body, Lloyd George would preside as chairman. Asquith equivocated and then turned the proposal down. Bonar Law soon had to face a rather critical meeting with his Conservative colleagues who rather resented the attempt to rearrange the Government over their heads for the benefit of Lloyd George and Carson. At this point, then, any hasty resignation by Lloyd George would merely have left him isolated with one or two mavericks like Carson and Churchill for company. However, he rewrote the proposal in a memorandum of 1 December which still excluded the Prime Minister from the new War Cabinet but emphasised that he could refer any of its decisions to the full Cabinet. To this Asquith replied at length, accepting the case for a new executive, but dissenting over the exclusion of the Prime Minister and the inclusion of Carson.

What interpretation should be placed on these manœuvres? Asquith's approach was essentially conciliatory, and he almost certainly expected a compromise to emerge in due course, subject to some jostling over personnel. Burdened with all the duties of the premiership in the Commons and in Whitehall, he could not expect to be a regular attender at the kind of body Lloyd George had proposed, and it was necessary only to find a formula that would save his dignity. Ultimately, no War Cabinet would be able to take controversial decisions without the approval of the full Cabinet, and its members might well take the blame if things continued to go wrong. This is almost certainly how Bonar Law and Lloyd George envisaged the new system. Though both were highly critical of Asquith's lackadaisical methods of running the war, neither wanted to displace him as *Prime Minister*. He remained a vital political figurehead under whose leadership controversial measures like conscription could be introduced without dividing either the country or the politicians.

Yet they still desired greater efficiency and speed in decision-making, and so they maintained the pressure. On 2 December Lloyd George composed a letter of resignation, making sure that news of his determination would be carried promptly to Asquith by Edwin Montagu. Then, on 3 December, Asquith had a visit from Bonar Law, who had had another awkward meeting with his own colleagues. He reported that the Conservative ministers had reached the conclusion that something more than an internal reorganisation of the Government was now necessary and that the Prime Minister and all his colleagues should tender their resignations. Although this decision had been incorporated in a written resolution which Law had in his pocket, he failed to show it to Asquith. It seems certain that he conveyed to Asquith a much more hostile impression than his colleagues actually intended. This may have been deliberate because Law was losing patience with Asquith's prevarication, and he resented the way in which the other Conservatives kept reining him in. Whether accidental or deliberate, the failure to let the Prime Minister see the resolution had a dramatic effect. If Asquith were losing the support of the Conservatives he had to back down; he thereupon summoned Lloyd George and the two men rapidly reached an agreement. While Asquith would not be chairman of the War Cabinet, he could attend whenever he wished, veto its conclusions, direct it to particular topics, receive the agenda, and see Lloyd George daily for a report.

Lloyd George, who essentially wanted a workable arrangement, not a disruption of the Government, seemed satisfied, and the whole affair ought to have ended there. However, the next day the Prime Minister began to change his mind. His excuse for this was an article in *The Times* which reported the proposals in detail and in terms that were unflattering to him. The leak, which Asquith attributed, not unreasonably, to Lloyd George, gave him a pretext for pulling out of the agreement. In fact it seems that Lloyd George only told Carson who informed the editor of *The Times*. However, the reason for Asquith's behaviour was that by Monday 4 December he believed his position to be much stronger than it had appeared on Sunday. Communications from several Conservatives corrected the impression given by Law by emphasising that their object had been to *strengthen* Asquith and expose Lloyd George's weakness; for if Asquith resigned and the Conservatives declined to serve under Lloyd George (and by implication Law too), then he would fail to form an administration and Asquith would be reinstalled to form a new government. A dismayed Lloyd George was told by Max Aitken that this was indeed the mood of the Tory meeting.[15] Asquith also had meetings with Liberal colleagues including Grey, McKenna, and Runciman, all resentful towards Lloyd George, who urged him to defy the plotters. It is easy to see why Asquith so readily accepted this vision of support on all sides; like most prime ministers he had come to believe in his own indispensability. He therefore boldly adopted the course suggested to him by going to Buckingham Palace to submit the ministers' resignations and gain royal approval for a reconstruction of his government. In a second letter to Lloyd George he repudiated the compromise reached on Sunday. His bluff having been called, Lloyd George responded with a letter of resignation clearly designed for publication: 'I am convinced that it is my duty to leave the Government in order to inform the people of the real condition of affairs.'

What saved Lloyd George at this point was simply the failure of the Conservative ministers to remain loyal to Asquith. There are three explanations for their behaviour. In the first place they were not wholly enthusiastic about either Asquith or Lloyd George or Bonar Law as Prime Minister; but they hoped to use their influence to maintain Asquith while instituting a more efficient approach to the war. It proved very difficult to achieve *both* of these aims. After Lloyd George had resigned there was a danger that Asquith would simply drift back into the old methods. Secondly, once Law made it clear that he would back Lloyd George if Asquith reneged on the compromise, the other Conservatives found themselves in an embarrassing position; the party would have found their determination to back Asquith bizarre. Thirdly, personal ambition inevitably entered into the question. A reorganisation of the Cabinet made all ministers nervous; and even Curzon, who had professed his contempt for Lloyd George, swiftly grabbed the chance of serving under him when it was offered. Asquith had miscalculated in relying heavily on the languid Balfour, who believed that Lloyd George should be given the opportunity to galvanise the war effort, while confining energetic figures like Curzon to peripheral, non-executive posts.

In spite of this, Lloyd George's accession to the premiership could have been blocked by Asquith. For the King adopted the proper course by initially inviting Law, who after all was the leader of the largest single party in the Commons, to form a government. However, the Government really needed a majority which required a new coalition, and this would materialise only if Asquith agreed to serve under Law. In fact Asquith declined to serve under anyone! Consequently Law rapidly gave up his half-hearted attempt, and on 6 December Lloyd George was at last invited to try. His Conservative support was by now clear, but Liberal and Labour attitudes remained doubtful. The existing Liberal ministers followed Asquith into opposition; Churchill, the only prominent Liberal willing to join, was unacceptable to the Tories. And so

Lloyd George made do with minor figures, one of whom, Addison, performed an invaluable function by organising a canvass of the Liberal MPs. This showed that 49 gave Lloyd George unqualified backing, while a further 126 would give support if he formed a government – a sign in effect of disillusionment with Asquith on the part of a majority of Liberal Members.

On 7 December Lloyd George held a formal meeting with the Labour Party's National Executive Committee. 'He was like a bit of mercury,' said Ramsay MacDonald, 'when you thought you had caught him on one point he darted off to something else.' But at this stage MacDonald was an embittered and peripheral figure; most Labour politicians felt inclined to take advantage of whatever opportunities presented themselves. In a virtuoso performance Lloyd George admitted that the war was being lost and could not be won without the backing of organised labour. He offered Labour a post in the new War Cabinet and two new ministries – Pensions and Labour. On an 18-11 vote Labour's leaders decided to accept his offer. Thus, at 7.30 that evening, Lloyd George was able to tell the King that he could form a broadly based administration capable of uniting the country against the threats which now made an Allied defeat seem a real possibility.

. . .

NOTES AND REFERENCES

1. Esher's Diary 23/7/08, quoted in Viscount Esher 1934 *Journals and Letters,* vol. II. Nicolson & Watson, pp. 329-30

2. W Tyrrell to Sir F Bertie 3/4/08, quoted in Fry M G 1977 *Lloyd George and Foreign Policy,* vol. I. McGill-Queen's University Press, p. 82

3. Esher's Diary 12/2/09, quoted in Esher 1934, p. 370

4. C P Scott's Diary 22/7/11, quoted in Wilson T (ed.) 1970 *The Political Diaries of C P Scott 1911-28.* Collins, p. 48

5. C P Scott's Diary 6/2/14, quoted in Wilson T (ed.) 1970, p. 80

6. C P Scott's Diary 27/7/14, quoted in Wilson T (ed.) 1970, pp. 91-2

7. Stevenson F 1967 *The Years That Are Past.* Hutchinson, pp. 73-4

8. Riddell's Diary 2/8/14, quoted in Lord Riddell 1933 *War Diary*. Nicholson & Watson, pp. 4-5

9. D Lloyd George to Margaret 11/8/14, quoted in Morgan K O (ed.) 1973 *Lloyd George: family letters 1885-1936*. University of Wales Press, p. 169

10. D Lloyd George Memorandum, 31/12/14, quoted in Gilbert M (ed.) 1972 *Winston S. Churchill*, vol. III *1914-16*, Companion vol. I. Heinemann, p. 350

11. Taylor A J P (ed.) 1971 *Lloyd George: a diary by Frances Stevenson*. Hutchinson, p. 50

12. Margot Asquith to D Lloyd George, undated, Lloyd George papers C/6/12/16

13. C P Scott's Diary 13-17/6/16, quoted in Wilson (ed.) 1970, p. 218

14. Sir D Haig to Lady Haig 13/9/16, quoted in Blake R (ed.) 1952 *The Private Papers of Douglas Haig 1914-19*. Eyre & Spottiswoode, p. 166

15. Stevenson's Diary 4/12/16, quoted in Taylor A J P (ed.) 1971, pp. 131-2; Vincent J R (ed.) 1986 *The Crawford Papers*. Manchester University Press, pp. 372-4

Chapter 5

THE GOVERNMENT OF NATIONAL EFFICIENCY 1916–1918

Critics and admirers alike considered that the system of government instituted by Lloyd George in December 1916 represented a watershed in British constitutional history. To some he was the Man Who Won the War, to others simply a dictator. Both saw in the concatenation of a national crisis and an unorthodox premier the origins of a revolution in government: Cabinet government gave way to prime ministerial rule; Parliament's role diminished, never to recover; even political parties lost their centrality in a government whose only guiding principle was national efficiency.

Yet to some extent the impression of Lloyd George as a dominating war leader is superficial exaggeration, the inevitable result of the excessive publicity he received, indeed cultivated, from the press; reputation is a poor guide to the realities of administration. Nor were Lloyd George's methods always novel ones; he is often credited with techniques which were practised regularly, if discreetly, by his predecessors. And although national efficiency was undoubtedly the ideal embedded within the centre of the new system by Lord Milner, the practice fell far short: 'we have not, after all, completely sloughed off the party skin', as Milner put it. In assessing Lloyd George's system two criteria should be kept in mind: first how efficient was his administration as a war machine; and second how powerful was he himself within the system? Like most prime ministers he had the power to survive and he exercised power to manipulate personnel; but he found his power to make innovations in policy far less tangible.

At the apex of the new system stood the five-man War Cabinet. It differed significantly from the scheme presented to Asquith in that Lloyd George presided over it, despite being

Prime Minister. However, his duties as Leader of the Commons were performed by Bonar Law, appropriately enough since the Conservatives provided the majority of the Government's support. As Chancellor, War Cabinet member, Leader of the House, and Conservative Leader, Law was overworked. However, none of the other War Cabinet members held departmental responsibilities. The deliberate exclusion of the heads of the Admiralty and the War Office reflected the belief that departmental obstructionism had to be overruled. However, the new system made little impact upon this particular problem. This was partly because Lloyd George chose the wrong individuals to preside over the Admiralty and War Office, and also because of the wide political support which the military professionals commanded.

The other War Cabinet members were Milner, Arthur Henderson, and Lord Curzon. This curious team had more to do with politics than with efficiency. While Law was essential as the leader of the party on which Lloyd George relied for his majority, Curzon was almost equally indispensable as a dangerous alternative leader to Law; however his huge appetite for work, so far unsatisfied in the war, made him an impressive choice. Lloyd George had never had a high opinion of Henderson, but as chairman of the Labour MPs and a reassuring figure among trade-unionists he symbolised the loyalty of the workers to the cause of victory. The most surprising choice was Milner who, in effect, displaced Carson. He and Lloyd George had been opponents in the Boer War and had only met twice. However, they were both Chamberlainites, the chief difference being that Milner had advanced much further down the Chamberlainite road. Having begun life as a rather authoritarian Liberal, Milner had become an apostle of imperial development, a cause which he combined with advocacy of state-sponsored social welfare. Thus Lloyd George could claim to Lord Riddell, 'Milner and I stand for much the same things.' Moreover, Milner had discerned in the patriotic conduct of the working class during wartime the possibility of a new movement which would harness British labour to the cause of empire, protectionism, and social reform. To this end he established the British Workers' League. This explains why Lloyd George found him a more valuable ally than Carson who represented only the dead-end of Ulster Unionism. In Milner's political vision he perceived a route which he himself might take out of the current political confusion. More immediately, Milner provided a further guarantee to the Tory right wing of the Government's determination to win the war whatever the cost; and as a ruthless schemer he was much safer inside the administration than outside it.

At first the War Cabinet met almost daily with a view to making the key decisions affecting the war effort, thereby effectively superseding the old Cabinet. It was serviced by the Cabinet Secretariat under Sir Maurice Hankey and four assistant secretaries, Thomas Jones, L. S. Amery, Clement Jones, and Mark Sykes. This originated with the Committee of Imperial Defence in 1902, but had been attached to the War Council and its successors since 1914. Under Hankey the functions of the Cabinet Secretariat were formalised: preparation of agendas, recording of minutes, circulation of decisions reached to the departments for action, arrangements for the attendance of ministers and advisers who were not War Cabinet members for certain items, and distribution of memoranda from the departments. Though this sounds unremarkable, the system did represent a major innovation and a gain in efficiency, for traditionally British Cabinets functioned entirely without the aid of minutes; and it was therefore not uncommon for ministers to be uncertain as to what decisions, if any, had been reached! The only formal record of Cabinet meetings was the weekly letter, usually scanty and inadequate, written by the Prime Minister for the King – a practice which Lloyd George abandoned as a waste of time!

However, the machine of government was only as good as the individuals who operated it. From his unique position at the elbow of the Prime Minister, Hankey gives a shrewd picture of the working of the new system. In his view, Lloyd George, far from being reluctant to attend to his papers, proved to be 'an omnivorous reader'. His practice was to wake up early and plough into the pile of official papers which were placed by his bedside, so that by breakfast he had mastered the contents and skimmed through much of the London and provincial press. Hankey confirms earlier ministerial experience in emphasising that the Prime Minister's supreme virtue lay in a capacity to obtain and use good advice; he built up his knowledge primarily by:

sucking the brains of the best men he could get on every

subject. This was a continuous process. At breakfast, lunch, dinner and between meals, whenever opportunity offered, Lloyd George was engaged in picking up knowledge from every sort and kind of person.[1]

This was a more remarkable habit than might be supposed; for unlike most major politicians, who grow narrower and more rigid in office, Lloyd George retained a good deal of his native tolerance. 'One can speak one's mind fearlessly', wrote Hankey, 'and, even if he is annoyed at the time, he bears no malice.' As a result of this confidence on the part of his colleagues, it seems not unreasonable to suggest that the *quality* of advice received by Lloyd George was probably superior to that of most prime ministers. His informality no doubt helped the flow of ideas, though it took time to get used to. As always, Lloyd George tended to mix business and pleasure in a way that was unsettling to more rigid minds. A dinner, for example, would suddenly take a serious turn as the conversation veered round to matters of political importance; Lloyd George would instantly summon officials or ministers, and before long Hankey or another secretary would find himself having to eat and take notes of the discussion. Lloyd George had never recognised a sharp line between social life and politics; when on the golf-course, as he frequently was, he always considered himself to be working if accompanied by an official or politician. This capacity to relax and enjoy himself undoubtedly helped him to bear up under the strain of his awesome responsibilities during 1917 and 1918.

Hankey's praise for Lloyd George gains plausibility from the fact that he was perfectly alive to the defects of the new Premier and his system. For example, he appreciated that the War Cabinet was, in practice, rarely as small as it was supposed to be. Balfour enjoyed the option of attending whenever he wished; and in 1917 Smuts and Carson were added. Sometimes as many as twenty non-members were invited to a meeting, thus reducing the proceedings to a 'beargarden' as one member put it. Even small meetings often degenerated into long rambling discussions as under Asquith, the chief difference being that Lloyd George now did much more of the talking! Consequently, by March 1917 Hankey had begun to complain that the business had become 'dreadfully congested – far worse than it ever was under the so-called 'Wait and See'

Government'. The weakness, as Hankey saw it, lay in the Prime Minister's unsystematic approach to work. All too often a carefully prepared agenda would be brushed aside as Lloyd George bounced in anxious to expatiate about his latest idea. As a result ministers and experts were kept waiting for hours for specific items, only to be sent away without being called. On occasions when Lloyd George felt too ill to attend, his colleagues felt they got through far more business. Another flaw lay in his habit of refusing to put his signature to the minutes, ostensibly on the grounds that they were misleading. This prevarication checked the transmission of decisions to the departments, though Hankey was allowed to circulate them, except where really major issues were involved.

A small Cabinet had to guard against the danger of becoming isolated from the information and practical expertise in the departments. Indeed Lloyd George's own experience, especially at the War Office, had made him sensitive to the capacity for obstructionism among the bureaucrats. He therefore determined to circumvent them by providing himself with an independent source of advice and information in the shape of a personal secretariat, known derisively as the 'Garden Suburb' because it occupied huts in the garden of 10 Downing Street. It comprised Professor W. G. S. Adams, Joseph Davies, Philip Kerr, Waldorf Astor, Lionel Curtis, and David Davies (later replaced by Cecil Harmsworth). Since several of these men were right-wing disciples of Milner they attracted criticism from Liberals such as H. W. Massingham who characterised them as 'a little body of illuminati, whose ... business [is] to cultivate the Prime Minister's mind ... and whose spiritual home is fixed somewhere between Balliol and Heidelberg'.[2] In addition to the personal secretariat, Lloyd George continued to enjoy the assistance of three private secretaries, Frances Stevenson, J. T. Davies, and Sir William Sutherland.

Beyond the War Cabinet and the secretariat stretched the vast apparatus of the ministerial departments. Lloyd George not only multiplied the number of posts to meet the special problems generated by the war, he also bypassed the regular party politicians by appointing a number of specialists and businessmen. This was the essence of national efficiency. However, the claims of the three parties could not be ignored. The commanding heights fell entirely to Conservatives, though this in part reflected Lloyd George's inability to find enough

Liberals of the first rank. He wanted to include Herbert Samuel and Edwin Montagu, who both refused, and also Churchill whom the Tories vetoed, which left him with relatively minor figures such as Dr Addison, Lord Rhondda, Sir Gordon Hewart, and Robert Munro. Two Labour MPs were also appointed, George Barnes (Pensions) and John Hodge (Labour).

The new ministries were Shipping, Food, National Service, Pensions, Labour, Air, and, later, Reconstruction. Disdaining the traditional amateur politician, Lloyd George deliberately gathered a phalanx of successful entrepreneurs and managers, notably Sir Joseph Maclay (Shipping), Lord Devonport (Food), Sir Albert Stanley (Trade), Eric Geddes (Admiralty), Lord Cowdray (Air), Lord Rhondda (Local Government and, later, Food), and Neville Chamberlain and Auckland Geddes who were successively responsible for National Service. Other experts brought their specialist knowledge or skills to bear: the historian and Vice-Chancellor H. A. L. Fisher (Education), the press barons Beaverbrook (Information) and Northcliffe (Director of Propaganda in Enemy Countries), and the patriotic trade-unionist John Hodge (Labour). 'Each department has been handed over to the "interest" with which it is concerned', commented Beatrice Webb, 'in this way, our little Welsh attorney thinks, you combine the least of political opposition with the maximum technical knowledge.' While some of these men proved their ability, notably Eric Geddes, Maclay, and Fisher, others such as Devonport, Chamberlain and Stanley were failures. However, the advantage of such novel appointments lay in the fact that they were largely Lloyd George's creatures and could be dismissed more easily than party politicians if their performance fell short.

. . .

FOOD AND THE SHIPPING CRISIS

During 1917 the central dilemma facing the new Government lay in four closely connected problems: merchant shipping, food supplies, manpower, and labour relations; failure in any one of these exacerbated the difficulties posed by the others. By late 1916 Germany had decided to extend submarine attacks on merchant shipping so as to sink 600,000 tons each month, deter neutrals from supplying Britain, and thus starve the British into submission. During April 1917 some 545,000 tons of British shipping was lost as a result. To meet this threat a twofold approach was adopted: the losses must be made good by more rapid building of replacements, and ways must be found to reduce the sinkings. Maclay managed to speed up construction by using a standard pattern, reduced the time spent unloading in port, and armed the merchant vessels. Even so, in May Lloyd George felt it necessary to impose another tier of administration in the shape of Eric Geddes as 'Controller of the Navy' who co-ordinated the competing claims of Maclay and the Admiralty for steel, skilled labour, and shipyards.

Meanwhile the Admiralty was managing to sink German U-boats at the rate of only one or two a month. Hankey urged the adoption of a convoy system, but the admirals feared that vessels would be even more vulnerable in large convoys and argued that they could not spare the ships to protect them. Carson, an unimaginative and uncooperative choice as First Lord, blindly backed up his admirals: 'They will not be interfered with by me and I will not let anyone interfere with them.' Lloyd George hesitated to antagonise Carson who was prone to resignation and capable of causing immense trouble in the Tory ranks. The situation exposed the limitations of the War Cabinet system: policy was not simply an abstract question of efficiency, but a matter of political clout. Eventually the Prime Minister held one of his famous breakfasts with Carson and the First Sea Lord, Admiral Jellicoe, to discuss convoys, and according to accepted myth, later descended upon the Admiralty in person to enforce the introduction of the new system. In fact his visit in late April was by prior agreement, and the admirals, having seen a successful experiment in carrying coal across the Channel by convoy, had already agreed to give it a wider trial. None the less his pressure was required to galvanise the hidebound professionals.

Lloyd George also wanted the navy to adopt a more belligerent role by attacking the German base at Heligoland. But after the Battle of Jutland both sides had become reluctant to take risks, and in Jellicoe caution verged on defeatism in Lloyd George's opinion. Again it proved difficult to separate Jellicoe from Carson; and the classic solution was found by promoting the latter to the War Cabinet and replacing him in July with Eric Geddes. With the extension of the convoy system shipping losses fell to 154,000 in November 1917. However,

Geddes still felt frustrated by Jellicoe's obstructionism, and in December Lloyd George finally sacked the Admiral, upon which Carson quit the War Cabinet. On balance the Government had scored a success by checking the shipping losses and maintaining the blockade of Germany; but it was achieved at the cost of some dangerous manipulation of personnel. Fortunately for Lloyd George the lacklustre performance of the navy during the war had robbed it of the prestige and influence enjoyed by the army and its leaders.

Shipping was vital because of Britain's dependence upon imported food without which, it was feared, the industrial workforce would grow weak and succumb to strikes. Who better to organise the supply of the nation's food than Lord Devonport the proprieter of a chain of food stores? However, Devonport proved a very tentative minister. He experimented inconclusively with meatless days and voluntary rationing, but hesitated to move further towards state enterprise. In June 1917 he was replaced by Rhondda under whom state subsidies were provided for basic food items like bread and potatoes. By the end of the war 90 per cent of food items were subject to maximum prices. The appearance of food queues early in 1918 paved the way for compulsory rationing which was much appreciated by the working class. On the output side the chief weapon was the Corn Production Act under which farmers were directed to meet specific targets by the County Agricultural Committees, backed by a threat to take over the land of those who failed to co-operate. In June the War Cabinet decided to stop the army taking any more men from agriculture and even secured the temporary release of 5,000 men for harvesting. Overall, both the production and the distribution of food supplies proved to be another success. It is now clear that although the composition of the British diet changed during wartime, the standard of nourishment did not deteriorate.[3]

· · ·

MANPOWER AND INDUSTRIAL RELATIONS

Food and shipping were but two aspects of the central dilemma about how to dispose of scarce manpower resources during the war. Logically the adoption of military conscription in 1916 should have led to *industrial* conscription; but all wartime governments feared the resistance of organised labour to this step. Consequently the tension between the insatiable demands of the army and the need to maintain the level of industrial output grew all the more severe. To grasp this nettle, Lloyd George appointed Neville Chamberlain, the younger brother of Austen and son of Joseph; but this was one gamble that did not come off. Though the idea of a minister for National Service had gained currency in the last days of the Asquith coalition, the new office was established hurriedly without clarification of the terms of reference. Although Lloyd George gave the impression that the proposal had been carefully thought out, he really expected the minister to improvise speedily as he had done at Munitions. He was consequently disappointed to find at a War Cabinet meeting on 12 January that Chamberlain had not yet produced a detailed scheme for manpower. In principle Chamberlain planned to recruit volunteer workers with the help of local authorities and then release them to industries and departments in need. In practice he found himself caught between the established ministries – Munitions, the War Office, the Admiralty, Agriculture, the Home Office – all fighting to retain their labour and trench upon that of others. Completely untried in this kind of situation, Chamberlain admitted to being bewildered. He protested that the War Cabinet failed to back him up when departments appealed over his head for extra men, and by August 1917 he had been driven to resignation. His successor, Auckland Geddes, produced a manpower budget in October which set an absolute limit of 450,000 additional men for the army in 1918. Although further troops could be drawn from the 350,000 recovering from wounds this still left the army far short of the 1.2 million the generals were demanding. The War Cabinet did agree to extend the age limit for conscripts from 41 to 51 and to review all exemptions from service, but Geddes largely succeeded in checking the drain of manpower from heavy industry and the land. He insisted that the country had reached the practical limits of its military effort, given the need to avoid enfeebling war production. This left Lloyd George dangerously exposed to the charge of undermining the army's capacity to resist the German offensive in the spring of 1918, but he was determined to take the risk.

Behind each of these problems stood the wider question of the British working man and his attitude to the war. Conscription had become necessary in part because the pool of men willing to fight had begun to dry up. Many preferred to remain at home to take advantage of overtime and higher wages, but they resented official interference with their right to change jobs. This is reflected in the wartime strike pattern. During 1915 and 1916 the number of stoppages fell sharply, but Lloyd George's accession to the premiership coincided with the reversal of this trend. In 1917 the number of working days lost through strikes doubled, and it doubled again in 1918.

Although the Government enjoyed extensive legal powers to direct labour under the Munitions of War Act, it hesitated to use them too freely, preferring to rely upon the co-operation and patriotism of the union leaders. They, however, were undermined in some areas by the emergence of shop stewards. Thus proposals to extend the dilution of skilled labour into private work provoked a rash of strikes among engineers in May 1917; and the plan was abandoned. Again conflict ensued when it was proposed to drop the trade card scheme which allowed key workers exemption from army service. After threatening to prosecute the strike leaders, the authorities backed down. Their hesitancy may be attributed to a fear that pacifist groups and other organisations such as the Rank and File Movement might lure dissatisfied workers into a general strike. In the excitement generated by the overthrow of tsardom in Russia in March 1917 such expectations gained credibility. And although British workers remained, on the whole, oblivious to ideological considerations, the Government could not feel confident that a few leaders would not be able to capitalise on the material grievances of the men as happened on Clydeside.

The efforts of Henderson, Hodge, and Addison, the ministers most directly involved, to maintain the co-operation of labour enjoyed no more than a limited success. In the atmosphere of crisis prevailing in 1917 Lloyd George failed to grasp the significance of the groundswell of self-confidence in the British labour movement. He thought he had done enough by entrenching the political leaders of labour in his government at the highest level. But he should have been warned by the behaviour of Henderson, an archetypal moderate, who was driven to resign from the War Cabinet in August 1917. His departure arose out of the proposal for a peace conference at Stockholm involving socialists from all the warring states. Initially the Cabinet accepted the idea of some British representation. However, after visiting Russia in the summer, Henderson became much more convinced about the need for both Russian and British delegates to go to Stockholm to counter the influence of the extreme left among the working class. When he returned, however, the War Cabinet had shifted its ground. It now argued that the Russian regime opposed the conference because to raise hopes of peace would be to destroy Russia's will to fight; this threatened to bring about a collapse of the Eastern Front. Greatly to Lloyd George's irritation, Henderson refused to put this view to the Labour Party Conference which voted in favour of representation at Stockholm. Consequently, on 1 August he and his colleagues kept Henderson waiting outside the Cabinet room for an hour while they discussed his conduct. Despite being thus rebuked, Henderson did not resign until 11 August. At the time Lloyd George clearly misunderstood the significance of the affair. Placing little value on Henderson, he believed he could safely humiliate him; another mediocrity was found in the shape of Barnes to fill Labour's place in the Cabinet. But Henderson's departure helped to reunify the patriotic and pacifist wings of the Labour Party; it led to a final break with the Liberals and set Labour's sights on becoming a governing party for the first time. In the post-war world Lloyd George was to be crippled by this development.

. . .

THE STRUGGLE OVER MILITARY STRATEGY

None the less, despite the frustrations and difficulties, the War Cabinet under Lloyd George achieved a great deal in its management of the war effort at home. Its major test lay in the military field where failure had already broken two administrations. It very nearly destroyed Lloyd George's too. He took over a month after the Somme campaign had finally ground to a halt with no gains of any strategic significance to justify the massive casualties. This seemed to him to underline that the war was being fought by the wrong methods and in the wrong place. Yet he had inherited the CIGS, Sir William Robertson, whose role was to advise the Cabinet on strategy. Robertson held stark and simple views: first, the chief theatre of war remained France and Flanders; second, the Allies could win here by a war of attrition since they enjoyed greater reserves than their opponents; third, the offensive must, therefore, be maintained during 1917. Though riddled with flaws,

Robertson's view could hardly be ignored. Paris did remain vulnerable to a German offensive. Moreover, Robertson reflected the attitude of the Commander-in-Chief, Sir Douglas Haig; to sack one would be to lose both, or so it seemed. Lloyd George had hoped to gain some influence by appointing a popular Tory, Lord Derby, to the War Office, calculating that a weak man would be more readily controlled by the War Cabinet. This proved to be a serious miscalculation. For Derby's weakness simply made him a willing prisoner of the generals. Thus any conflict between the War Cabinet and the military threatened to drive Derby to resignation along with the generals, and this was something the Conservative Party would not tolerate. As a result of this dilemma, the story of the next two years was the story of Lloyd George's devious and debilitating efforts to influence military strategy by roundabout means.

In January 1917 he advocated the transfer of troops to Salonika, reinforcements for the Russians, and the dispatch of heavy guns to the Italian Front. All of this was rejected by the military, backed up by Lord Northcliffe who threatened to use his newspapers to smash the Government if it overruled the generals. Robbed of a positive role, Lloyd George turned to a negative approach: how could he prevent another disastrous offensive on the Western Front in 1917? Experience suggested that, as with ministers, the best way of changing policy was to find new men. Unfortunately, Lloyd George never came across a British general with imagination or enterprise. But he liked the French generals immensely. One, General Nivelle, visited him in London and explained his ideas for recovering the advantage of a surprise attack. This involved using preliminary bombardments to mislead the enemy about the true direction of the offensive. Lloyd George was enchanted, particularly as Nivelle expressed himself in fluent English, an accomplishment of which Haig and Robertson seemed incapable. He therefore arranged with the French Premier, Briand, that at a conference at Calais in February the French would propose a new system of command involving the subordination of Haig to Nivelle for the forthcoming campaign. Though embarrassed, the French eventually presented the plan at Calais to the outrage and disbelief of Haig and Robertson. Lloyd George claimed that the proposal had the support of the War Cabinet, and according to Frances Stevenson's account, he warned Haig that refusal to accept it would lead one or other of them to resign. However, Hankey, who was present, insisted that Lloyd George had not received the full authority of the War Cabinet, and that the matter had been discussed in the absence of both Robertson and Derby.[4] In the event Lloyd George readily accepted a compromise formula which saved face for both parties. However, his relations with Haig never recovered from this episode.

Subsequently Nivelle's offensive failed to get off the ground, and as a result the French had stopped fighting by May, thus presenting Haig with the opportunity to initiate an offensive of his own. His plan was to try to turn the German's right flank in Belgium with a view to advancing up the coast. At the time this seemed compelling because of the Admiralty's insistence that it could not counter the submarine threat without depriving the Germans of their bases along the Channel. In addition, Haig argued that the mutinies in the French army made it imperative to draw pressure off them by a British offensive. Early in June the War Cabinet considered all this, but neither Lloyd George, Bonar Law, nor Milner felt persuaded that Haig was likely to do any better than he had in 1916. To them common sense suggested a holding operation until 1918 when the arrival of fresh American troops would give the Allies a better chance of success. Meanwhile the Italian Front offered a more promising chance of a breakthrough against the Austrians. Still casting around for alternative military advice, Lloyd George hit upon the figure of General Jan Smuts, one of the colonial premiers whom he had summoned to join the Imperial War Cabinet. Smuts was now placed on the War Cabinet itself in the hope that as a soldier he would strengthen the civilians in argument with the professionals. Alas, Smuts merely advised that Haig's plan had a good prospect of success. Thus, on 20 June the Cabinet reluctantly consented to the campaign, influenced primarily by the fear that refusal would provoke Haig and Robertson's resignations and a consequent revolt by Conservative back-benchers. In this way began the disastrous Passchendaele campaign.

Against this background Lloyd George felt distinctly insecure by the summer of 1917. As yet he had no tangible military successes to his credit and had entirely failed to get his way with the generals. His Liberal opponents understandably anticipated that his alliance with the Conservatives would disintegrate sooner or later, leading to Asquith's return to power. Such apprehensions help to explain why he took the risk of bringing Churchill into his government in July. At this point three crises were gathering around him: the conflict with Carson and Jellicoe, the dilemma over Haig's proposals, and the prospect of the emergence of a full-blooded parliamentary opposition led by Churchill. He could not expect to win all three challenges. By backing down over Haig's plans he at least deprived the Liberals of an opportunity to destroy his government in co-operation with the Tories. But he urgently desired to weaken the Asquithians by giving jobs to Churchill and Montagu. Since Lloyd George had already offered Churchill the Air Ministry, only to withdraw it, and then the Duchy of Lancaster, only to have it rejected, it seems clear that he felt desperate to hook his man. His appointment to Munitions duly provoked an outcry throughout the Conservative ranks; but the rumpus gradually subsided. 'I confess I am surprised', commented the lugubrious Bonar Law, 'that after six months during which nothing has gone particularly well in the war the unpopularity has not become greater than it is.'

In giving its approval to the Passchendaele offensive the War Cabinet had stipulated that it should be called off if its objectives were not being attained. By September the campaign appeared to be bogged down in the Flanders mud and on the 18th Bonar Law suggested to Lloyd George that the time had come to call a halt. Yet he did not feel strong enough politically to take the risk, and the fighting continued until November, producing 300,000 British casualties against under 200,000 German. Meanwhile Lloyd George pressed once more for the transfer of 300 guns to the Italian Front, but eventually backed down, saying to Hankey, 'I do not think this is the moment for a row with the soldiers.' Then in October the Italians suffered a major defeat at Caporetto which Lloyd George felt could have been prevented by proper co-ordination of the Allied war effort. As a result he became, in Hankey's words, 'restless and neurotic, unstable and rather infirm of purpose, neuralgic and irritable, exacting and difficult to please'.[5] His understandable sense of failure and of outrage at Haig for making 1917 merely a repetition of 1916 explains why, by the winter of 1917-18, he was determined to impose some check on the Commander-in-Chief. To this end he began to rely more upon General Sir Henry Wilson, Director of Military Operations (DMO). An inveterate schemer, Wilson gladly co-operated with Lloyd George's wish to find some means of bypassing the CIGS. They therefore took up the question of the central direction of the war, arguing, plausibly enough, that the resources and strategies of the four governments ought to be co-ordinated. Lloyd George felt that Passchendaele and the Italian rout after Caporetto proved the point conclusively. He was even emboldened to make a public attack on the Flanders campaign in November – a rare step for him. This provoked the predictable flurry of criticism in the press and coincided with Northcliffe's return from the United States. Lloyd George, anxious to deflect his anger, promptly offered him the Air Ministry, but without telling the incumbent, Lord Cowdray, who was outraged to learn in *The Times* that Northcliffe had declined to be gagged by the offer of his job! Cowdray thereupon resigned and Lord Rothermere, who was Northcliffe's brother and proprietor of the *Daily Mirror* and *Sunday Pictorial*, accepted the post. Such were the convoluted consequences of the Prime Minister's attempts to influence military policy! However, he won the support of the French for an inter-Allied war council, and at Rapallo in November the Italians added their agreement. On the new Supreme War Council (SWC), as it came to be called, the French were represented by Foch, the Italians by Cadorna, and Britain by Wilson. Here was one alternative source of military advice to that provided by Robertson.

Meanwhile Lloyd George brought into play his ultimate weapon in the struggle to check Haig – the withholding of troop reinforcements – an expedient capable of blowing up in his own face as the events of 1918 were to show. By the winter Haig's resources were already stretched. In September, before the establishment of the SWC, he had agreed to extend the British share of the line from 100 to 128 miles in order to relieve the French. After some prevarication, the extension was carried out at the beginning of 1918. Haig meanwhile had asked for 615,000 class A men for the new year, but the Cabinet's committee on manpower offered only half this number including only 100,000 class A men. On 7 January Haig blindly resorted to his usual argument that the Germans were too weak and demoralised to attempt an offensive, and he must therefore resume the attack upon them. However, a dispute between him and Marshal Pétain over the appropriate strategy for 1918 presented an opportunity to Wilson and Lloyd George. It was agreed with the French to wait and see what the Germans would actually do, and meanwhile to create an Inter-Allied Reserve Force of thirty divisions including nine British ones. This body would be under the control of a special executive on which the British representative would be Wilson. Viewing this as a serious setback, Robertson tried to insist that he should be the British representative. Lloyd George countered that he could not be in France and in London advising the Cabinet: he must choose one or the other. Robertson's refusal to choose was taken as a resignation, and Wilson took over as CIGS while Sir Henry Rawlinson went to Versailles.

Lloyd George fully appreciated that the loss of Robertson might bring his government down. Revelations appeared in the press giving a detailed account of the creation of the Reserve Force at the SWC. This was the work of the *Morning Post's* military correspondent Colonel Repington who had probably been briefed by General Sir Frederick Maurice, now DMO. The Government successfully prosecuted Repington and his newspaper under the Defence of the Realm Act. Somewhat surprisingly, Haig chose not to go with Robertson which saved Lloyd George from a worse crisis. Derby handed in his resignation as Secretary of State, but was persuaded to stay on for a while before being moved to Paris as ambassador. Northcliffe agreed to accept a new post as Director of Propaganda in Enemy Countries. Milner replaced Derby at the War Office, and Austen Chamberlain, who had become a dangerous back-bench critic, joined the War Cabinet. Thus by some frenetic exercise of prime ministerial patronage Lloyd George managed to score a victory over the military. However, the victory had little substance; for it made no practical difference to the war or to his influence. The Reserve Force was not set up simply because Haig refused to part with any of his divisions. Moreover, the rest of the war was about to be dominated by two things, first the arrival of American troops, and second, the new German offensive which Haig had pronounced impossible.

It was on 21 March that Ludendorff launched his massive attack on the Fifth Army. Haig's reserves were in the wrong place, and, as the Allies retreated, a wedge was driven between the British and French forces. 'I fear it means disaster', Lloyd George told Riddell, 'they have broken through, and the question is what there is behind to stop them.' The crisis at least led to the appointment of Foch as Commander-in-Chief of both the Allied armies; he stopped the retreat of the British to the Channel and the French to Paris, and as the German advance slowed down Lloyd George began to take heart. By the beginning of May, he was actually contemplating making Haig Commander-in-Chief of the Home Forces in place of Sir John French.

This plan was interrupted, however, when the military struck back at him on 7 May in the form of a letter to the press by General Maurice the former DMO. In this letter Maurice accused both Lloyd George and Bonar Law of misleading the House of Commons in answers they had given to questions about the situation on the Western Front. In particular the Prime Minister's statement on 9 April that the army in France was stronger on 1 January 1918 than on 1 January 1917, and Law's assertion that the extension of the British line had not been discussed by the Supreme War Council were fallacious. Maurice clearly intended to demonstrate how Lloyd George, not Haig, had been responsible for the current disasters by keeping the army short of men. When Asquith took up the allegations in the Commons Bonar Law unwisely offered to appoint an inquiry by two judges which, it is now clear, would probably have vindicated Maurice. But Asquith, equally unwisely, rejected this, insisting on a select committee of MPs. In this dire situation Lloyd George amply proved his capacity for survival by his daring and perception. Shrewdly disdaining inquiries of any sort he decided to treat the matter as a political challenge which he would rebut in the Commons. The Cabinet agreed to this after an assurance that the manpower figures he had given were correct. Asquith's motion for a select committee was simply treated as a vote of confidence.

After a legalistic Asquithian speech on the relative merits of judicial inquiries and select committees, Lloyd George tackled the substance of the charges. The decision to extend the British line, he said, had been taken *before* the establishment of the SWC; Maurice had not even been present at the SWC meetings at which he claimed the question had been discussed – as the minutes proved. As to troop numbers Lloyd George pointed out that his figures had been supplied by the department of the DMO – Maurice himself at the time! If there was any error it must be Maurice's. However, he insisted that the figures were correct and quoted a note by Maurice's deputy to that effect.

In fact, the truth was more complicated. The original War Office figures showed 1.25 million men for January 1917 against 1.29 million for 1918. Subsequently, however, it was discovered that the 1918 total included 86,000 men who were in Italy, which meant a reduction of 41,000 between 1917 and 1918. Also the figures for both years included some non-combatants. When the totals had been revised in the light of this it emerged that the full decline in numbers stood at 88,000.

It now seems certain that Lloyd George knew at least that corrections had been made before the Maurice Debate. However, the Opposition in the Commons had not been briefed by Maurice, perhaps because they wished to avoid a charge of having joined a military conspiracy against the Government. Consequently they made no detailed reply to Lloyd George; the debate fell flat and the Government won by 293 votes to 106. The Maurice controversy proved to be of very considerable significance for Lloyd George. Three days afterwards Milner and other ministers tackled him about the revised War Office figures, but he merely brushed them aside. Milner felt disgusted by this, and thereafter the two men drifted apart. The affair also exacerbated, though it did not cause, the split in the Liberal ranks. While 71 Liberals had voted for Lloyd George, 98 voted against him. Subsequently this provided him with a pretext for his proscription of the Asquithian Liberals in the general election. Finally, although Maurice failed to make his charges stick, it appears that his initiative was prompted by the fear that Lloyd George was about to sack Haig. Any such intention had been decisively checked. Haig's resignation would inevitably have reopened the investigation of manpower on the Western Front. Lloyd George had had an extremely narrow escape; he could hardly expect to be so lucky a second time. Many Tory MPs, though very appreciative of the spirit and energy he had brought to the conduct of the war, regarded him as an inveterate liar. They would readily have accepted that General Maurice had not, after all, been wrong. Thus, in exchange for another superficial political triumph Lloyd George found himself shackled to his military masters for the remainder of the war.

His chief consolation was that none of this mattered very much by the summer of 1918. Although the Germans had come within 60 miles of Paris, their offensive steadily lost momentum and discipline as they advanced over the broken terrain of earlier battles. By July they began to face an Allied counter-attack, and at Cambrai on 8 August they retreated in the face of the British tanks. Though no one expected victory within a few months it was clear that the pressure had been lifted from the Allies.

While contending with the generals, Lloyd George had also devoted much effort to the management of civilian morale and the consolidation of his own support during 1917 and 1918. Unfortunately for him, he succeeded to the premiership at a point when war-weariness was becoming a serious problem. By late 1916 a man as patriotic as Lord Lansdowne had reached the conclusion that, in view of the unlikelihood of a military victory, Britain ought to seek a negotiated peace. On several occasions the American President, Woodrow Wilson, attempted to mediate by asking the two sides to state their terms for peace. Now Lloyd George's obvious strength as a war leader was that he personified the rejection of such notions. 'The fight must be to a finish – to a knockout' as he had told an American journalist in a famous interview in September 1916. He undoubtedly inspired the people with the will to win. Robert Graves, a grudging admirer, heard him speak in the summer of 1916:

> Lloyd George was up in the air on one of his 'glory of the Welsh hills' speeches. The power of his rhetoric amazed me. The substance of the speech might be commonplace, idle and false, but I had to fight hard against abandoning myself with the rest of his audience. He sucked power from his listeners and spurted it back at them.[6]

However, by 1917 a simple reiteration of the knock-out blow was insufficient. Pressure groups like the Union of Democratic Control had gained support and authority in their advocacy of a negotiated peace, and some MPs demanded a clear statement of Britain's war aims. Now neither Asquith nor Lloyd George had given much thought to war aims, largely because Britain's essential objective was an intangible one: the restoration of the balance in Europe. But Lloyd George felt obliged to give some indication of British aims both in January 1917 and in January 1918. These amounted to the restoration of Belgium and Serbia, evacuation of France and Russia, self-determination for the peoples of Austria-Hungary, and the dismemberment of the Ottoman Empire. He avoided laying claim to the German colonies, knowing President Wilson's aversion to fighting a war for Anglo-French imperialism. But within the Government the Milnerites were insistent on acquiring the colonies and on using tariffs to preserve the commercial gains Britain had won through the interruption of German trade.

Lloyd George's tough stance on the war itself was complemented by a conciliatory approach to civilian living standards and aspirations. In May 1917 he appointed a number of commissions to inquire into the causes of industrial unrest which identified food prices, wage-rates, restrictions on labour mobility, and the calling up of men previously exempt from military service as the chief concerns. By 1917 the war had had the effect of raising civilian expectations so that it was necessary not only to make immediate improvements in living standards, but also to hold out a vision of a better society once victory had been attained. This received practical expression in the idea of reconstruction. Lloyd George also had a personal motive. Embarrassed by his acute dependence on the Conservatives, he badly wanted to make the relationship respectable in Liberal eyes. This could best be done by seizing the initiative on social reform and proving that he had not forfeited his radical credentials. He greatly multiplied the committees working on aspects of reconstruction, drawing in an impressive group of advisers including the Milnerites, Seebohm Rowntree, and Sidney and Beatrice Webb, all united by their belief in the necessity for state intervention in social welfare. Eventually a Ministry for Reconstruction was established under Addison, though unfortunately it lacked executive powers. Under its aegis much constructive thinking was done, though Addison found that the War Cabinet repeatedly postponed a decision on housing legislation. H. A. L. Fisher, on the other hand, had accepted office only on condition that a major reform of education was taken up. His 1918 Act extended compulsory education to 14 years and envisaged a complete system from nursery school to adult education classes, to be financed by a 50 per cent grant by Government to local authorities. Another characteristic expression of reconstruction thinking was the idea of Whitley Councils which were joint committees of employers and unions. Under the Ministry of Labour they were set up in twenty industries by 1918.

But by far the most sweeping and conspicuous domestic reform of the wartime coalition was the 1918 Representation of the People Act which transformed the pre-war electorate of under 8 million to one of 21 million including 8.4 million women voters. The origins of this lay in 1916 when Asquith's Cabinet had thrown the apparently insoluble question of parliamentary registration into the lap of a conference under the Speaker, James Lowther. In January 1917 Lowther reported to Lloyd George that his all-party group had agreed on a comprehensive set of proposals covering franchise and redistribution. This presented the Prime Minister with a ticklish problem because some Conservatives alleged that their representatives on the Speaker's Conference had been persuaded to make too many concessions. A Bill might well provoke a Tory revolt on the grounds that Lloyd George's coalition had been formed specifically to win the war not to dabble in domestic party controversies. On the other hand, the report presented a great opportunity. Conscious that he might have to face an election at any time, Lloyd George badly wanted a comprehensive and accurate electoral register which would give men in the armed forces an effective vote. Fortunately, several Conservative colleagues, notably Walter Long, supported him in this, and the result was a government Bill embodying the Speaker's proposals, though with a free vote on several controversial issues. Lloyd George wisely left it to two Tories, Long and Sir George Cave, to steer the measure through the Commons. Conservatives were mollified with several concessions in the Bill and a promise of reform of the House of Lords which, of course, was never honoured. As a result Lloyd George succeeded in resolving the tangled question of the franchise which had repeatedly frustrated Asquith's pre-1914 government. It gave some substance to his boast that he dictated terms to his Tory colleagues, not the other way round. His consequent credibility as a radical helped him to retain a body of Liberal MPs in 1918 and thus to bargain with the Conservatives over the terms of the general election.

Another issue that had perennially baffled Lloyd George's predecessors was Ireland. The rise of Sinn Fein in the aftermath of the Easter Rising of 1916 made a measure of Home Rule all the more urgent. With this in mind, and encouraged by the success of the Speaker's Conference, the Government appointed an Irish Convention representing all opinions in May 1917. Although Lloyd George undertook to introduce legislation if substantial agreement was reached, he undoubtedly hoped that the Convention – an unwieldy body of 95 – would simply take Home Rule off the agenda for the duration of the war. Contrary to expectations, the Nationalist, Southern Unionist, Liberal, and Labour delegates did achieve a considerable measure of agreement. Only the intransigence of the Ulster Unionists held matters up; and in December 1917 the majority petitioned Lloyd George to assist them by demonstrating his willingness to put pressure on Ulster. This he declined to do, fearing the consequences of forcing a Bill upon his Tory colleagues. Thus by April 1918, when the convention finally reported, the Government had effectively dropped the whole enterprise; indeed, by deciding to impose conscription upon Ireland they made certain of alienating the Nationalists and thus torpedoing the fragile measure of agreement.

Lloyd George's timidity in handling Home Rule is a reminder that any assessment of his personal wartime rule must take account of his underlying political weakness. In a sense, he enjoyed much less authority than a normal prime minister because he was neither the leader of the majority party in Parliament, nor even the leader of any party. He owed his premiership strictly to a coup engineered at Cabinet level by a handful of men and sustained for a limited reason – the need to hold the nation together behind the war effort. His survival for two years reflected less a conviction that the war was being won than an appreciation that the alternative – Asquith – might mean defeat or a negotiated peace. The influence of party had . by no means been eliminated by the crisis, and the most crippling result of Lloyd George's dependence on Bonar Law was his inability to impose himself upon the military sphere. Although he achieved some changes in military personnel, at great risk, he cannot be said to have made much impact on policy except in the navy. Indeed the Asquith Government had exercised rather more influence over strategy than he ever did.

On the other hand, there was surely something, not dictatorial, but distinctly *presidential* about Lloyd George's regime. Like the American President he appeared to be the dynamic centre of the vast apparatus of government. Like the President, he relied more upon his extensive and expanding powers of patronage than upon a disciplined party base. Indeed, his links with Parliament became unusually slight. He descended only occasionally to address the Commons, spending his time ensconced within the Cabinet Secretariat and the

Garden Suburb. In this machine he built up a government within a government, bypassing the Civil Service and the regular Cabinet. His choice of ministers from outside the ranks of the party regulars also echoed American practice. Most of the new recruits bowed to British tradition by taking a peerage or accepting a seat in the Commons; but three important appointees escaped even this formal link with Parliament. Maclay served for five years as Shipping Controller without sitting in either House. Neville Chamberlain did not become an MP until 1918, after he had left office, and in 1917 Lloyd George actually discouraged him from seeking a seat. Finally, Smuts, though not a departmental minister, sat in the War Cabinet without being in Parliament.

This represented an unusual departure from the British idea of the executive as responsible in a formal and direct sense to Parliament. However, to conclude from this that parliamentary government ceased in this period would be a considerable exaggeration. It is true that, with many MPs absent from the House on war work, attendance in the division lobbies was often low and the whipping ineffective. Asquith largely neglected to play his role as Leader of the Opposition, and criticism from Liberal and Labour Members, though fierce, was sporadic and uncoordinated. Yet the House still acted as the ultimate check on Government because it could never be relied upon to produce a majority. The party composition of the Government's majority in a major measure such as the Represention of the People Bill fluctuated wildly from one clause to the next.[7] The practice of patching up *ad hoc* majorities is much more typical of the American Congress than of the British Parliament, and it obliged the Government to work much harder for its support than was usual.

Lloyd George's reputation as the man who won the war can only be assessed in the light of those factors or decisions which were crucial to victory. Had he experienced defeat on the Western Front, as seemed likely for a time in 1918, he and his system would doubtless have been held up to execration as Asquith's has often been. Some of the key decisions, over munitions and conscription for example, *preceded* his premiership, though as he was invariably responsible for them he deserves some of the credit. As Premier his chief contribution to victory lay in his success in the maintenance of food supplies, the allocation of manpower, the stimulation of production, and the preservation of shipping. As a result, Britain won the real war of attrition. Her industry and the morale of her soldiers held up until superior Allied resources were finally brought to bear in 1918. Lloyd George could hardly be given credit for the military victory, if such it was; no more could Sir Douglas Haig, though some writers have devoted much futile effort to presenting him as a great general. Haig, too, survived long enough to preside over victory, but he had not discovered the answers to the problems that had baffled him since 1916. The German armies were not comprehensively beaten in battle, rather, they were pushed back almost to their own frontier by French, American, and British forces alike. The demoralised French and the inexperienced Americans performed as effectively as the British. Luckily for the Allied commanders, the Germans decided against fighting on their own soil which would have made 1919 another costly year. Ultimately, Lloyd George was to be vindicated by the Second World War. Many of his methods and policies in such matters as rationing, manpower, and munitions were adopted more rapidly and more thoroughly than in the First World War; and Churchill applied the key lesson of the First World War by subordinating the defence chiefs more effectively to prime ministerial authority.

. . .

THE COUPON ELECTION

Although Lloyd George could never dispense with Parliament, he hoped to render it more amenable by changing its composition. Whenever troubled by criticism in the House he felt inclined to invoke the Prime Minister's ultimate weapon – a general election. He anticipated winning an election comfortably by seeking a simple mandate to get on with the war. Since the last election had been held in December 1910 he could reasonably argue that the House no longer reflected public opinion. In fact, by the summer of 1918 he had decided to conduct an election during wartime on the assumption that the fighting would continue throughout 1919.

However, it proved difficult to decide on what practical basis Lloyd George should and could go to the country. In 1918 he had no more than the rudiments of a party. Between a quarter and a third of the existing Liberal Members regularly supported him, but it was not clear whether even they would be renominated by their constituency associations. For a long time the relationship between the supporters of Asquith and Lloyd George remained unclear, both sides being reluctant to formalise the split. While Asquith claimed to be supporting the Government, Lloyd George avoided repudiating the Liberal Party formally until December 1918. However, the two sides issued separate whips in the Commons, and issues such as the disfranchisement of conscientious objectors and Irish conscription steadily divided the party even before the Maurice Debate which Lloyd George chose to take as the criterion of loyalty to him. In this process the right-wing Liberals, who felt that nothing should be allowed to stand in the way of victory, gravitated to Lloyd George, which left Asquith leading the centre and radical left of the party – an odd outcome which illustrates the confusion the war introduced into British politics.

There is in fact little basis for the charge made by some historians and many contemporaries that Lloyd George was to blame for splitting and destroying the Liberal Party. Primary responsibility lay with Asquith for his stubborn refusal to serve in Lloyd George's coalition in 1916. Thereafter he led the Opposition, and the fact that he did so ineptly and unenthusiastically hardly exonerates him. Lloyd George's last-minute overtures to Asquith in November 1918 to join his Cabinet as Lord Chancellor were only made to be rejected, of course; for they enabled Lloyd George to put Asquith firmly in the wrong. By this time he had already committed himself to an alternative strategy involving an alliance with the Conservatives.

This emerged during the summer when a wartime election was seriously in contemplation. Detailed negotiations got under way between Lloyd George's whip, F. E. Guest, and Sir George Younger, designed to allocate the constituencies to Conservative, Lloyd George Liberal, and National Democratic Party (NDP) candidates all standing in the name of the coalition. By 20 July the Conservatives had agreed to give an unopposed run to Liberals in 114 seats. Though this was not a large number, it did not reflect a lack of generosity on the Conservatives' part so much as the difficulty Guest experienced in producing candidates and existing MPs willing to stand as Liberals in the Prime Minister's name. Eventually the coalition fielded 159 Liberal, 373 Conservative, and 18 NDP candidates, though a further 75 Conservatives stood independently.

Official coalition candidates were to be furnished with a letter of endorsement signed by Bonar Law and Lloyd George – the famous 'coupon' as Asquith called it in his only memorable utterance of the campaign.

As these plans matured during August and September, the Allied armies made steady advances on the Western Front, but the politicians were taken by surprise when, in early October, the Germans sought terms of peace. Now Lloyd George grew alarmed, for he could not reasonably hold the election until a new register of voters had been prepared to include all those recently enfranchised. This proved to be a slow and complicated affair involving novel arrangements for soldiers to vote by post and by proxy. Lloyd George chose to blame Hayes Fisher, the minister responsible, for the delay, and unceremoniously sacked him. Meanwhile hostilities came abruptly to a halt. When Lloyd George attended the Lord Mayor's banquet on 9 November the entire august company stood on their chairs to cheer him. 'Well', said Balfour, 'the little beggar deserves it all.' Two days later, with the armistice signed, Lloyd George told the jubilant crowds in Downing Street that the war was officially at an end.

Now what had been intended as a wartime election necessarily became a post-war one in which Lloyd George sought a further term of office in order to settle the terms of peace. This was rather worrying; for, with the crisis now over, did the Conservatives need him any longer? In November 1918 the party's leaders believed they did. For Bonar Law, Balfour, and others, working with him had become a congenial habit. But there were wider considerations. The Conservatives had not won an election since 1900, and by 1918 the political landscape had changed in ways apparently disadvantageous to them. The trade unions had enrolled 6 million members, over three times the 1900 figure, while the Labour Party, having cut free from the Liberals, was fielding sufficient candidates to win a majority of seats for the first time. With a huge new electorate, many of whom were young men of unknown political views, who could be sure Labour would not succeed? When Law confronted his own party members on 12 November he therefore emphasised that Lloyd George's immense prestige and popularity in the constituencies would be essential in checking any sudden lurch to the left. He also reassured the doubtful that it was safe to continue the alliance with him:

By our own action we have made Mr Lloyd George the flag
bearer of the very principles upon which we should appeal
to the country.

This claim was partially borne out by the coalition manifesto
which, though vague and platitudinous, committed the new
Government to several Conservative causes such as colonial
preference and House of Lords reform. Such issues had to be
suppressed by Lloyd George when he met his Liberal
colleagues before the election, which took place on 14
December. To them he painted an entrancing picture of the
coalition proceeding from a fair peace treaty to tackle reforms
for housing, health, land, and minimum wages while
defending free trade and Home Rule.

Having been starved of elections since 1910, Lloyd George
now became obsessed with the voters, according to Hankey: 'He
seems to have a sort of lust for power.' Such disdain came easily
enough to Hankey whose job was not at risk. Yet Lloyd George
has continued to suffer much criticism for his supine approach
to popular xenophobia during the coupon election.
Unfortunately the war had ended so abruptly that the country
had not had time to readjust before the election occurred. After
the initial brief euphoria of the armistice, emotions turned to
sorrow for those who had been lost, thence to bitterness against
those responsible for the war. Lloyd George's defenders argue
that he did not *intend* to fight the election by pandering to such
emotions, but put forward a constructive domestic programme.
This, however, is scarcely an adequate defence, and, in any case,
is only *partially* true, for he prepared for a chauvinistic appeal
as well as a liberal one. As early as 5 November when the
Cabinet discussed the treatment of the Kaiser, he showed
himself more belligerent than many of his colleagues: 'Lloyd
George wants to shoot the Kaiser', declared Henry Wilson. The
Cabinet did agree that the Kaiser could be tried for treason
against humanity, and consequently, when popular support
for such a proposal emerged, he was already predisposed to
capitalise upon it.

As to the punishment of Germany itself, the American
President had already proposed that compensation should be
paid to Belgium both for the physical damage done and for the
cost of resisting the invasion; France, however, would be
entitled only to the cost of the physical destruction. This left

Britain, who had suffered hardly any direct attacks, with no hope of significant compensation. In the event, the terms of the armistice excluded any general claim for the cost of waging war, and Lloyd George told the Cabinet it would be wrong to demand an indemnity. However, this view was promptly challenged by the Australian Prime Minister, Billy Hughes, and when some MPs tackled Bonar Law on the point in the Commons he gave no answer. Although Parliament was dissolved on 25 November, Lloyd George's colleagues in the Imperial War Cabinet led him rapidly along that path that he had declared closed. Originally, the Treasury had estimated Germany's capacity to pay compensation at £2 billion; but Bonar Law now declared that the war had cost Britian £8 billion. Thereupon Lloyd George appointed a Cabinet committee including Walter Long, Mr Justice Sumner, and Lord Cunliffe, a former Governor of the Bank of England, to investigate the matter. After deliberating for exactly one day, the committee pronounced Germany capable of paying £24 billion! This was simply guesswork fortified by prejudice. However, it gave the Prime Minister a measure of insurance against the vagaries of public opinion.

During November he had been subject to repeated and increasingly wild demands from Northcliffe's *Daily Mail* to the effect that 'the Huns must pay'. By now a complete megalomaniac, Northcliffe insisted that he be made a Cabinet minister, be allowed to approve the names of new ministers, and be made a delegate to the peace conference. All this was refused, and as a result Northcliffe endeavoured to punish Lloyd George by making trouble during the election. At his first public meeting at Wolverhampton on 24 November, he launched his programme to 'make Britain a fit country for heroes to live in'. But his audience lost interest and began to heckle him on the subject of enemy aliens and whether they were to be expelled. Such experiences, combined with a flood of excitable letters engineered by Northcliffe, thoroughly rattled Lloyd George. He soon fell back on his line of defence, and at Newcastle on 29 November he announced that 'Germany must pay the cost of the war up to the limit of her capacity to do so', and that the Kaiser was to be prosecuted. Northcliffe thereupon demanded to know what he meant by 'her capacity to pay'. The débâcle culminated at Bristol on 11 December when the Prime Minister publicly endorsed the figure of £24 billion; the

Germans, he said, should pay to the uttermost farthing: 'we will search their pockets for it'. In spite of the undoubted pressure upon him, he was certainly not obliged to descend to these depths of irresponsibility. After all, electors who wanted a punitive peace could hardly have voted for Asquith or for Labour; they had no alternative to the coalition. Lloyd George might have used his prestige in the hour of his victory to give a lead by puncturing the crude prejudices on which men like Cunliffe and Northcliffe thrived; he chose instead the easier and lower path.

In the event, the Government won an unprecedented victory, with no fewer than 526 seats to 181 for all the opposition parties. In a competition to prove hatred for all things German most Liberal and Labour candidates had been hopelessly outclassed. The 'coupon', despite complaints from Asquithian Liberals, had effectively protected Lloyd George Liberals, of whom 133 were elected, by sparing them from Conservative opposition. The 75 Conservative and Unionist candidates who stood without the 'coupon' did nearly as well as those who had it. At the time the arrangement appeared to have succeeded in its underlying object of checking Labour, which won 22 per cent of the vote but only 61 seats. 'Lloyd George can be Prime Minister for life if he wants', said Bonar Law. In the event he was to enjoy less than four years at the top of the greasy pole.

. . .

NOTES AND REFERENCES

1. Lord Hankey 1961 *The Supreme Command 1914–18*, vol. II. Allen & Unwin p. 576.
2. Quoted in Turner J 1980 *Lloyd George's Secretariat.* Cambridge University Press, p. 1.
3. Winter J M 1985 *The Great War and the British People* Macmillan, p. 213–48.
4. Haig's Diary 26/2/17, quoted in Blake R 1952 *The Private Papers of Douglas Haig 1914–1919*, p. 201.
5. Roskill S 1970 *Hankey: Man of secrets* vol. I *1877–1918.* Collins, pp. 435–45.
6. Graves R 1929 *Goodbye To All That.* Cape (1971 edn), p. 168.
7. Pugh M 1978 *Electoral Reform in War and Peace 1906–18.* Routledge & Kegan Paul, p. 194.

Chapter 6

THE FAILURE OF THE CENTRE PARTY 1918–1922

'George thinks he won the election', remarked Walter Long shortly after the results of the coupon election came in. 'Well, he didn't. It was the Tories that won the election, *and he will soon begin to find that out.*' Many years later an equally shrewd observer, Harold Macmillan, echoed Long when he chararacterised Lloyd George as 'the prisoner of the Tories' after 1918.[1] However, historians have not usually seen him in quite these terms, influenced, perhaps, by the depth of contemporary feeling during 1919–22 that the Conservatives themselves had become trapped by Lloyd George rather than the other way around: 'a dynamic force is a terrible thing', in Stanley Baldwin's famous phrase. Yet the fact is that by 1922, and for years thereafter, Tory Party interests required that he should be portrayed as a virtual dictator. Had he not continued to bypass the Cabinet and exclude the Foreign Office from the making of foreign policy? Did he not attempt to shore up his personal regime by creating a docile press and by the flagrant sale of honours to disreputable men? The more dominant the Prime Minister, the less blame could be attached to the Conservatives for the record of the coalition government when they abandoned him abruptly in 1922.

In fact no prime minister who lacks a party majority of his own, as Lloyd George did, can be dominant for very long, especially when his obvious assets – in this case his war record and his hold over the new voters – appeared to be diminishing steadily. Throughout 1918–22 the 383 Tory MPs, on whom his government depended for its existence, kept Lloyd George on a short lead. It is true that within this range he operated ruthlessly and often successfully; but he had always to risk being reined in by the Conservative leadership if the party rank and file refused to back him. This check worked effectively, as we shall see, and culminated dramatically in 1922 when the Conservatives denied Lloyd George the use of the ultimate weapon of a British prime minister: the right to dissolve Parliament at a time of his own choosing. Of course, after 1918 Lloyd George did enjoy a party of a sort in the shape of the 133 coalition Liberal MPs. However, the by-elections of this period rapidly suggested that these politicians could not hold on to their seats except in the special conditions of 1918, and they proved to be an insecure and inadequate counterpoint to the Tory hosts. No doubt they retained a major hold on Cabinet posts including the Home and War Offices, Health, Education, India, Scotland, and Ireland. But, apart from Churchill, they were second-rank figures who steadily lost influence within the coalition. Those who survived to 1922 like Churchill, Hamar Greenwood, or Sir Alfred Mond did so by moving emphatically to the right and thereby weakening their *raison d'être* in the coalition.

Yet although Lloyd George lacked the power to dominate his government he undeniably exuded the aura of a great despot. Even as sympathetic and perceptive a participant as Maurice Hankey considered that he *behaved* increasingly like a dictator. To some extent this was a reflection of the fact that after thirteen years in office, mostly at the centre of events, he had begun to feel tired and jaded. To his colleagues this showed itself in his increasing irritability; he had aged, become unfit, succumbed to minor illnesses, and resorted more frequently to holidays at home and abroad. In spite of his superficial bonhomie, Lloyd George had always been detached, making few close friendships, 'He neither likes you nor dislikes you', commented Beatrice Webb. 'You are a mere instrument, one among many.' It is not surprising that he became alienated from colleagues like Curzon, or even fellow Liberals like C. P. Scott, Addison, and Montagu between 1918 and 1922. But more telling was the coldness that entered his relations with Milner and Churchill who were, if anyone was, his natural political allies by 1918. A growing tendency to insult such figures publicly was a sure sign of Lloyd George's partial loss of touch and of the coarseness which the prolonged experience of power inevitably fostered in him. As friends and colleagues drifted away he found himself marooned more and more with a handful of advisers like Lord Riddell and Philip Kerr, with the faithful Frances, and with his wife and daughter, Megan, both of whom played a more active role in his public work after 1918.

Another reason for the persistence of the aura of dictatorship around Lloyd George lay in his own reluctance to adapt to peacetime conditions. His penchant for finding solutions and his will to implement them quickly made him a natural leader in an emergency; but in attempting to govern as though the wartime crisis still existed he ran into opposition. Even before the election, several colleagues had pressed for the restoration of normal Cabinet government; Churchill particularly resented a system in which he, as Secretary of State for War after 1918, was excluded from the Cabinet; and Chamberlain refused to serve as Chancellor unless he was included. In spite of this dissatisfaction Lloyd George maintained his five-man War Cabinet until October 1919. He hoped to restrict the new Cabinet to fifteen members, but this proved impossible, given the acute competition for places in a coalition government. Though many of the new ministries were abolished, several such as Labour, Pensions, and Health survived, and when formed in November the new Cabinet numbered twenty. However, he governed as far as possible by frequent meetings of four or five ministers summoned *ad hoc* so as to bypass the full Cabinet. The Cabinet Secretariat was a permanent legacy of the war, and Lloyd George maintained a substantial personal entourage to help him circumvent the Whitehall administration, though it was in foreign affairs that this worked most effectively.

Lloyd George's success in riding the Tory tiger for four years must in part be attributed to his skill and energy in delivering the country from a particularly difficult phase in 1919–20 when industrial militancy reached its peak. But his survival also reflects the accident that during these years the Conservatives were led by two men – Bonar Law and Austen Chamberlain – each of whom was a natural second-in-command. These grey, competent figures were the perfect foil for the Premier's more original and volatile qualities. Ultimately, like most politicians in office, they thought relatively little about the future; the day-to-day reality of holding power was enough. Even for Lloyd George, who was perfectly alive to the need to take out some insurance for his long-term political career, it seemed either more congenial or simply imperative to concentrate upon the succession of problems confronting his government, in the belief that the resolution of each issue would, in itself, somehow settle the broader political strategy. Darting from one issue to another, and throwing himself into a series of international conferences, Lloyd George seemed to impart a frenetic, convulsive quality to his administration, an impression memorably captured by Asquith's daughter, Lady Violet Bonham-Carter, in 1922 when she described it as a government suffering from St Vitus's dance! For the first seven months the settlement of the peace treaty provided central direction, but thereafter Lloyd George was always too busy to devote himself fully to re-establishing a broad sense of purpose which, in the circumstances, could only mean the development of a new centre party from the political chaos of war.

. . .

THE PARIS PEACE CONFERENCE

From the very beginning of his premiership until August 1919 Lloyd George was an absentee Prime Minister, returning to London from the peace conference periodically in response to ominous messages from Bonar Law to make brief and dramatic appearances in the Commons. He took up residence in January in a flat in the fashionable Rue Nitot in Paris, with an entourage that included Frances Stevenson, who was treated as his unofficial wife, along with Megan Lloyd George, Maurice Hankey, Philip Kerr, and Lord Riddell. The British Empire delegation, some 200 strong, occupied the Hotel Majestic near by, and Balfour, the Foreign Secretary, had a flat above Lloyd George's.

At the outset it was agreed that the task of producing a treaty would be handled by a Council of Ten whose work would be largely conducted in private through a series of commissions investigating each problem. By March, when this system had become hopelessly bogged down, Lloyd George char-acteristically proposed to President Woodrow Wilson, Georges Clemenceau, and the Italian President, Orlando, that they, as the Big Four, should bypass the formal peacemaking machinery. To this they readily agreed.

Wilson had attempted to determine the broad lines of the peace in advance of the conference by means of his famous Fourteen Points which included such principles as national self-determination, absolute freedom of the seas, the impartial adjustment of colonial claims, and establishment of a League of Nations. Neither Lloyd George nor Clemenceau understood what all this meant, and regarded themselves as entirely uncommitted to the President's grand scheme. A major disagreement arose over the terms on which occupied territory was to be restored. Wilson clearly distinguished between Belgium and France in this respect. The former should receive full compensation for physical damage resulting from the invasion *and* for the costs of resisting it. But since the invasion of France was not an illegal act, Germany was liable only for the physical damage. After his rash commitment to an indemnity at the recent election, Lloyd George was dismayed to find Wilson resolutely committed to his original idea. To represent Britain on the Reparations Commission he had chosen Lord Cunliffe, Mr Justice Sumner, and Billy Hughes, the Australian Premier. This was his first and worst error in peacemaking. He doubtless calculated that their reputation for toughness would insure him against criticism at home. But when the three adopted a narrow, vindictive approach to German payments and stuck obstinately to it, Lloyd George could not risk provoking their resignations; for as early as February he began to be challenged by MPs who doubted his sincerity over reparations. He could only reply that the commission was at work and the Government would stand by its pledges. Back in Paris he found a complete deadlock over the indemnity by March. With typical ingenuousness he confessed to Colonel House, Wilson's special adviser, that the British claims were absurdbly high as a result of an election stunt perpetrated by others! But he could not throw over the claims, and therefore must secure a large sum for Britain, even if its actual collection were to be pushed into the distant future.[2]

Thus there were two objectives for Lloyd George: to settle on a respectably large total sum for German liability, and to ensure that Britain won a major share of it. The Big Three (Lloyd George, Clemenceau and Wilson) soon settled on a figure of £6 billion, but Cunliffe and his colleagues insisted on £21 billion! The Big Three went up to £8 billion, and Cunliffe, with great reluctance, came down to £12 billion and stuck. At home rumours of a Lloyd George climb-down, fanned by the Northcliffe press, led to a virtual vote of confidence in the House of Commons on 2 April. Bonar Law was badly rattled by this, and claimed afterwards that nine out of ten Conservatives were now disgusted with him. On 8 April an ominous telegram, signed by over 200 coalition MPs, arrived for Lloyd George reminding him of his election pledges – an extraordinary experience for a Prime Minister within four months of his great triumph. He now appeared to be trapped between the irresistible force of the Conservative rank and file, which could break his government, and the immovable obstinacy of Cunliffe. But Lloyd George found an escape route. First, he shrewdly prevailed upon General Smuts, whom Wilson liked and admired, to persuade the President to agree to include the cost of British disability pensions and allowances for dependants of the dead and disabled in the claim for reparations; this would double Britain's share. Second, he and Clemenceau sought to establish that their right to compensation was practically unlimited. Under the strain, the American President fell ill and matters were settled with the more flexible Colonel House. At Lloyd George's suggestion, they decided to incorporate into what became Article 231 of the treaty an acknowledgement of war guilt on the part of Germany. Given this acceptance of unlimited liability by the Germans, both Lloyd George and Clemenceau felt they could dispense with a precise figure; this could be left to a commission which would report in two years' time. Woodrow Wilson reluctantly acquiesced in this. He even agreed to the trial of the Kaiser. 'Now I understand why you are Prime Minister', an American delegate told Lloyd George afterwards.

Armed with the war-guilt clause, he boldly returned home to face the House of Commons on 16 April. Flourishing his triumph without going into details, he teasingly asked his critics whether they wanted him to return to Paris to complete the task or not, and made fun of Lord Northcliffe's pretensions at great length. At one point he tapped his forehead and referred to the 'diseased vanity' of the press baron at which the House laughed heartily. As a result the opposition collapsed. Lloyd George had sprung from the trap that appeared to be closing on him.

His approach to the rest of the peace settlement reflected his proposals in the Fontainebleau Memorandum which he had drawn up in March when the conference had practically ground to a halt. By this time, as Clemenceau observed, the British had already won the points that were of vital concern to them such as the surrender of the German fleet, and the disposal of

German colonies. Naturally Wilson resisted the dismemberment of colonial territory for the benefit of the old imperial
powers. But, once again, Lloyd George enlisted Smuts to
persuade him to adopt a system of 'mandates' to facilitate the
transfer of Tanganyika, South West Africa, and other German
territories. Wilson was also placated by the ready acceptance of
his proposals for a League of Nations. Lloyd George and
Clemenceau thought this a concession of no great significance
beside the immediate and tangible objects they desired.

By and large the Fontainebleau Memorandum aimed to force
the French to compromise on their demands. Reappearing in
liberal guise, Lloyd George now warned against punitive
treatment of Germany; this would only invite a war of revenge
in the long run, or, in the short run, might even push Germany
into the hands of the Bolsheviks. In particular he opposed any
permanent detachment of the Rhineland from Germany. The
French none the less obtained a fifteen-year occupation of the
Rhineland and accepted Lloyd George's offer of an Anglo-
American guarantee to come to France's aid in any future
unprovoked aggression by Germany. In eastern Europe Lloyd
George deplored the French desire to exclude Upper Silesia
from Germany. Since it contained more Germans than Poles,
he successfully insisted on the holding of a plebiscite there, but
in the meantime it was in fact included in the new Poland.
Similarly, he thought that French ideas on a Polish corridor
would place too many Germans under the Poles. He accepted
the need for Polish access to the sea, but drew the line at Danzig
with its 400,000 Germans. Eventually Danzig became a Free
City.

In spite of such modifications, the treaty remained a severe,
even humiliating one for the Germans, who, to the
consternation of the Allied leaders, rejected the terms. This once
again threatened Lloyd George's position, for it might become
necessary to take up arms again. Yet by now the Northcliffe
press was demanding that the troops be brought home.
Therefore Lloyd George summoned his entire Cabinet to Paris
where he entertained them to dinner on 31 May. Conservative
and Liberal ministers alike found the terms vindictive and
unjust towards Germany. Thus, with their encouragement, he
tried to persuade Wilson and Clemenceau to make further
concessions. But they were now disgusted by the opportunism
and shiftiness of the British and refused to move. Consequently

the settlement stood and the Germans reluctantly acquiesced.

In the settlement as a whole Lloyd George had clearly played the key role. He had worked with the French President over the central question of reparations, and then with Wilson in order to limit the punitive demands of Clemenceau. Meanwhile he had successfully defended British interests, narrowly defined in terms of the German navy, the colonies, and her share in compensation for the war. There is justice in the view that whereas Wilson and Clemenceau had both worked from principles, albeit very different ones, Lloyd George had been guided by expediency. Nor was his expediency justified by the results, for it left the French sulky and detached, and the Germans with a burning sense of injustice. His failure was a moral one; he had never attempted to use the immense prestige and authority he had won in the war to defy his critics at home and insist on a just and honourable peace. No sooner was the treaty made than most British politicians agreed, as H. A. L. Fisher put it, that it 'should be modified ... there will be an appeasement'. It is to his credit that Lloyd George entirely agreed.

'What a wonderful time it has been', Lloyd George observed as he left Paris with Riddell in August. Diplomacy by conference was indeed addictive. Most prime ministers, even in the late twentieth century, find it appealing to strut on the international stage, putting aside for a time the exhausting and intractable problems of the domestic economy. How much more attractive, then, to concentrate on diplomacy at a time when Britain really counted in world affairs. Lloyd George, with his natural talent for patching up compromises, had found his apotheosis in the international conference. The very fact that the Versailles settlement was defective required him to keep up his involvement in world affairs, and as a result he began to dominate British foreign policy to an unusual degree. For him foreign policy was a matter not of reading boring ambassadorial reports in London, but of holding a series of great conferences in exotic locations aided by Philip Kerr and his own genius for compromise. He regarded the mandarins of the Foreign Office as slow and blinkered; they and their political master were simply bypassed. Balfour, languid and detached, had cheerfully confessed to his own irrelevance in Paris; and though his successor, Curzon, bitterly resented being ignored and undermined, he swallowed his pride until 1922.

It must be acknowledged that Lloyd George's objectives were widely supported as sane and honourable: to seek disarmament, to restrain the French, to limit German reparations, to withdraw troops from Russia and restore relations, and finally to disengage from the Japanese Alliance and co-operate more closely with the United States in naval and Pacific affairs. Even Curzon had little disagreement on the substance of policy except over Russia. With Churchill at the War Office Britain adopted the Ten Year Rule – an assumption that she would not be involved in war with a major power for the next decade. Expenditure on the armed forces therefore fell from £600 million in 1919 to £110 million by 1922; and at Washington in 1921 Britain concluded an agreement on naval disarmament with the world's leading naval powers.

Other policies proved more complicated, however. Keen as he was to restore relations with Russia, Lloyd George found it difficult to unravel Britain's involvement with the opponents of the Bolshevik regime. In 1919 her troops were scattered around the country supporting the rebel commanders Kolchak, Deniken, and Yudenich. This commitment to a reactionary, and losing, cause must, in the Prime Minister's view, be terminated; but the reversal of policy could only be accomplished over the noisy and vitriolic opposition of Churchill, and a group of back-bench Tory die-hards who saw the hand of Bolshevik subversives throughout the Government and the Civil Service. After many verbose Churchillian memoranda and some stiff clashes in Cabinet with Curzon and Churchill, Lloyd George got his way, and by the end of 1919 British troops had left Russia. The next step was to restore commercial relations between the two countries, for Russia was regarded as a huge potential market for manufactured goods which, especially after the slump in the mid-1920s, must be exploited. To this end Lloyd George was prepared to overlook Russian debts and the claims of the British bondholders for compensation, at least for the time being. He did not, however, receive full credit for this approach. This was partly because his ministers sympathised with the Poles who were currently waging a successful war against the Russian regime, and advocated assisting them by sending arms and ammunition. Their intentions appeared to have been confirmed in 1920 when the trade unions intervened by refusing to load a ship, the *Jolly George*, which was destined for Poland with a cargo of arms. In fact Lloyd George found this pressure helpful, on balance, in resisting the demand for British involvement, which would only have killed his policy of *rapprochement* with Russia. Eventually a trade agreement was signed in March 1921, and though it did not generate much trade, Lloyd George rightly saw it as a step towards a realistic relationship.

Meanwhile he actively sought the appeasement of Germany at a succession of international gatherings culminating in the conference at Genoa in 1922. Blithely condemning the demand for heavy reparations as absurd, he set himself to overcome the obstinacy of the French in the first meeting at San Remo in April 1920. Here he began the long process of whittling down Germany's payments, and also managed to hustle the French into withdrawing their troops from Frankfurt and other recently occupied German towns. At Boulogne in June of that year he and Millerand, the new French President, settled on a modest figure of £4.5 billion as the indemnity which the Germans would pay over thirty-five years. At Spa in July it was agreed that Britain would enjoy a 22 per cent share of reparations payments, and France 52 per cent. Discussions over the terms of the German payments continued at Brussels in December and at London in March 1921. Lloyd George also pursued the Silesian question. The plebiscite of November 1921 produced a 7–5 vote in favour of Germany, and as a result Upper Silesia was partitioned under League of Nations auspices in 1922 so as to restore much of the urban German population to their homeland. Yet for all his efforts Lloyd George won little thanks. The central German grievances remained intact, while the French increasingly felt betrayed. He recognised that after the refusal of the American Senate to ratify the peace treaty and the consequent lapse of the Anglo-American guarantee to France, she was bound to be apprehensive about any revival of German power. In spite of the constant friction with the French he kept this point well in mind. At home his critics looked askance at his attempts to revise the Treaty of Versailles; it was, in Dr Lentin's words, 'too much like Satan rebuking Sin'.[3] However, until the crisis over Chanak in 1922 Lloyd George retained the support of his colleagues for his foreign policy. It was not the substance so much as the style that attracted their criticism. His personal approach involved too much hustling and bullying, albeit for sound objectives. One consequence, as Lord Robert Cecil complained, was a neglect of the more open diplomacy of the League of Nations. The fact is that Lloyd George had never shown any interest in the League. However much it suited him to complain of the secretive pre-war British diplomacy, he himself proved a traditionalist in this respect. As a result an opportunity to invest the League with real authority and support immediately after the war was decisively missed.

. . .

DOMESTIC REFORM AND RETRENCHMENT

On the home front Lloyd George proved to be a far less dominant figure. His post-war coalition had been launched as a vehicle for social reconstruction and during the first two years of its life it achieved a good deal in this field. In education, for example, H. A. L. Fisher began to put into effect the central proposals of his 1918 Act by means of a programme of school-building and evening classes. Even the vexed question of teachers' salaries was resolved in 1921 by the Committee under Lord Burnham which raised them to more than twice their pre-war level, though Fisher rather feebly declined to give women teachers equal salaries with their male colleagues. In addition there were some major extensions of the social welfare schemes with which Lloyd George had been associated before 1914. The old-age pension was raised from £26 5s. od. a year to £47 5s. od. For the unemployed the special out-of-work donation, due to end in mid-1919, was extended to March 1920. Meanwhile a new Bill to extend the 1911 scheme of unemployment insurance was introduced. Although farm labourers and domestic servants were excluded, some 12 million workers now joined the scheme. After the summer of 1920, when the post-war economic boom sharply collapsed, unemployment rose rapidly. By April 1921 it stood at 1.6 million, and by December at 2 million. Since a worker was supposed to have made six weeks of contributions for every week of benefit, many men now failed strictly to qualify under the scheme. However, because the Government wished to save them from being thrown on to the Poor Law they modified the rules and introduced a range of 'uncovenanted' and 'transitional' benefits. Inevitably insurance became much more costly than had been anticipated.

But it was housing which attracted the most attention among social reforms of the coalition. By 1919 it appeared to be a matter of agreement between all parties that the Government should encourage local authorities to undertake a major construction programme. At the Ministry of Reconstruction Dr Addison had endeavoured to get precise plans and targets, but had largely been frustrated by the Local Government Board. At last, in January 1919, Addison himself took over the Board which was effectively replaced by the new Ministry of Health in June. His Housing Bill, which was passed in July, placed a duty upon local authorities to build houses and send up their schemes to the ministry. Since the houses were not expected to produce enough in rent to cover the capital cost, the Government agreed to make up the difference. Some authorities sent up purely token plans, but even the co-operative ones often found the task difficult. As a result of the post-war inflation, building materials rose sharply in price; skilled labour did not return to the building industry, and private firms found it more profitable to construct commercial property. Consequently, house-building was so slow that in November the Cabinet agreed to offer private builders a subsidy of £100 per house, and eventually 170,000 houses were constructed under Addison's scheme. By comparison with previous housing policy this was a great achievement, and the use of subsidies became common practice in the inter-war years. At the time, however, it was a disappointment in that it fell far short of the promises made in 1918.

The explanation for this lies in the impact of the slump from 1920 onwards and in the political pressure for a deflationary policy which had been building up within the coalition. In the aftermath of war the Exchequer faced the problem of a hugely swollen National Debt, the payments on which absorbed much of its revenue and competed with new social welfare policies. Consequently there was widespread support in all three parties for a special levy on capital designed to cut the debt to manageable proportions quickly and thus give future governments more room for manoeuvre. In February 1920 a Select Committee on War Wealth was set up, but the most favourable opportunity had already passed. Austen Chamberlain, a very narrow, unimaginative Chancellor, firmly rejected any idea of a special levy. Lloyd George himself made little or no contribution in these vital years. He contemplated the abolition of his famous land taxes of 1909 in the budget of 1919 without concern. While the country enjoyed the post-war restocking boom the pressure on the Government was slight. Chamberlain imposed an excess profits tax in 1919, increased it in 1920, and maintained the standard rate of income tax at a high level: 6s. in the pound. But with the collapse of British export markets, the loss of revenue to the Exchequer and the growing cost of unemployment, Chamberlain shifted to an orthodox policy. By April 1920 bank rate had been raised to 7 per cent, which deterred local authorities from borrowing money; Chamberlain came under pressure to lighten the burdens on industry and taxpayers by reducing the Government's spending. His object was to balance the budget and to use any surplus to pay off the National Debt. Lloyd George's contribution to this was to improvise a new Cabinet committee on unemployment which met – a typical stunt – on Christmas Day 1920. His reply to a deputation of Labour mayors in 1921 was to the effect that the remedy for unemployment lay in waiting for better times – an attitude for which he would deride Baldwin and MacDonald in years to come. But in 1920–21 Lloyd George had simply not thought about the economic problem. In any case, his attention was concentrated less upon the protests of working men than upon the explosion of discontent from his middle-class followers.

During 1920 criticism of excessive government expenditure built up within the Conservative ranks under influential figures like Lord Salisbury. The burgeoning cost of housing was a natural target; in addition, Conservatives widely believed that workers were refusing to take jobs because of the attractions of the 'dole'. It was even argued that no benefits should be paid to women whose husbands were in work. Such sentiments were crystallised in January 1921 when Lord Rothermere set up the Anti-Waste League. This body promptly fielded a candidate in a by-election at Dover and defeated the coalitionist comfortably. Anti-Waste campaigners went on to triumph at St George's and at Hertford in June. In the Westminster (Abbey) by-election in August the official Conservative candidate managed to hold on only by offering himself as a 'Constitutional and Anti-Waste' candidate! With the Conservative rank and file apparently lurching in this direction the Cabinet was dragged along behind. As early as February 1921 Addison agreed to limit expenditure on housing and withdraw his targets. Then in March Lloyd George moved him from Health to become Minister without Portfolio. He thought this a neat move.

Addison would now resign and the critics would be happy with their victim. Instead the Opposition in Parliament fixed upon Addison's new salary: why was he being paid £5,000 to do nothing? A motion – in effect one of confidence – was tabled to reduce his salary by £2,000. Both Chamberlain, who was by now the Conservative Leader, and the Coalition Liberal Whip, McCurdy, advised the Prime Minister that to resist the revolt might well lead to a defeat. It is also clear from Lloyd George's correspondence with Chamberlain in June that he was badly rattled by the middle-class revolt against high taxation. Before the debate on 23 June he actually cancelled all his appointments for a week, claiming ill health, and retired to Chequers. In the event he gave a performance that was as shabby as it was inept. He tried to disarm criticism by announcing that Addison's new appointment would last only to the end of the session. He made a feeble job of defending his minister: 'I know that his unfortunate interest in health has excited a good deal of prejudice.'[4] As a result the Government survived the debate but Lloyd George himself had been humiliated. It was another reminder that his huge majority was a cause of weakness as much as of strength for him. In the exchanges in this debate one may see the central political failure of the coalition; for Lloyd George was attacked both by the Left and by the Right for his feebleness. In fact many Conservatives were willing to speak up for Addison, and did so, which only underlines the point that Lloyd George threw away the chance to make a stand as a reformer. The summer of 1920 was the last opportunity to cut adrift from the Coalition whose job was now done, and to develop the new Centre Party.

Instead he merely vented his exasperation on Addison for not having the decency to resign quickly. His successor, Sir Alfred Mond, though a Liberal, was keen for economy. He readily agreed to wind down the housing plans, and Addison at last left the Government. Sir Robert Horne, the new Chancellor, appointed a committee under Eric Geddes to recommend cuts in expenditure as a further sop to 'Anti-Waste'. Geddes recommended economies of £76 million of which £46.5 million fell on the armed forces. On the social side, education was the chief target. Lloyd George himself urged that classes should be allowed to rise to sixty or seventy children and that the Burnham Committee's new salary scales should be abandoned. Fisher, however, resisted so strongly that eventually education bore only a third of the cut originally proposed by Geddes. But improvement had been checked and the Government had been driven decisively off the high ground of social reform by its own supporters. In the 1922 budget Horne reduced income tax to 4s. By then the Anti-Waste campaign had withered, but its political effects proved to be lasting.

Whatever criticisms Conservatives had of the financial policies of the coalition, they could not fault Lloyd George's handling of industrial affairs. From the start, trade-union militancy dominated the Government's term of office. For three years the level of strike activity was unparalleled. During 1919 35 million working days were lost, compared with 6 million in 1918; this figure fell to 26 million in 1920 and leapt to 86 million in 1921. As Lloyd George settled down to work in Paris in January 1919, strikes were building up among engineers, miners, railway and shipbuilding workers, on the London Underground, and even among the police. Partly because he was absent, and thus influenced by rather excitable communications from his colleagues, Lloyd George adopted a belligerent stance towards the strikes. In February he set up a Cabinet committee on industrial unrest under the Home Secretary, Edward Shortt, charged with maintaining essential services such as food, coal, electricity, and transport during major strikes. Later, under Eric Geddes, this became the Supply and Transport Committee under whose aegis successive governments evolved methods for coping with a general strike.

Attention was concentrated on the dramatic events on Clydeside where the movement led by Willie Gallacher, Emmanuel Shinwell, John Maclean, and David Kirkwood was interpreted as a Bolshevik conspiracy by the authorities. It resulted in the imprisonment of the strike leaders and the appearance of armoured cars on the streets of Glasgow. However, the underlying cause of militancy lay less in ideology than in the experience of wartime which had raised the expectations of working-class families. In the inflationary boom of 1919-20 many workers made further gains. Yet the war had also stimulated the argument for the nationalisation of coal and the railways, for the workers' objectives were more readily attainable under the wartime system of state control. Both Churchill and Geddes supported railway nationalisation, and the latter introduced a Bill for the amalgamation of railway companies and state purchase in 1919. This, however, was withdrawn because of opposition within the coalition, and the nine-day rail strike in September was essentially over wages and differentials in the industry. Lloyd George denounced the strike as an 'anarchist conspiracy' – an unlikely description of a movement led by the genial, patriotic Jimmy Thomas who had almost become a member of the War Cabinet in 1916! Inevitably Lloyd George talked with Thomas, as of old, and made concessions to maintain the real value of wages. His ministerial colleagues poured out their gratitude to the Prime Minister. Similarly, a strike by dockers in 1920 brought concessions in the shape of a forty-hour week, a national minimum wage, and the registration of dock labour. Lloyd George seemed to have the knack of satisfying his colleagues by adopting a tough stance, while also bringing strikes to an end through giving ground on the men's demands. He certainly inspired the confidence that he could manage the situation.

Only in the case of coal was his cleverness obviously overdone. The miners greatly appreciated the wartime system of state control which was to last until August 1921. In February 1919 their leaders, Bob Smillie, Herbert Smith, and Frank Hodges, asked for a 30 per cent wage rise and nationalisation. In response Lloyd George established a Royal Commission under Mr Justice Sankey to investigate both wages and the long-term organisation of the industry. In March it recommended a 2s. per shift rise in wages. In July it issued four reports on organisation, though a majority supported nationalisation. The evidence thrown up of the inefficiency and inhumanity of the coal-owners, added to the experience with state control, seemed to provide a perfect opportunity to take over the industry. Five ministers did support nationalisation: Addison and Montagu from the Liberals, Barnes and Roberts for Labour, and, significantly, Lord Milner. But Lloyd George adhered to his Tory colleagues and rejected Sankey's proposals in August. Now the miners felt Lloyd George had tricked them by prevaricating until the demand for nationalisation and the mood of militancy had subsided somewhat. Their suspicions were stirred again when the Government announced that decontrol of the industry would be brought forward from August to March 1921. The owners were thus left to face a situation in which the export markets upon which the industry relied for a third of its sales had collapsed and in which cheap German coal was available as part of the reparations payments.

By this time Lloyd George had largely lost any sympathy for the miners. 'I think we had better have the strike', he commented on 13 April. Two days later on 'Black Friday' the miners found to their dismay that their colleagues in the Triple Alliance, the railway and transport unions, had decided not to join them. They struck regardless, but their wages began a steep downward slide that led to the General Strike in 1926.

. . .

EMPIRE AND THE IRISH TREATY

Lloyd George's loosening hold on patriotic labour and social reform was not unconnected to the diminishing role played by Lord Milner in the coalition. For Milner, more than any other Conservative, combined an ideology of interventionism at home with imperialism abroad. Until 1921 he served as Colonial Secretary with L. S. Amery as his Under-Secretary. The British Empire now stood at its height territorially, and Milner and Amery hoped to initiate a great programme of constructive imperial development. In this they certainly had Lloyd George's sympathy, but apart from a measure of imperial preference in the 1919 budget little was achieved. Essentially the white colonies were too insular and the British Government lacked the resources to promote development. During 1919-22 the priority seemed to be to reduce military commitments, especially in the Middle East where we were tied down in Transjordan, Mesopotamia, and Palestine. Britain found herself both supporting a new Arab state and, since the Balfour Declaration of 1917, protecting Jewish settlements. During 1919 she gave military assistance to Persia and held down a Nationalist rising in Egypt. Neither Milner nor his successor Churchill were primarily interested in the Middle East, and they willingly began the process of military withdrawal in Persia and Mesopotamia. In 1920 Milner recommended conceding internal self-government in Egypt. It is significant that in the ensuing Cabinet debate Lloyd George found himself on the Conservative side in resisting this proposal. To him, Egyptian nationalism mattered not at all; he saw Egypt simply in terms of imperial strategy and communications. But by 1922 he felt obliged to accept Milner's advice.

Much the same applies to his view of India. The Liberal direction of coalition policy in India owed nothing to Lloyd

George and everything to the appointment of Edwin Montagu as Secretary of State in 1917. Montagu appreciated that pre-war reforms under Morley and Minto has disappointed the moderate Indian Nationalists, and during the war the growing co-operation between Congress and the Muslim League threatened British control. Montagu's Declaration of 1917, which established Indian participation as the goal of official policy, was therefore very timely. He followed it up in unprecedented fashion for a Secretary of State by visiting India to gather advice on reform. The result was the Montagu–Chelmsford reforms of 1919 which gave Indians partial self-government at provincial level. Unhappily the impact of this initiative was diminished by Gandhi's non-cooperation movement and by the Amritsar Massacre at which nearly four hundred Indians were shot by the troops under the command of General Dyer. Dyer's conduct was condemned by an official investigation and he was dismissed. However, all this was too much for Tory back-benchers who accepted Dyer's plea that he had averted a revolution in India. They attacked Montagu in the Commons, and in July 1920 129 of them voted against the Government over his treatment of Dyer. Caught between reaction at home and non-cooperation in India, Montagu bravely stuck to his policy but he became isolated in Cabinet, supported only by Fisher and Addison. Lloyd George evinced not the slightest sympathy for what was a triumph of Liberal policy; on the contrary he took the side of Curzon and Churchill in deriding Montagu for 'behaving not so much as a member of the British Cabinet but a successor to the throne of Aurangzeb'.[5] As with Addison, he declined to support a minister under attack for his Liberalism. In March 1922 Montagu too, quit, though not without some acrimonious exchanges in which he publicly denounced the Prime Minister for the 'absolute disappearance of the doctrine of cabinet responsibility'.

Lloyd George had long since lost any sympathy for the cause of nationalism in Ireland, but he was keen to settle the problem which he had so nearly solved in 1916. In 1918 he and Bonar Law had promised Home Rule with separate treatment for Ulster, and during 1919 a Bill along these lines made its way through Parliament. However, during the war British tactics had succeeded in completely discrediting the Irish parliamentary leaders who might have accepted such a scheme. The coupon election had seen the demise of Redmond's party and its replacement by Sinn Fein, whose members refused to attend at Westminster, preferring instead to set up their own Dáil Eireann in Dublin.

Under the Lord Lieutenant, Sir John French, Ireland was now under virtual martial law. In May 1919 the Irish Secretary declared the Dáil illegal and Sinn Fein a proscribed organisation. Soon the British army and the Royal Irish Constabulary found themselves fighting a war against the Irish Republican Army (IRA) throughout the southern and western counties. Sir Neville MacCready, the Commander-in-Chief, stepped up the retaliation against the IRA by employing auxiliaries, often drawn from unemployed ex-servicemen. These so-called 'Black and Tans', as they were named after a well-known pack of County Limerick foxhounds, became involved in guerrilla warfare in which the civilian population suffered heavily. It was not until mid-1920, by which time the government forces were pursuing a counter-terrorism of their own, that Lloyd George began to take an interest in the situation. Rejecting advice from all sides in favour of seeking a truce, he held out for a military victory. 'We have murder by the throat', he gloated in a notorious speech in November 1920. As a result of this delusion the war continued until the summer of 1921 when he finally accepted the folly of an indefinite military conflict in Ireland. By July a truce had been agreed and Eamon de Valera arrived in London with four colleagues for negotiations. Lloyd George's task was facilitated by the change that had come over several leading Tories, notably Birkenhead, once an uncompromising supporter of the Union. As an insurance against Conservative rejection of a deal Lloyd George carefully included Chamberlain, Birkenhead, and Worth-ington-Evans in the negotiating team. He genuinely feared that Bonar Law, now on the back benches, might lead a revolt in the Commons; but typically he exploited his weakness in bargaining with the Sinn Fein delegates. He virtually convinced them that failure to reach an agreement with him might lead to his resignation and replacement by a militarist regime under Law. Hence they accepted the appointment of a boundary commission to separate Ulster from the rest of Ireland, a concession which helped the Conservative leaders to defend themselves successfully at the party conference which took place at Liverpool that autumn. By 5 December the parties had agreed on the establishment of the Irish Free State which, to save face for the British, was to be called a Dominion under the Crown.

Here was a triumph indeed. Lloyd George had succeeded where generations of British statesmen had failed. He felt sufficiently buoyed up to contemplate holding a general election early in the next year. Yet in this he completely misunderstood his achievement. There was no political credit for him in the Irish settlement on the Right or the Left. The Unionists' bitterness at his willingness to negotiate with the 'murder gang' was only deepened in 1922 when the IRA assassinated Sir Henry Wilson on his doorstep in London. The Left, on the other hand, could not forget the Black and Tans, the episode which finally and irretrievably alienated Lloyd George from his old ally C. P. Scott.

. . .

PERSONAL GOVERNMENT

Thus, as he successfully surmounted one crisis after another, Lloyd George actually grew less secure and more isolated. As the war receded, his anomalous position as a great Premier without his own majority party became starker than ever. And the personal nature of his rule was exaggerated by his increasingly idiosyncratic working habits. Age seemed to exacerbate both his predilection for working at odd times and in odd places, and his notorious reluctance to commit things to paper. Hankey complained that he slept too long after lunch and then kept his subordinates up late at night, that he constantly interfered in the work of others but would then withdraw from the disorder he had created. Even allowing for the civil servant's natural resentment for the dilettante politician, it cannot be denied that Lloyd George's tendency to mix long absences abroad with lightning interventions made government an unusually erratic business. The farcical situations which sometimes resulted are well illustrated by Lloyd George's holiday at Gairloch on the west coast of the Scottish Highlands between late August and October 1921. Having ensconced himself at this remote holiday retreat he detained large parts of the Government there without a telephone, with only one car, and with a railway line no nearer than 30 miles. Since this holiday coincided with the critical Irish negotiations, he decided in September to summon the entire Cabinet to a meeting at the town hall in Inverness! After this he succumbed to a severe toothache and developed an abscess on the jaw which required a period of convalescence. Meanwhile a deputation of Labour mayors who had arrived to see him about unemployment were kept waiting for four days, as were no fewer than five ministers whom he required to assist in his deliberations.

Ultimately the façade of personal autocracy was no substitute for effective power; and Lloyd George compensated for the absence of a firm party base by the standby of the eighteenth-century chief minister – patronage. Yet even here his reputation outran his achievement. He was widely accused of creating a subservient press by awarding jobs and honours to newspaper proprietors and editors. In fact he bestowed peerages on Lord Beaverbrook (*Daily Express*), Northcliffe (*The Times* and *Daily Mail*), Lord Rothermere (*Daily Mirror* and *Sunday Pictorial*), Lord Burnham (*Daily Telegraph*), Lord Riddell (*News of the World*), Sir Henry Dalziel (*Daily Chronicle*), and Sir Edward Russell (*Liverpool Post*). Yet despite his undoubted concern to manipulate the press Lloyd George ended up with most of it against him by 1922. Apart from the *Daily Chronicle*, which he bought, even the Liberal and Labour press regularly opposed him.

The purchase of a major national paper was made possible by the amassing of a huge political fund from the sale of honours. When he became Prime Minister Lloyd George was already familiar with the practice of raising money from wealthy businessmen for special political purposes; he had irritated the Liberal whips in 1909, by his success in diverting donations into the coffers of the Budget League. As Prime Minister, he had free access to an accepted and traditional source of funds through his power to recommend men for honours to the King. However, in 1917 he did not have a *party* to which the donations might be directed. Yet this made his need all the more acute. The honours touts of 1917-18 used the argument that the coalition Liberals urgently wanted to build up their machine. And the Conservative success in the general election, by dwarfing Lloyd George's own organisation, only strengthened this case. Thus, his unrestrained expansion of the traditional sale of honours was, in part, another reflection of his political weakness. One of Lloyd George's secretaries, Sir William Sutherland, was well known for touting baronetcies around the London clubs, but by 1918 it was felt necessary to put the whole enterprise on a more organised basis. However, the use of, in effect, a formal tariff for honours put the Chief Whip, who traditionally channelled the recommendations to the Prime Minister, in an embarrassing position. Therefore Freddie Guest, the coalition Liberal Whip, acting on the advice of Alexander Murray, an ex-whip, chose to distance himself a little from the process by employing one Maundy Gregory to act, in effect, as a broker. Gregory organised the touts, whom the snobbish Guest described as 'grubby little men in brown bowler hats', and took his cut on the proceeds; this helped to expedite sales and keep Guest's hands clean.

Under this management the fountain of honour spewed forth its tawdry rewards. In 1917 Lloyd George persuaded the King to institute the Order of the British Empire (OBE) for wartime service at home or at the front. By 1919 some 22,000 OBEs had been awarded, thereby giving rise to the popular chant 'Lloyd George knows my father, Father knows Lloyd George' on the appearance of each new recipient. The real prizes, however, were the knighthoods which cost £10,000–£12,000, baronetcies for £35,000–£40,000, and peerages which were still more expensive. Of course many of the recipients, who were shrewd businessmen, managed to bargain for a lower price. But they were themselves vulnerable to the methods of Gregory and his men. In a debate in the House of Lords in July 1922 the Duke of Northumberland quoted a letter from one tout: 'There are only 5 knighthoods left for the June list . . . . It is not likely that the next Government will give so many honours, and this is really an exceptional opportunity.'[6] Altogether, Lloyd George was responsible for the creation of some ninety peerages. The sheer volume might not have attracted much criticism had not the quality of many of the newly ennobled been so dismal. They included Sir William Vestey (a barony) a wartime tax-dodger; Rowland Hodge (a baronetcy) convicted for food hoarding; Sir John Drughorn (a baronetcy) convicted for trading with the enemy; and Sir Joseph Robinson (a barony), the South African gold millionaire who had been convicted for fraud and fined £500,000.

As early as October 1917, Lord Curzon tried to reassure the House of Lords that the Prime Minister would satisfy himself that no money had changed hands in return for honours. But Lloyd George himself simply claimed to be in ignorance of such matters. No doubt he remained unaware of the details of each case, though the system worked by his approval and authority. In his candid moments he rationalised the practice. 'You and I know that the sale of honours is the cleanest way of raising money for a political party', he told J. C. C. Davidson. 'The worst of it is you cannot defend it in public.'[7] He contrasted British practice with American. In the USA donations were given for actual policy pledges, whereas in Britain only worthless and harmless titles exchanged hands. The flaw in this was that peerages carried some power through membership of the Upper House. But the argument certainly reflects Lloyd George's contemptuous view of the British peerage. If it were devalued by a huge influx of dubious characters so much the better in the long run. His chief line of defence, however, lay simply in the fact that the sale of honours went back to the 1880s and that every party was equally implicated. This did not prevent his Tory opponents raising the question, especially in 1921 and 1922. In this there was a large element of hypocrisy. What angered the Party Chairman, Sir George Younger, and the Chief Whip, Leslie Wilson, was to find a man like Rowland Hodge, who had already approached them for an honour and been refused, being snapped up by the Lloyd George machine! They did not so much disapprove of the system as resent the fact that through systematic poaching they were not getting a big enough share of the proceeds. This, however, did not prevent Baldwin grasping the high moral ground by blaming Lloyd George for the corruption that entered politics, and there is no doubt that by 1922 this manœuvre was playing its part in discrediting him. He was obliged to propose a Royal Commission to investigate the honours system which led to the 1925 Honours (Prevention of Abuses) Act under which Maundy Gregory was caught in 1933.

. . .

THE FALL OF THE COALITION

Of course, considered as a fund-raising exercise, the sale of honours was an immense success from which Lloyd George benefited for the rest of his career. It provided the financial base on which to construct a new political party. It proved, however, far more difficult to build the superstructure. As early as July 1919 Churchill had floated the proposal for a centre party and there is no doubt that Lloyd George saw this as the eventual way out of his dilemma as prisoner of a Tory majority. It is therefore important to consider why this strategy eventually failed to reach fruition.

At the heart of the explanation lay the Conservatives, a deeply divided and directionless party after 1918. Of course, there were many who never evinced any sympathy for working with Lloyd George. Against this the bulk of the Conservatives accepted their leaders' argument that in the exceptionally fluid conditions of 1918 co-operation with him was necessary. And it must not be forgotten that the survival of the coalition for four years reflected an appreciation of Lloyd George's achievements in foreign affairs and, crucially, in steering a safe course through industrial militancy. This, combined with the evident loyalty of their leaders, Bonar Law and Austen Chamberlain, made the coalition look more secure than it was. Whether Law and Chamberlain really wished to go beyond co-operation to create a new party is doubtful. Law, in particular, eventually began to see clearly that the Conservatives did not really need to go any further towards fusion, and only an imminent Labour government would have justified the step. Distinct from them were a group of leading figures like Birkenhead, Beaverbrook, Sir Arthur Lee, Robert Horne, Sir Laming Worthington-Evans, and A. J. Balfour, all of whom were somewhat detached from their party. At the extreme stood Birkenhead, who had only contempt for the party and showed it, and Beaverbrook, essentially an adventurer in politics. These mavericks occupied common ground with Churchill and Lloyd George on the Liberal side. But a party formed from such material would have been the product of personality and temperament; impressive at the parliamentary level it would hardly have survived in the constituencies. However, an ideological basis for a centre party existed in men like Milner and Eric Geddes – Conservatives who favoured state interventionism in economic and social affairs. The special blend of a strong, patriotic imperial and foreign policy with a bold constructive social programme undoubtedly seemed attractive in the immediate aftermath of war and held an appeal for men who found themselves uncomfortably caught in the Conservative, Liberal, and Labour Parties.

However, it proved difficult for Lloyd George to develop this ideological and programmatic basis for a centre party while he himself remained at the head of the Government. Daily detail simply blotted out the broad vision. The more he came adrift of Milner the further this strategy slipped from his grasp. The coalition Liberals, who broadly reflected the emphasis on patriotism abroad and reform at home, ought to have provided a solid core for the new party. Even Churchill continued to support social welfare during these years. However, they soon lost coherence, some quit the Government in disgust, others took offence at protectionism and began to rediscover their liberalism. Others went very far to the right, notably Churchill, Greenwood, and Mond. All were rattled by their loss of support in the country and the growing threat posed by both Labour and the Asquithians. For them, a centre party was essentially only a refuge in the coming storm.

To be credible a centre party also needed a Labour element. This was not impossible. Milner had perceived the sheer patriotism of the working class in the war, and the essentially pragmatic approach of most union leaders in domestic affairs. Since Labour was not expected to become a governing party for many years, a number of Labour politicians still found Lloyd George's mastery of practical reform highly attractive. Unfortunately the steady shift of his government to the right made co-operation less and less respectable for Labour; it exposed more sharply the fact that the underlying rationale for the coalition had been as a bulwark against the rise of Labour. Lloyd George, who lost Barnes and Roberts from his government in 1920, failed to place much significance on the Labour leaders, but as a result he was left somewhat cut off from potential support.

On the other hand, there are signs that he detected another large building block for his new party in the 8 million women voters. In the coupon election he had been alone among political leaders in addressing a major meeting for women chaired by Mrs Fawcett. He had secured the coupon for Christabel Pankhurst in 1918. He also supported Nancy Astor's nomination in 1919 and acted as one of her proposers when she took her seat in the Commons, for the politics of the Astors made them perfect material for a Lloyd George party. He also stimulated the Duchess of Atholl to take up a political career in 1921. In the immediate post-war years it was not clear whether women would behave as a single voting bloc, but Lloyd George had placed himself so as to tap their support should they eventually do so.

After his return from Paris in August 1919 Lloyd George took up Churchill's advocacy of a centre party. First he tried to persuade his coalition Liberals that the Liberal Party itself was fossilised; but, although many of them were not very good Liberals, they showed the politician's reluctance to give up their party label too quickly. Meanwhile, on the Tory side Younger drew the line between *coalition* by two separate parties and *fusion*; he doubtless expected to absorb coalition Liberals into the Tory Party in due course. Thus, he and Talbot, the Chief Whip, resisted such proposals as the introduction of a joint Coalition Whip which would have been a step towards a new party. The one serious effort at fusion came in the spring of 1920. In February Lloyd George asked Fisher to draft a speech setting out the aims of a centre party which he hoped would then be advocated by Balfour. Meetings were planned for 16 and 18 March at which Lloyd George would commend the plan to his Liberal ministers and then to his Liberal MPs. Bonar Law would then endorse the idea of fusion at a Conservative meeting. In the event this carefully laid scheme fell rather flat. At his first meeting with the Liberal ministers Lloyd George presented fusion as an anti-socialist crusade. In one whose antennae were usually so finely tuned this was a sign that he had absorbed too much of the colour of his political surroundings. By 1920–21 he had become a rather Conservative politician. As a result the ministers recoiled, and a dismayed and surprised Lloyd George promptly climbed down. At his second meeting he spoke of closer co-operation, not of fusion. Consequently, Bonar Law, somewhat relieved, declined to push the Tories where Lloyd George's own men would not go. March 1920 was thus a major turning-point. The escape route of a new centre party virtually collapsed and from then on the coalition itself was on a slippery slope.

Although most of the public criticism of the coalition came from the right-wing Tories, usually known as 'die-hards', they were numerically too insignificant ever to bring the Government down. What diminished the loyalty of the ordinary Conservative Member was the gradual realisation that the coalition was no longer necessary and might even be a danger. This was the message of the by-elections of 1919–22. Within months of the coupon election the opposition parties had bounced back, Labour taking seats at Rothwell, Widnes, and Spen Valley, the Asquithian Liberals at West Leyton, Hull, and Central Aberdeenshire. In addition Labour enjoyed sweeping gains in the local elections of that year. However, this success was not maintained and the coalition managed to hold many of its seats. The real flaw lay in the evident inability of the coalition Liberals to retain urban, working-class territory. Their demise would destroy the underlying *raison d'être* of the alliance with Lloyd George. In 1922 the coalition candidates suffered some very heavy losses, and Conservatives chose to place much significance upon the Independent Conservative who fought Newport in October. In a three-cornered contest he won the seat from a coalition Liberal. Clearly it was now an advantage *not* to be associated with the coalition, and Conservatives might expect to do well independently of Lloyd George, whereas the longer they remained loyal the more they would be tarnished by him.

None the less, this feeling would probably not have sufficed to topple the coalition but for the retirement of Bonar Law in March 1921. His successor, Chamberlain, proved to be a cold and aloof leader quite unable to guide the party through a difficult period. Even so, he might well have succeeded but for the fact that Law's health returned. By autumn he was back in the House of Commons. Thus the Conservatives could feel that in throwing over their party leader they were not taking a great risk, for a superior alternative was available to them. This confidence manifested itself in the party's refusal to be bounced into an early general election. After the Irish settlement Lloyd George hoped to go to the country at a January or February election. But when the Party Chairman, Younger, was confidentially sounded out about this he denounced the idea in public as 'pure opportunism' and declared that he and many other Tories would refuse to stand as coalitionists. This successfully blew Lloyd George off course.

Next he hoped to retrieve the situation by a new triumph of international diplomacy at the conferences in Cannes and Genoa. He aspired to restore both Russia and Germany to a respectable role in world affairs, though even here his wish to recognise the Russian Government was frustrated in advance by a threat of resignation from Churchill. In the event his strategy was completely wrecked by the dramatic announcement of the Rapallo Agreement by the Germans and Russians, which made the efforts of the statesmen at Genoa superfluous.

Lloyd Georgian diplomacy was now exhausted, but it had at

least brought him credit. Now in the last months of his regime he dissipated much of this by one reckless and belligerent act which nearly culminated in war with Turkey. Lloyd George had enough Gladstonianism still in him to sympathise with the Greeks in their attempts to seize territory from the 'unspeakable Turk' after the war. He encouraged their aggression despite the opposition of both Liberal and Conservative colleagues who reasoned that the new Turkish State represented a viable barrier to Russian expansion. During 1921 the Greek army retreated and by August 1922 when the Turkish leader, Kemal, was nearing the Dardanelles, Lloyd George wished to give military assistance to the Greeks. On 27 September the Cabinet agreed to reinforce the small British force at Chanak under the command of General Tim Harington, and thus try to keep Kemal out of the European mainland. Thanks to Harington's restraint a truce was patched up in October. Although Lloyd George claimed this as a triumph, Britain had been on the verge of a war in which no one in Europe or the Empire was willing to support her. This was the result of his reckless and autocratic style of government, so it appeared. Bonar Law in an ominous letter to *The Times* declared that Britain could not longer act as 'policeman of the world'.

Meanwhile the disintegration of the coalition during the summer and autumn proceeded apace. After Montagu's resignation as Secretary of State for India no fewer than three peers – Derby, Devonshire, and Crawford – declined to take the job. Even the power of patronage was losing its force. By June the Prime Minister was on the defensive over the honours scandal again. In July two meetings between the junior Conservative ministers and Austen Chamberlain were handled tactlessly. He and Birkenhead simply expected to restore discipline by calling for an early election, but this only antagonised senior ministers like Curzon and Baldwin. Blindly Chamberlain revealed the proposal for an election on 16 October and agreed to a full meeting of Conservative MPs on the 19th at the Carlton Club. This meeting debated a proposal that the party should fight an election on an independent basis. Most of the rank and file were ready to continue the coalition *after* the election providing the party's independence had been reasserted. However, instead of accepting this, Chamberlain adopted an uncompromising line, thus forcing the moderates to vote against him. The motion was carried by 187 to 87.

Although Baldwin derived much of the credit for this by his bold denunciation of Lloyd George as a 'dynamic force' who would soon shatter the party, the key speech was that of Bonar Law, now clearly available as leader once again.

After the Carlton Club vote Chamberlain went straight to Number 10 Downing Street. 'We must resign LG', he said, 'Baldwin has carried the meeting.' But Lloyd George already knew and lost no time in resigning his office. However, he acted as Prime Minister for four more days because Bonar Law refused to take office until he had been elected leader by the Conservatives. They had outwitted Lloyd George completely. Having capitalised upon his prestige in 1918, they had now ditched him before his failings could drag them down. Since 1916 Lloyd George had wandered far from his original course in politics. It was to prove difficult to find his way back.

. . .

NOTES AND REFERENCES

1. Macmillan H 1975 *The Past Masters*. Macmillan, p. 53.
2. In this section I rely upon Lentin A 1985 *Guilt At Versailles*. Methuen.
3. Lentin 1985, p. 144.
4. HC Deb. 23/6/21 c. 1600.
5. Morgan K O 1979 *Consensus and Disunity: the Lloyd George Coalition 1918-22*. Oxford University Press, p. 124.
6. HL Deb. 17/7/22 c. 505.
7. James R R (ed.) 1969 *Memoirs of a Conservative: J C C Davidson's memoirs and papers 1910-37*. Weidenfeld & Nicolson, p. 279.

Chapter 7

THE REDISCOVERY OF RADICALISM
1922–1945

The loss of the premiership left Lloyd George initially elated; he even spoke enthusiastically of regaining his freedom after seventeen years in Cabinet. Yet this reflected more than a natural effervescence on his part, for he assumed, as did nearly all contemporaries, that his exclusion from office would be strictly temporary. He continued to be surrounded by a prime ministerial entourage. To Frances Stevenson and Sir William Sutherland was added a new secretary, the formidable A. J. Sylvester, poached from the Cabinet Secretariat, whom Hankey declared to be worth two or three ordinary typists. Styled 'Principal Secretary' Sylvester usually accompanied Lloyd George abroad and helped to mediate in his increasingly complicated private life. After their return from Paris, Lloyd George and Frances had found the parting particularly painful, though they remained close as long as he was Prime Minister. But when he left Downing Street their relationship was interrupted, and there are signs that he himself expected it to dwindle steadily in the 1920s. He certainly saw more of his family than hitherto. Though still largely absent from Wales, he visited Margaret at Brynawelon for several weeks each summer and regularly appeared at the Eisteddfod. During the war Margaret had been involved in national charitable work and she continued to be prominent in public life. She handled constituency matters in Caernarfon, and conducted election campaigns on her husband's behalf, notably the Cardigan by-election in 1921 when a Lloyd George Liberal fought an Asquithian, and the 1931 general election when he was too ill to campaign in the Boroughs. Moreover, they frequently took holidays abroad together in the inter-war years and their relationship seemed calmer and more secure than it had ever been.

Lloyd George's dealings with his children were, however, much stormier. Richard, the eldest son, was antagonised by the treatment of his mother; the two had never been close, and eventually Lloyd George cut him out of his will. Meanwhile, Megan, his youngest child, became more prominent in Lloyd George's life from 1919, when she accompanied her father to Paris and began to receive a fine political training. As other colleagues drifted away, he relied more and more on Megan as a political companion, though this was not without complications. Megan also resented Frances, nor was she entirely sure that she wanted to play the role her father had mapped out for her. In 1923, in a show of independence, she spent a year in India much against his wishes. However, Megan was undeniably a political animal and had inherited much of Lloyd George's shrewdness, charm, and eloquence. From 1924 she found herself drawn inexorably into his career. A frequent speaker at Liberal bazaars and rallies, she represented Lloyd George and thus spared him much of the burden of travelling as he grew older. By 1927 she was being spoken of as a potential MP herself, and it gave Lloyd George great pleasure when she was elected for Anglesey in 1929 at the age of 26. Her brother Gwilym had been a Member since 1924.

In spite of this, Lloyd George's relations with Frances survived and eventually strengthened. By July 1922 his new house at Churt was ready for occupation. Set high up among the heather not far from Hindhead in Surrey, Bron-y-de and its estate became Lloyd George's real home for twenty years. Here Frances continued her work as private secretary throughout the years in opposition. Thus, by the 1920s his career was sustained by *three* women each operating in a different sphere: Margaret at Criccieth, Megan at Westminster, and Frances at Churt.

Although Lloyd George never recovered office after 1922 his career is not lacking in interest and general importance. He remained a professional politician with his health and vigour unimpaired until 1931. He was the key figure in the fortunes of the Liberal Party. And contemporaries took it for granted that he would return to government: the only question was in what shape and form. Conservative and Labour leaders believed him to be perpetually plotting a new coalition which would divide their own parties, and in Stanley Baldwin and Ramsay MacDonald this fear bordered on an obsession. Consequently their own tactics during the 1920s and 1930s were powerfully influenced by Lloyd George's behaviour – actual and anticipated. Above all, he still had a major constructive contribution to make to British politics. In facing up to the problems of managing the economy in an era of mass unemployment he did more than any other politician to launch the Keynesian revolution whose fruits were to be seen after 1945 in economic progress and social stability.

In October 1922, however, it was sobering to see how widely his fall was celebrated in the press. It was as though in dismissing Lloyd George the country was also putting the war behind it and making a fresh start. As the reaction against the Treaty of Versailles gained ground he found it hard to accept that his past achievements were not quite the political asset he believed them to be. In 1922 he consoled himself by mocking his successor, Bonar Law, now attempting to patch up a Cabinet, from unpromising and inexperienced material, in the absence of a considered policy. Yet his own dilemma was an equally complex one. While Prime Minister his strategy had largely been dictated by events; now he had to think it out again. It was comforting that a group of Conservatives – Chamberlain, Birkenhead, Horne, Balfour, and Worthington-Evans – held aloof from Law's government in loyalty to Lloyd George. His other assets included 120 coalition Liberal MPs, the *Daily Chronicle*, and a party headquarters at Abingdon Street. But, deprived of office and patronage, these elements would not hold together for long. No sooner had he resigned than Fisher and Mond urged him to drop coalitionism and call himself a Liberal pure and simple. Although he felt naturally reluctant to renounce the possibility of a new coalition so soon, the choice began to be made for him by his opponents. Bonar Law, anxious above all to restore normal party politics, held an immediate general election on 15 November.

Unquestionably, the 1922 election came too soon for Lloyd George to organise, or even to decide what to say; it was, he confessed, 'a most difficult and baffling fight'. Wherever he went, the press and the crowds flocked to see him, but this was a misleading guide to his popularity. They were drawn by the spectacle, the unpredictability, and the aura of power that he trailed behind him; but they voted for his humdrum rivals. Bonar Law won comfortably with 344 seats, Labour came second with 142, and the Liberals secured 117, of which 60 were held by Asquithians and 57 by coalitionists. His enemies gloated that he had been cut down to size so emphatically. Now the Conservatives appeared set to govern for five years with no opportunity for a coalition. What was Lloyd George to do in this situation? He himself saw little option but to retrace his steps to the Liberal Party. Throughout the 1920s, therefore, he rebuilt his credentials as a progressive, despite occasional deviations towards coalitionism as opportunity offered.

. . .

LIBERAL REUNION

However, the Asquithians professed to regard Lloyd George and his associates as unclean, and insisted that they should prove their opposition to the Conservatives in Parliament before gaining readmission to the Liberal Party. In no hurry to allow his rival back into the leadership, Asquith determined to wait for the Lloyd George Members to dwindle while his own followers increased. Yet rank-and-file Liberals soon showed their impatience with this prevarication and vindictiveness. In March 1923 several MPs led by J. M. Hogge, an Asquithian, published a memorandum signed by 73 members, urging Liberal reunion, and the parliamentary party formally advised Asquith and Lloyd George to get together to devise a common Liberal programme by a 4-1 vote. For his part Lloyd George publicly supported reunion, but pointedly remarked that 'progressive minds are by no means confined to the Liberal Party', doubtless out of a genuine wish to keep open his line to the Conservative coalitionists as long as possible. During 1923 he continued to hold meetings with Birkenhead, Churchill, and Chamberlain, ostensibly with a view to establishing a new 'progressive' group. Nor was he incapable of reciprocating the vitriol of the Asquithians. In a draft speech he wrote of one of them: 'I don't know why Sir Herbert Samuel has such a grudge against me, I have never done him any injury. After all, I made him the first Procurator of Judea since Pontius Pilate.'[1] On Gwilym's advice he cut out this remark, as well he might in a speech to promote Liberal reunion!

In view of the stalemate in the party Lloyd George decided to disappear on a six-week tour of the United States, so that by autumn 1923 reunion had still not been accomplished. His return early in November coincided with the dramatic announcement that Parliament was to be dissolved and the country plunged into a new election. This was precipitated by the new Prime Minister, Baldwin, ostensibly to obtain a mandate to introduce tariffs in order to reduce unemployment. Having been elected repeatedly as protectionists, most Conservatives were scarcely in need of such a mandate; the real motive was political. As Baldwin admitted later, he saw it in part as an anti-Lloyd George tactic; for he felt so apprehensive about the prospect of Lloyd George winning back the Tory coalitionists by launching a tariff policy, that he decided to anticipate him and thus reunify the Conservatives. Baldwin's conduct in holding an election for narrow partisan purposes when he enjoyed both a large majority and a four-year term of office was a shameless abuse of prime ministerial power. But even on partisan grounds the tactic was probably unnecessary. There had been some press speculation about Lloyd George's intentions, and Robert Donald of the *Daily Chronicle* told Churchill that he would declare for protection on his return from America. Yet this is the only slight corroboration for Baldwin's claims. The idea was not entirely implausible, for he had always adopted a very pragmatic view of free trade, and his 1918 programme had included an element of protectionism. However, no firm evidence has been found that Lloyd George planned to adopt tariffs in 1923; and Baldwin's decision is significant only as proof of his concern to reunite his party and of the exaggerated role Lloyd George occupied in his thoughts. Indeed, several men close to Baldwin such as Tom Jones, Deputy Secretary to the Cabinet, P. J. Grigg, his private secretary, and J. C. C. Davidson, the Party Chairman, all used the word 'obsession' when describing his feelings on the subject. It seems beyond doubt that for Baldwin the exclusion of Lloyd George from office represented a major objective throughout the inter-war period.

Politicians naturally expected Lloyd George to follow up his triumphant return from the United States with some startling initiative. But for once he had nothing particular to say. Whatever his real views on tariffs he could hardly have adopted such a policy at a time when he was presenting himself as a good Liberal keen to return to the party. In the event, even before he left ship at Southampton, he was greeted by Sir Alfred Mond who secured a pledge of loyalty to free trade. Although he did meet with Birkenhead, Beaverbrook, and Chamberlain on 12 November, there was no serious bid to renew the coalition.

On the 13th he met Asquith and Liberal reunion was officially proclaimed. In this way Baldwin accomplished what the Liberals had failed for a year to achieve. Lloyd George wound up his separate organisation, he and Asquith drew up a programme, and the Liberals joyously threw themselves into the defence of free trade, though Lloyd George insisted on retaining the option of retaliating against governments who imposed tariffs against Britain.

Reunion was only skin deep, however. Having returned to Parliament at a by-election at Paisley in 1920, Asquith showed no sign of giving up the leadership, despite his lack of ideas and drive. He surrounded himself with men like Sir John Simon, Viscount Gladstone, and Vivian Phillips, not to mention his wife, Margot, still anxious to punish Lloyd George for the coupon election, and suspicious, not without reason, that if the party fell into his hands he would simply use it as a platform to raise himself to the premiership again. Equally, Lloyd George regarded them as narrow and out of touch, clinging to the empty shell of their party. Yet in the diminished Liberal Party of 1923 such men bulked large. Many of his natural allies had already departed to join Labour. Radicals like Charles Masterman, once bitterly hostile, now relented, seeing salvation in Lloyd George's dynamic leadership, though others like William Wedgwood Benn still found him repugnant. There was much work to do in untangling the knots the First World War had tied in Liberal politics.

At first, however, things went well. Lloyd George dipped into his funds to assist a large field of Liberal candidates, and only two seats saw a clash between his supporters and those of Asquith. Unopposed in Caernarfon, he was free to tour the country, even appearing on Asquith's platform at Paisley: 'I have rarely felt less exhilaration', was the typical Asquithian reaction! But, as the press noticed, Lloyd George rapidly began to look like the *de facto* party leader. And though the party grandees professed to find his style lowbrow and a shade vulgar, even they admitted that he had brought the Liberals back to the centre of attention again. The result was almost a triumph. Liberal representation rose to 158 while the Conservatives fell to 258. But the gross Liberal gains of 83 were cut to 42 net because of further losses of ex-coalitionist seats to Labour.

No sooner had the votes been counted than even this modest success began to fall apart. Though holding the balance of power, the Liberals could not capitalise on their position. In view of the issue on which the election had been fought they were obliged to join with Labour in voting Baldwin out of office. Their next object should have been to secure terms for co-operation with Labour, or to make a bid to govern themselves. This was frustrated by the obduracy of MacDonald and the weakness of King George. Since MacDonald had only 191 MPs it was obvious that he could not expect to govern for long without Liberal support; and his defeat might precipitate a *third* election in three years. The King, however, neglected to invite MacDonald to form a majority government as Lloyd George had done in 1916, largely because of apprehension about the reaction of the working class; he wished to give no ground for suspicion that Labour was being denied its chance to rule. For his part MacDonald evinced no interest in getting Liberal backing for a definite legislative programme; his mind did not work in that way. Hampered by an inferiority complex, he found it hard to cope with criticism from Lloyd George, and especially feared his dominating presence within his administration. Tom Jones recorded that when at his official residence, Chequers, MacDonald invariably hid the photograph of Lloyd George in a drawer because it upset him so much! This behaviour was comparable to that of Baldwin who was known to deface photographs of Lloyd George in an album.[2] Yet behind the emotion there also lay a shrewd calculation. In 1923 the popular vote showed the Liberals and Labour neck and neck. No one could be sure the Liberals would not overtake their rival especially if Lloyd George were seen to be dictating a progressive policy. To MacDonald, therefore, it seemed axiomatic to exclude the Liberals from power for as long as possible, thereby destroying their credibility as a rival for working-class support. Nor was his total non-cooperation with the Liberals in Parliament as risky as it appeared. Though the Conservatives alone could have outvoted the 191 Labour Members, they carefully avoided doing so for nine months, for Baldwin wanted a respite to consolidate his hold on his own party; and he fully shared MacDonald's desire to make the Liberals irrelevant.

These calculations left Asquith and Lloyd George little room for manoeuvre. Asquith, naturally suspicious of any coalition involving Lloyd George, felt inclined to let MacDonald try to govern. It is more remarkable that so

incorrigible a coalitionist as Lloyd George did not press harder
for a deal. But he was not yet Liberal Leader, and hesitated to
provoke accusations of disloyalty by negotiating with Labour
himself. In any case he expected that MacDonald would come
round in due course. In this, however, he was mistaken.
Perhaps he failed to appreciate that the Labour Leader lacked
his own penchant for tackling concrete problems, or that his
principal strength lay in his grasp of broad political strategy. In
this sense both MacDonald and Baldwin were more able
politicians than Lloyd George, if his inferiors in the art of
government. However, Lloyd George quickly saw that it would
be futile in 1924 to attack Labour for threatening socialism:
'They are all engaged in looking as respectable as lather and
blather will make them', he told Megan. He concluded that the
best tactic was to play up expectations of reform in order to
expose the hollowness of MacDonald's radicalism. But as
reform failed to materialise he grew more aggressive. When the
Liberals opposed the naval estimates in March the Government
was saved by Conservative votes; and in April the Liberals
engineered a government defeat on the Rent Restriction Bill. By
the summer Lloyd George seemed ready to force MacDonald
out of office, given half a chance. This alarmed many Liberal
MPs who shrank from another election; but he contemplated
the prospect with some equanimity, believing that a purge of
the Asquithians would facilitate his own control of the party.
Eventually he fastened upon the issue of MacDonald's treaty
with the Soviet Union, on which he put down a critical motion
which the Tories could hardly refuse to support. However, they
seized upon another question – the Government's failure to go
ahead with the prosecution of J. R. Campbell, the editor of a
Communist journal, for incitement to sedition. This trivial
matter was adopted by both Baldwin and MacDonald to achieve
the showdown which, by the autumn, they both wanted. By
treating the Campbell case as a matter of confidence,
MacDonald secured a defeat and release from office without
having to face the more serious attack prepared by Lloyd
George over his Russian policy. In the subsequent election
Liberal support was severely squeezed, and the acute shortage of
money stirred up fresh controversy over Lloyd George's
personal fund. Though the Asquithians usually denounced his
fund as immoral earnings, they wanted access to it, and bitterly
resented having to go cap in hand to him. The fund was

nominally controlled by trustees appointed by Lloyd George, and he used it to promote any cause or campaign of his choice. Since it remained his strongest bargaining point he flatly refused to pool it with party funds. In 1924 he took the view that no more than 300 candidates should be fielded rather than the 500 urged by Viscount Gladstone. Eventually 339 stood and Lloyd George contributed £50,000; but no amount of money could save the Liberals from a heavy defeat, and they returned with only 42 MPs.

Although Lloyd George had not expected to do so badly, the result was in line with his calculations. For in the débâcle Asquith himself lost his seat and was translated to the House of Lords. Subsequently Lloyd George was elected chairman of the Parliamentary Party by 26 votes to 7, and he began to travel the country rallying the faithful as though he were their leader in the full sense. Nine of the surviving Asquithian MPs stubbornly resisted the Lloyd George take-over, and organised themselves as the 'Radical Group', under Walter Runciman, claiming to preserve the independence of Liberalism.

. . .

THE NEW RADICALISM

After 1924 Lloyd George began to see his political strategy more clearly. MacDonald and Baldwin plainly intended to restore a two-party system by stoking up a bogus debate between capitalism and socialism which would leave no room for the Liberals. It was not in Lloyd George's nature to occupy the soggy middle ground. Instead he intended to make a bid for radicalism by contrasting his constructive approach to the economy with the common conservatism and passivity of his rivals. He frankly contemplated the inevitability of achieving his programme by reaching an agreement with another party eventually; but he would only be able to bargain from a position of greater strength, which underlined the immediate necessity of restoring the Liberal Party to something of its former vigour.

The first harbinger of the new course had appeared in July 1924 with *Coal and Power*, the report of an inquiry into the coal industry financed by Lloyd George. It recommended nationalisation of coal royalties, the appointment of Royalty Commissioners empowered to close pits and amalgamate collieries, more representation for the workers, and the use of royalties for a welfare fund, better housing and pit-head facilities for the men. Though there was nothing particularly original in these proposals, they comprised a realistic formula for economic efficiency and humanitarian improvement. More striking was the second investigation into the land, begun in 1923 and completed in 1925. The land had always been an issue dear to Lloyd George. His Edwardian schemes had been lost in the war; the food shortages of 1916–17 and the post-war insolvency of many farmers made agricultural improvement seem even more necessary; after 1918 his government had pioneered a scheme to help demobilised servicemen settle on the land; and he himself was now pursuing the vision of self-sufficiency with his market gardening at Churt. At the centre of *Land and the Nation* (the 'Green Book') lay a proposal that the State should become the ultimate proprietor of all land and enjoy certain rights and carry certain duties towards the individual owner-cultivators. The State would regulate the use to which the land was put and assist farmers financially with drainage, reclamation, advice, and marketing facilities. It would also guarantee a living wage to labourers and provide cottages and substantial gardens. Clearly the unifying theme in all this was the intervention of the State where private enterprise was unable or unwilling to satisfy economic and social objectives. Though bold, the vision was unlikely to be a vote-winner; for even in wartime government regulation had been barely tolerated. Well might Lloyd George say: 'If I want to know how to treat a field here I ought to be able to send into Guildford and get an agricultural expert out at once.' This reflected the fact that for him farming amounted to a serious hobby rather than a profession. The average farmer was less enthusiastic about visitations by officials anxious to tell him his business; and the only form of intervention he relished was subsidies and guaranteed prices. Nevertheless the 570-page report formed a major step forward in Lloyd George's rediscovery of radicalism. He launched a campaign with a mass rally at Killerton Park in Devon in September 1925, where 25,000 people stood in the rain to hear him for one and a half hours. While Sir Alfred Mond condemned the report as socialism, his old collaborator Masterman was more appreciative: 'I have to confess, when Lloyd George came back to the party, ideas came back to the party.'

Certainly by 1926 Lloyd George's initiatives had gone some way to making him and his party a serious and credible alternative to the Baldwin administration, entrenched behind a large majority but becalmed amid a sluggish economy and high unemployment. For Baldwin, the key to economic recovery lay in a restoration of world trade and thus of the export markets of British industry. Effort was therefore concentrated upon trying to restore the pre-1914 financial system, return to the Gold Standard, reduce wage levels, and balance the budget. Lloyd George instinctively espoused the alternative strategy which relied upon the deliberate development of internal resources and stimulation of the domestic market for the products of industry, rather than waiting upon a world economic recovery which was now largely beyond the powers of a British government. In some highly effective parliamentary interventions he voiced his mounting contempt for the aimlessness with which Baldwin approached unemployment. When Churchill introduced an Economy Bill to reduce expenditure on health and unemployment insurance he virtually led the Opposition attack. 'The Labour Party listened enraptured', commented the *Sunday Times*, 'One could almost see the Labour Party holding out its hands to him in invitation, so full of acclamation were they.'[3] Even allowing for hyperbole he does seem to have gained the initiative by his sustained defence of working-class interests. So much so that there was renewed speculation about an alliance with Labour during 1926.

This impression gained credence from the General Strike in May, which Frances Stevenson believed had helped him to move further towards the consolidation of the forces on the left. When the strike began Lloyd George criticised Baldwin for breaking off negotiations with the miners and forcing a confrontation. But other Liberals saw it differently. Sir John Simon, with all the dessicated majesty of the lawyer-politician, pronounced the strike to be illegal and a threat to the Constitution, an interpretation which Asquith accepted. In view of this divergence Lloyd George avoided a meeting of the Liberal Shadow Cabinet on 10 May, saying, 'there'd only be a row'. But in an article for the American press he flatly denied any revolutionary purpose on the part of the trade unions, and urged a settlement. This encouraged the clique of men around Asquith to write to Lloyd George rebuking him, apparently in the belief that this might drive him out of the party. For once, he returned a mild reply which dwelt on the need to avoid a split. Asquith, however, blundered on with a public accusation that his absence from the party meeting was tantamount to resignation, and a threat to resign himself if Lloyd George failed to withdraw. In this way he put himself firmly in the wrong in the eyes of most Liberals who saw merely a crude and contrived attempt to drive Lloyd George out. The Liberal press largely praised him for his conciliatory approach to the strike and indicated that Asquith was out of touch. Resolutions passed by constituency associations, the Candidates' Association and even the Parliamentary Party referred to the need for unity and for a constructive industrial policy. As a result, it was Asquith who felt obliged to give up, thereby delivering the party into Lloyd George's hands at last.

Yet he had succeeded too late. During the vital decade from 1916 to 1926 the Liberals had suffered the steady attrition of their grass-roots organisation and lost a generation of radicals, male and female, to Labour. Indeed speculation mounted in 1926, fuelled by Beatrice Webb and others, that Lloyd George might join them. His friendly relations with George Lansbury and Philip Snowden in the late 1920s compounded this impression; and his appeal grew with the failure of Labour activists to pin MacDonald to any definite economic strategy, which seemed necessary if a repetition of the barren experience of 1924 was to be avoided. Yet although Lloyd George undoubtedly anticipated greater co-operation with the next Labour government, his tactics were less convoluted than contemporaries often believed. Having just succeeded in wresting the Liberal Party from Asquith's palsied hand he was keen to maximise his new asset. In any case he fully appreciated the furious reaction which any direct overture to the Labour Party would provoke. His wartime and post-war record was always used as a stick with which to beat him; and it allowed his opponents to adopt a high moral line in denouncing him as 'this discredited down and out political adventurer' in the words of the *Daily Herald*.

By 1927 he had begun to re-create the Liberal Party in his own style by appointing a new chief whip, making Herbert Samuel Party Chairman and planning for 500 candidates at the next election. The electoral tide also seemed to turn with a Liberal victory in the working-class seat of Leith and gains from Labour at Southwark and from the Conservatives at

Bosworth. Baldwin's drift and Labour's lacklustre performance made Lloyd George look like the coming force for a time. Attracted by the scent of power, the press barons, Rothermere and Beaverbrook, began to support him in the belief that he might have the second largest party after the next election and thus be able to form a government. Wherever Lloyd George appeared victory seemed to follow. His arrival at a by-election with a great entourage of aides, publicity, and pressmen in tow invariably proved to be the dominating event in the campaign particularly as, in this period, Cabinet ministers still abstained from appearances at by-elections. His financial resources were freely poured out for the benefit of his supporters. According to the successful candidate at Bosworth Lloyd George put thirty paid organisers into the constituency and spent £10,000 there over a six-month period.[4] However, this quick injection into the tired veins of constituency Liberalism was no substitute for real growth. The by-election victories, usually won very narrowly and with a modest turnover of votes, were unlikely to be sustained at a general election.

Yet Lloyd George's appeal was not merely a matter of public relations. Behind the circus lay an impressive grasp of the substance and the details of policy. This is emphatically underlined by the third of his great investigations, the Liberal Industrial Inquiry, which was set up in the summer of 1926. The origins of this lay in the early 1920s when a group of Manchester radicals – Ramsay Muir, Ted Scott, E. D. Simon, and Philip Guedalla – anxious to maintain the progressive tradition when their leaders were losing their grip, began to formulate policies for a capital levy, direct taxation, minimum wages, profit-sharing, publicly financed housing, and nationalisation of the mines and railways. From 1921 such ideas were regularly discussed at the Liberal summer schools whose participants included an impressive array of economists and social investigators such as J. A. Hobson, William Beveridge, Walter Layton, Hubert Henderson, J. M. Keynes, L. T. Hobhouse, Seebohm Rowntree, and Sir Josiah Stamp. However, the potential of the summer schools was not fully realised until later in the 1920s when Lloyd George was drawn into co-operation with the leading figures. He had been pointed in this direction in 1924 by Philip Kerr who challenged him to get to grips with the question of the economy and unemployment on the grounds that until he did so he would never be able to cope with the rise of Labour. After this, Lloyd George dwelt much more on unemployment, reaching almost instinctively for a 'public works' solution. An interventionist approach was not, of course, new for him. His 1909 budget had included provisons to establish a Development Commission, a body intended to utilise surplus revenues for investment in those capital projects not widely undertaken by private entrepreneurs, like afforestation and land reclamation, or more appropriate to the State like road-building. In this sense, though lacking the intellectual rationale, he was naturally predisposed towards Keynesianism.

Collaboration between Lloyd George and the summer school did not materialise until 1925 when Simon, Muir, and Masterman participated in his land inquiry. Towards the end of 1926 he decided to advance £10,000 from his fund so that Muir and Simon could launch what became known as the Liberal Industrial Inquiry under the chairmanship of Walter Layton. The inquiry operated in five subcommittees under Keynes (industrial and financial organisations), Lloyd George (unemployment), Simon (labour and trade unions), Muir (the function of the State in relation to industry), and E. H. Gilpin (worker status and remuneration). Their labours culminated in a 500-page document, *Britain's Industrial Future*, better known as the 'Liberal Yellow Book', and published at the end of 1928 at 2s 6d. The Yellow Book started from the empirical position that Britain was no longer simply a capitalist economy, but rather a private enterprise system with significant elements of state control. The question was how to establish the most beneficial form of government intervention so as to maximise both efficiency and living standards. To this end the authors urged the establishment of a Board of National Investment to channel more capital into industry. They advocated a deliberate state strategy of managing credit so as to raise the level of economic activity, and extensive expenditure on welfare for the benefit of those who were likely to spend their extra income and thus swell demand. In industry they recommended profit-sharing schemes and worker shareholders, backed up by minimum wages and family allowances. The immediate means of tackling unemployment lay in state finance for a vast programme of public works including road-building, slum clearance, house-building, electrification, afforestation, drainage and renovation of docks and harbours.

Though bold, the report was well considered and perhaps too detailed and academic to have an immediate popular appeal. Yet it remained by far the most serious attempt by British politicians to get to grips with the inter-war depression. Conscious of the seriousness of the challenge, Lloyd George's opponents rushed to condemn it as 'socialism' or as traditional individualism. Yet their haste only underlined his achievement in seizing the initiative just as the Government was seen to be running out of steam.

The year 1928 also proved to be a critical one in Lloyd George's personal life. At the age of 65 he decided to start a new family. Frances had always longed for a child, notwithstanding her devotion to Lloyd George's career; and it seems that in February 1915 she had had a miscarriage after which she gave up the idea for some years. Now approaching 40 herself, Frances wanted a family before it was too late. Between December 1928 and early January 1929 they spent several weeks together, and their letters make it clear that the pregnancy which followed was a deliberate choice by both of them. On 4 October 1929 Frances gave birth to a girl who was named Jennifer. She registered the birth, naming herself as mother, but not Lloyd George. Then she took out an adoption certificate, telling everyone that Jennifer's parents had been killed in China. The little girl was not allowed to call Lloyd George her father, but, since Frances acquired a house near Churt, he spent a good deal of time with her.

Although there was no general Liberal revival, 1928 brought enough Liberal victories at by-elections in places as diverse as Lancaster, St Ives, Middlesbrough, and Carmarthen to justify optimism in the Liberal camp. By the start of 1929, with a general election now imminent, Lloyd George feared only a repetition of 1923 and an ineffective, minority Labour government. He attempted to maintain the pressure on Labour by demonstrating his readiness to do a deal with the Conservatives through talks with Churchill. But this was never a convincing threat, and nothing came of his friendly meetings with Snowden. All he could hope to do was to retain the initiative in the country, to which end he launched the Liberal campaign on 1 March, before the date of the election was known, by issuing a pledge that he was ready with schemes which 'will reduce the terrible figures of the workless in the course of a single year to normal proportions'. This was followed up by a 6d. pamphlet under the arresting title, 'We can conquer unemployment', which provided a readable summary of the Yellow Book ideas. His opponents endeavoured to disparage this as a typical stunt from the man who had promised to build homes for heroes; but they were alarmed that he had determined the chief issue of the election for them. There was nothing inherently unrealistic in Lloyd George's claim in 1929; for unemployment stood at 1.1 million, a substantial but far from unmanageable figure. To reduce this to 'normal proportions' meant cutting the figure by 600,000. The Liberal case rested on the argument that £250 million, spent in certain specified ways, would generate 600,000 jobs lasting two years.

Later in March, as the Liberals gained Conservative seats at Eddisbury and Holland-with-Boston, Lloyd George and Samuel embarked upon extensive tours in the hope that they were on the verge of a sweeping triumph. However, the Liberal effort probably reached its peak too soon. The Government played for time and delayed polling day until the end of May, three months after the Liberal campaign had begun. By then Lloyd George was tired and his proposals had lost something of their novelty and impact. He spent the campaign itself largely in Caernarfon, making visits to other parts of Wales. In his absence the Liberal attack elsewhere in the country inevitably flagged. He had done enough to concentrate the election on ground unfavourable to Baldwin, but could not prevent MacDonald reaping the benefit, in that voters who accepted Lloyd George's case invariably saw Labour as the more efficacious vehicle for defeating the Conservatives. Some who liked the message remained sceptical about the messenger, heavily compromised as he was by his own record. Though, at 66, only slightly older than Baldwin and MacDonald, he seemed to represent an older generation, an impression which was enhanced by his style; the florid passages and heavyweight gloom of the lay preacher contrasted sharply with the vapid optimism of his rivals.

In the event the Liberals increased their share of the poll to nearly a quarter, but won only 59 seats. One consolation for Lloyd George was the election of his daughter, Megan, for Anglesey. From 1929 she became his constant companion when at Westminster. Every afternoon the pair could be seen taking tea together on the terrace of the House of Commons. Though an infrequent speaker, Megan delighted the House with the charming duet between herself and her father. Lloyd George would sit on the bench in front of her beaming proudly each time she mentioned him, and in one speech in 1931 he 'hear-heared' so frequently that she leant forward to declare her pleasure that 'my Rt. Hon. Friend supports his follower'.

. . .

MACDONALD AND THE NATIONAL GOVERNMENT

However, though Lloyd George held the balance of power, his position was ultimately as profitless as it had been in 1924. Both sides were determined not to indulge in bargaining with him; and Baldwin resigned promptly to allow MacDonald unimpeded access to office. Lloyd George, however, spelt out his terms for supporting Labour: bold economic innovations and reform of the electoral system. Since Labour, with 288 Members, was not far short of a majority it was more difficult than in 1924 to clip their wings. Moreover, co-operation with the Conservatives proved complicated because at this stage the party was so racked by internal divisions over issues like India and Empire Free Trade which were being used to challenge Baldwin's leadership. At least the divisions provided Lloyd George with collaborators inside the House, like Churchill, and allies such as Beaverbrook and Rothermere outside it.

Naturally enough the collusion between these men and Lloyd George was interpreted less as undermining MacDonald than as a plot against Baldwin, and as further proof of his incorrigible opportunism. More seriously, however, his tactics tended to deflect Lloyd George from his post-1922 course to the left. This was all the more obvious as imperial questions came to the fore, drawing out the illiberalism in him much as Ireland had done in the early 1920s. By 1929 India stood on the brink of a new campaign of civil disobedience led by Gandhi, which the Viceroy, Lord Irwin, hoped to avert by a bold declaration offering dominion status to India. But if Congress were to take this seriously it would require the endorsement of all three parties. Baldwin took the risk of backing Irwin only to be undermined by Tory back-bench rebels led by Churchill. Lloyd George threw his weight behind the die-hards too. Advised by Lord Reading, an ex-Viceroy, and Sir John Simon, he condemned Irwin's declaration; and in a speech in November he pronounced Indians too backward politically and too diverse to be capable of self-government. This reflected both his ignorance of the progress Indians had already made towards self-government, and also his instinctive imperialism. Lloyd George's biographers have never sufficiently noticed the oddity of his position in such matters. The Liberal tradition of Morley and Montagu was now being upheld by Baldwin and MacDonald. His stance in 1929 only underlines the long-term consistency of his politics – the combination of patriotic and imperial attitudes with progressive interventionism in domestic affairs.

It was not long before Lloyd George succeeded in putting Labour on to the defensive. During the passage of the Coal Mines Bill he repeatedly took the bulk of the Liberals into the anti-government lobby, though the impact was blunted a little by the abstention of some Liberals, fearful of precipitating an election. By the spring of 1930, with unemployment steadily mounting, MacDonald felt obliged by the dissatisfaction among his own supporters to adopt a more conciliatory approach to Lloyd George. Some Labour back-benchers saw in the Liberal Leader's pressure a means of shaking the stubborn passivity of the Cabinet, and urged MacDonald to overcome his personal dislike by accepting co-operation on a bold economic programme.

By March secret meetings were taking place in which Samuel and Henderson acted as go-betweens. The Liberals linked co-operation on the economic front to the adoption of proportional representation. Though widely supported by Labour politicians before 1914, proportional representation had always been resisted by MacDonald who saw, correctly, that it would undermine his whole political strategy by ensuring a firm Liberal base of 100–150 MPs. Now that Labour was so close to winning a majority of seats, he hoped to maintain the squeeze on the Liberal vote by sticking to the single-Member system. But he backed down to the extent of setting up a new Speaker's Conference as a result of which a Bill was introduced in 1930 for the adoption of the alternative vote system. MacDonald's chief motive in all this was tactical. He feared that, if decisively rebuffed, Lloyd George would scheme with the Tories to defeat the Government; wiser, then, to keep him entangled in negotiations. This is borne out by the talks on the economy. After the resignation of Sir Oswald Mosley in May

1930 in protest at the Cabinet's inaction, Lloyd George agreed to engage in consultations with the Economic Advisory Council. He soon realised, however, that his frustrating sessions with civil servants and ministers were achieving nothing. He seemed genuinely surprised at the impotence and lack of urgency at the top. 'Sisyphus is not in it with me,' he lamented, 'I am trying to roll a melting, slushing snowball up the hill.'

However, MacDonald's tactics succeeded in keeping Lloyd George away from the Tories, and during 1931 speculation began to grow that the Prime Minister would sack Snowden and make him the new Chancellor. It seems unlikely that the vain and prickly MacDonald would ever have made himself a latter-day Asquith, but Lloyd George, perhaps buoyed up by the admiration of younger Tory and Labour members, evidently felt that his moment was coming at last. He told Frances that MacDonald looked 'tired, jaded, spiritless. The fizz is out of him. I did my best to pump oxygen into this poor, limp creature.'[5] In the summer opinion began to polarise on the economic crisis, and when the Tories put down a censure motion the Government defeated it with the help of 30 Liberal votes. Thus events appeared to be conspiring to bring Lloyd George into formal co-operation with the Government.

Yet it was not to be. Towards the end of July he fell ill and on the 29th underwent an operation for the removal of the prostate gland. By chance this coincided with the climax of the crisis. For in August the May Committee presented the Cabinet with proposals for expenditure cuts of £96 million and tax increases of £24 million, designed to produce a balanced budget. Eventually the Cabinet split in half over this and broke up on 23 August. Lloyd George, still recovering from his operation, was kept informed by Herbert Samuel of the discussions which he and Baldwin had with the Prime Minister and in which they offered support for certain emergency measures. To this Lloyd George had no objection. But when MacDonald accepted the King's invitation to form an all-party administration things grew more complicated. While Samuel, Reading, and Donald MacLean took office, Lloyd George was not fit enough to do so, though Gwilym's acceptance of a junior post suggested that he would come in when he had recovered. Before long, however, the National Government took steps to put itself on a permanent footing. Under Conservative pressure MacDonald readily agreed to hold an election which would have the effect both of giving the new Government a five-year lease and, significantly, of making Lloyd George's inclusion unnecessary. From his bed, Lloyd George denounced the election plan as an 'incredible act of reckless and criminal folly', and called upon the Liberal Members to resign at once. 'If I am to die', he told Samuel rather melodramatically, 'I would rather die fighting on the left.' However, for the time being the Liberals preferred to cling to the National Government, counting on the protection it would give them at the election. Some 68 Liberals were, indeed, returned, but they merely turned Liberalism into a debilitated centre-right force. Lloyd George himself was left with a little family group of MPs including Megan, Gwilym, and Goronwy Owen, and even after the Samuelites had quit the Government in 1932 he abstained from all formal relations with his old party.

Now nearly 69 years of age, Lloyd George sensed that his last chance of returning to office had passed. In obvious need of rest and inspiration, he wisely departed in November 1931 for a holiday in the warmth of Ceylon. Thereafter he was in semi-retirement, making only occasional speeches in Parliament. He spent much more of his time at Churt in the company of Frances who had become, by this time, his wife in all but name. She played a central role, as secretary and archivist, in his new absorbing interest – the writing of his memoirs which began in 1932. Lloyd George's practice, in the 1930s, was to start work at six in the morning by reading a draft of an article or part of his memoirs; this would be typed up later while he made excursions to inspect the farm and the crops, and then revised again. He enjoyed a long sleep in the afternoon, and retired to bed at 9.30 with a good supply of shilling shockers. The publication of two volumes of memoirs in 1933 and a third in 1934 brought him the pleasure of refighting old battles, especially as some of his victims took to the correspondence columns of the press to defend themselves. On the domestic front he derived great encouragement from the work of the American President, Franklin Roosevelt, after 1932, so much so that by 1935 he had launched his own 'new deal'. With the praises of the press and men in all parties ringing in his ears he even went back on the stump again. Just as in 1930, the Cabinet offered confidential talks about his proposals, but as before it was all a charade designed to minimise his capacity for making mischief. As they prepared for a general election in 1935 the leaders of the National Government did what they could to isolate the trouble-makers, Lloyd George and Mosley, from their following. Although he created the Council of Action for Peace and Reconstruction, its role, when the election came, amounted to little more than scrutinizing the views of the party candidates rather than running its own campaign. When the Government was returned with a reduced but still comfortable majority, Lloyd George promptly disappeared for another holiday, this time in Morocco.

Meanwhile, the economic depression was steadily losing ground as the central issue of politics to the increasingly bitter duel being fought between Churchill on the one hand, and Baldwin and Neville Chamberlain on the other, over national defence and the British response to Fascism. Until 1937 Lloyd George showed himself more inclined to accept Baldwin's reassurances than Churchill's alarmism. He tended to make excuses for the illiberal aspects of the Nazi regime, such as its attitude towards the Jews, on the grounds that a period of revolutionary change inevitably involved some harsh and arbitrary consequences. He sympathised with Germany's withdrawal from the Disarmament Conference and the League of Nations in the face of French rearmament, he supported the idea of restoring her colonial territory, and he was not unduly disturbed by the remilitarisation of the Rhineland in 1936. Hitler's rise to power in no way weakened the belief in appeasement that he had adopted in the 1920s. Indeed, he clearly admired Hitler as a bold, constructive statesman who could achieve the regeneration of Germany. After several invitations Lloyd George eventually succumbed to the temptation to visit the Führer in September 1936. Accompanied by Megan, Gwilym, Sylvester, and a Welsh academic, Dr T. P. Conwell-Evans, he travelled to Berchtesgaden where Hitler entertained him to afternoon tea on two successive days. As usual on such occasions the Führer was at his most charming and flattering, and according to Sylvester, Lloyd George was 'spellbound by Hitler's astonishing personality and manner'.[6] When he wrote an article about his visit for the *Daily Express* it was so enthusiastic that it had to be toned down before publication.

On the other hand, Lloyd George adopted a far more hostile view of the Italian Fascist leader, Mussolini, whom he regarded as a bully. In 1935 when Abyssinia became threatened by Italian troops he had no hesitation in urging British support, including military support, through the League of Nations. In the summer of 1936, when the conquest of Abyssinia was an accomplished fact, and the Foreign Secretary went to Geneva to advocate the abandonment of sanctions against Italy, Lloyd George delivered one of his last great speeches in Parliament, saying of Anthony Eden: 'I have never before heard a British Minister ... come down to the House of Commons and say that Britain was beaten.' And he threw the brave but hollow warning against a cowardly surrender which Chamberlain had made in 1935 back at its author: 'Tonight we have had the cowardly surrender – and *there*,' he gestured towards the Government front bench, 'there are the cowards.'

But this was a rare display of his old fire. As winter approached in 1936 he took himself off to Jamaica: 'it is exactly like a tropical Wales', he enthused. As was often the case on his foreign holidays, Frances accompanied him at first, but departed so that Megan and Margaret could join him. On one occasion the local minister invited the congregation to pray for a safe voyage for Dame Margaret and to sing 'For those in peril on the sea'. Frances was evidently a little thoughtful at this, for Lloyd George roared with laughter: 'You should have seen your face', he teased her. Back at Churt, he occupied himself with writing lucrative articles for the newspapers, and building up his estate to 500 acres on which he raised pigs, poultry, and fruit. Fond of fresh fruit since childhood, he took particular pleasure in having bred a new raspberry, named after himself, which is still grown for its fine flavour. Margaret, meanwhile, tended her garden at Brynawelon as well as his constituency. In 1938 they celebrated their golden wedding anniversary at Cannes. A lesser man might have found it humbling to contemplate such an extraordinary married life, but not Lloyd George:

> We have lived together in perfect harmony for fifty years. One of us is contentious, combative and stormy. That is my wife. Then there is the other partner, placid, calm and patient. That is me.[7]

The year 1938 also brought the Munich settlement which provoked a bitter and contemptuous denunciation of Chamberlain by Lloyd George. But as war approached his thoughts seemed to turn increasingly not towards politics, but back to the scene of his youth. In the summer of 1939 he purchased a 37-acre farm, Ty Newydd, between Llanystumdwy and Criccieth. Now aged 77 he declared himself ready to serve in government once again, but his only significant contribution to the war came in the Commons debate on the fiasco of the Norwegian Campaign on 8 May 1940. Lloyd George had not been present in the Chamber to hear the Prime Minister's maladroit appeal to his 'friends' to support him; but Megan, sensing the opportunity, ran out to fetch her father. He appeared to deliver a stinging twenty-minute speech which culminated in the reminder to Chamberlain that he had appealed for sacrifice:

> The nation is prepared for sacrifice so long as it has leadership . . . . I say solemnly that the Prime Minister should give an example of sacrifice, because there is nothing which can contribute more to victory in this war than that he should sacrifice the seals of office.[8]

Following Chamberlain's resignation and the succession of Churchill, he had a medical examination and seemed to be holding himself in readiness to take office. But he made it clear that he would not serve with Chamberlain and Halifax, a condition which enabled him to spurn the rather tentative offers made to him by Churchill.

Early in 1941 Margaret suffered a fall and fractured her hip. Although her condition did not improve, it was not until 19 January that Lloyd George left to be with her at Criccieth. Unhappily the weather deteriorated badly so that he was prevented by snow-drifts from reaching her before she died. After her death, he began to age rapidly; he lost weight, his face became lined, and his formerly thick white hair grew thin. Now was the moment to fulfil the promise he had given to Frances thirty years before. But he hesitated for two years, no doubt because of the friction the marriage would cause with Richard and Megan. In January 1943 he celebrated his eightieth birthday and appeared in the Commons to record a protest vote against the failure of the Government to adopt the Beveridge Report. It was a fitting finale to his parliamentary career. At last, in October, he married Frances in the Register Office at Guildford. After a relaxing year of marriage he seemed to grow weaker, and Frances had him examined by two doctors who confirmed that he had cancer. Though he was not told of this, Lloyd George evidently sensed that the time had come to return home; and in September 1944 he moved to his new farm at Ty Newydd. Though ostensibly paying a visit, the reluctance with which he tore himself away from his beloved Churt showed that he did not expect to return.

He found Llanystumdwy much as he had known it. Some of his boyhood friends still lived there. The River Dwyfor still splashed through the village, and he pointed out to Frances the spot beside it where he wished to be buried. Though very loath to give up as Member for the Boroughs, he was scarcely fit enough to face a difficult three-cornered contest. Sylvester, who now carried out his duties in the constituency, made sure the Prime Minister was apprised of the situation. The result was the offer of an earldom in the New Year Honours List for 1945. He accepted, reluctantly, but never took his seat in the House of Lords. Sadly this expedient proved unnecessary, for he did not live to the general election. By February he had become confined to his bed in the library at Ty Newydd. During March he became very weak, and on the evening of the 26th he passed away peacefully with Frances holding one hand and Megan the other. He was buried simply, as he had requested, in a tree-shaded spot on the banks of the Dwyfor, his grave marked by a huge boulder of Welsh stone.

. . .

NOTES AND REFERENCES

1. Macmillan H 1975 *The Past Masters*. Macmillan, p. 55.
2. Campbell J 1977 *Lloyd George: the goat in the wilderness 1922-31*. Cape, p. 86; see also Middlemas K 1969 (ed.) *Thomas Jones: Whitehall Diary*, vol. I *1916-25*. Oxford University Press, p. 256.
3. Quoted in Campbell 1977, p. 132-3.
4. Campbell 1977, p. 163.
5. Campbell 1977, p. 280-1.
6. Sylvester A J 1947 *The Real Lloyd George*. Cassell, p. 202.
7. Rowland P 1975 *Lloyd George*. Barrie & Jenkins, p. 748.
8. HC Deb. 8/5/40 c. 1283.

CONCLUSIONS: LLOYD GEORGE AND THE CENTRIST TRADITION IN MODERN BRITISH POLITICS

I was seated at dinner one night at 10 Downing Street beside a distinguished Liberal. 'What a wonderful bust of Chamberlain that is in the hall,' I said. 'Ah,' he replied, 'you mean the bust of Pitt. Yes, it is marvellously like Chamberlain. I wonder,' he went on, musingly, as though the question fitted in with his train of thought – 'I wonder what will happen to Chamberlain's successor?' I looked up. 'Chamberlain's successor? You mean ––' 'Lloyd George, of course.'

There was a faint hint of reproof in the 'of course', as though I had asked solemnly for an explanation of the obvious. I looked down the table to where Mr Lloyd George himself sat, his face lit with that smile, so quick and sunny, yet so obscure, his light voice penetrating the hum of conversation, with its note of mingled seriousness and banter, his whole air, at once so alert and self-poised, full of a baffling fascination and disquiet. Yes, here was the unknown factor of the future, here the potentiality of politics.[1]

Down the decades commentators on Lloyd George have echoed A. G. Gardiner's feeling that he presents a fascinating puzzle: 'obscure', 'baffling', 'the unknown factor'. Yet all too often contemporary observers solved the puzzle they had posed, merely by pointing to defects of character. What made Lloyd George difficult to pin down, they suggested, was his nimbleness of thought and speech, his opportunism, his lack of fixed principle and moral sense, his detachment from party and individual friendship, his perpetual search for the expedient of the moment, his ultimate rootlessness. In all this they were not, of course, *entirely* wrong, though they depicted only a part of the man. Any politician with a career as long as Lloyd George's must be vulnerable to charges of inconsistency; his 16 years in opposition, followed by 17 in office, and then 22 in opposition again, inevitably involved ceaseless manœuvring, broken friendships, principles infringed, and policies jettisoned. His years in opposition left Disraeli with a similarly exaggerated reputation for opportunism.

But Disraeli's positive achievements have been kept alive by successive generations of followers. By and large it has been in no one's interest to defend the reputation of Lloyd George. British politics is perversely intolerant of those men who show a lack of proper regard for party; and on this charge Lloyd George has been found guilty. Ever since 1922 he has provided both Conservative and Labour Parties with a splendidly tawdry backcloth against which to display their own virtue. But Liberals, too, never really freed themselves from the feeling that he was the prime cause of their downfall. Writing in 1930 Sir Charles Mallet pronounced: 'The best hope for the character and independence of Liberalism in future is to dissociate itself from the political fortunes of Mr Lloyd George.[2] By and large this strategy has been followed, perverse as it is. To historians it has become much clearer that the primary responsibility for triggering off the decline of the Liberal Party lies with Asquith, in so far as it lies with any individual, for alienating radicals over the suffrage issue before 1914, and for his crassitude in refusing to serve in any government but his own in December 1916. By stubbornly clinging to the party leadership for years after 1918, when he had nothing to offer, he only exacerbated the difficulties in effecting a recovery. Had Lloyd George been able to take over, even as late as 1922, party fortunes in the inter-war period would have been rather different. Moreover, Lloyd George can hardly be made to bear responsibility for the party's further demise after the revival he achieved in the late 1920s. In 1931 the bulk of the Liberal MPs insisted on remaining in the National Government and fighting a general election under its wing. Thereafter, almost half the party was permanently lost to Liberalism, as, under Sir John Simon, the National Liberal Members disappeared into Conservatism. Even the other half of the Parliamentary Party which, under Sir Herbert Samuel, belatedly quit the National Government to re-establish its independence, decisively forfeited the historic position of the Liberal Party on the radical left in Britain. From the 1930s Liberalism was hopelessly marooned as a bland centre-right force, while Labour completely occupied its natural ground. From this condition the Liberal Party was not effectively rescued until 1956 when Jo Grimond attained the leadership. Even at this point, however, Lloyd George's daughter, Megan, was on the point of joining the Labour Party, while Asquithianism remained influential both in spirit, and, in the shape of Asquith's daughter and grandson, in body too. Thus, even when in the process of re-establishing themselves as a party of the reformist left, Liberals largely failed to invoke the memory and the achievements of their greatest radical leader. It is of some significance, in the present writer's view, that the advent of the alliance between Liberals and Social Democrats in the 1980s has led to a warmer appreciation of him.

Modern historians, however, have presented an altogether more flattering interpretation of Lloyd George, assisted by the easy availability of the collections of material which came, via Frances Stevenson and the Beaverbrook Library, to the House of Lords Record Office, as well as that held at the National Library of Wales which is still being added to by members of the family. The writing of Kenneth Morgan, John Grigg, John Campbell, and A. J. P. Taylor, to name only a few, has helped to establish Lloyd George's reputation as the greatest constructive statesman of the twentieth century. No doubt distance lends enchantment to the view, especially to the vista of British governmental achievements in the modern period. But, standing as we do, a century after the effective start of Lloyd George's political career, we can also now begin to bring, not just the governmental aspects, but the tangled party political significance of Lloyd George into truer perspective.

In his heyday, Lloyd George personified the winning strategy for the left in Britain. His essential case, during the Edwardian period, consisted in the claim that if the British working class were to improve its conditions of life significantly under a parliamentary system, it would have to accomplish this not through a one-class party, but by some form of co-operation with men of the middle classes, businessmen, farmers, and others, those who shared with the manual worker a common interest in creating the wealth of the country. This meant some form of progressive alliance under the aegis of Liberalism to sustain a Parliament committed to reform and social harmony. It is sobering to reflect that in the elections of 1906 and 1910 the Conservatives suffered three defeats on the basis of a *high* share of the popular vote: from 43.4 to 46.8 per cent. Only by effectively harnessing the natural liberal majority in the country by means of electoral co-operation did the parties of reform manage to hold power.

Historians tend to share with contemporaries a certain reluctance to take Lloyd George seriously from the point of view of ideas and ideology. They regard him, understandably, as a man of action and expediency, but not one who fits into any coherent party tradition or intellectual system: 'he is a very ignorant man. And he will ever remain so owing to his inability to read', as F. S. Oliver put it in 1915.[3] Straight-laced Liberals and condescending Tories alike decided early on that he was rather lowbrow, with his taste for 'shilling shockers', his preference for conversation over detailed memoranda, and his fondness for newsprint and the superficialities of journalism. While the claim that he did not read is palpably false, it is true that he seems to have had little interest in literature for its own sake; he read for strictly utilitarian purposes. Whether, however, some of the great scholarly politicians like Curzon and Asquith, products of Oxford cramming, were really very different, seems doubtful; the difference is the difference between Lloyd George's shilling shockers and Asquith's P. G. Wodehouse. Undoubtedly Lloyd George displayed a lifelong fascination for the press. He perceived correctly that Asquith's failure to cultivate and feed even the sympathetic press weakened the Liberal Party; and he himself readily supplied them with copy in return for the contact they gave him with opinion in the country. But one can see how this easy familiarity with journalists compounded the impression of him among politicians as lacking refinement and dignity; he seemed more like the hustling American politician, breezing into the sophisticated world of Westminster.

No one was more unsettled by the slightly alien quality of Lloyd George than John Maynard Keynes, who gave vent to his feelings in a remarkable outburst:

How can I convey to the reader who does not know him, any just impression of this extraordinary figure of our time, this syren, this goat-footed bard, this half-human visitor to our age from the hag-ridden magic and enchanted woods of Celtic antiquity? ... rooted in nothing ... a vampire and a medium in one.[4]

Keynes, of course, despite his collaboration with Lloyd George in the 1920s, could never quite forgive him for his part in the settlement of reparations after the First World War. But above all his reaction to Lloyd George reflects the baffled irritation of the highly educated, slightly supercilious academic when confronted with an unsophisticated, intuitive intelligence. Before 1914 Keynes was not a Keynesian; he eventually became one through a good deal of thought and industry. How strange it must have been to discover that Lloyd George, cheerfully unread in economics, had got there, in a rough-and-ready sort of way, via simple Hobsonian ideas about under-consumption, years before.

Yet acknowledging, as one must, the flexibility, opportunism, and detachment from party in Lloyd George, does his career really defy coherent interpretation? 'Who shall paint the chameleon, who can tether a broomstick?' Can we not answer Keynes's question? Historians have a responsibility not to encourage an easy cynicism about politicians. Yet this is sometimes difficult to avoid, especially from the standpoint of high politics. Perhaps the clearest example of the cynical, empty statesman is Lord Randolph Churchill. Roy Foster's biography of him confirms one's impression of him as a man rooted in little but ambition, for whom party, policy, or philosophy represented convenient rungs on life's ladder. But a little consideration surely suggests that this is a highly unusual case. Are any twentieth-century politicians at all comparable? F. E. Smith perhaps? If Lloyd George were to be treated in the same way, would one have an adequate explanation of his life and significance?

Certainly there is a case for interpreting him as a dynamic force, an explosive cocktail of talents set off by ambition and opportunism, and quite unattached to principle, morality, ideology, party, or any long-term aim. Yet such a view must be considered, at the very least, inadequate, because of the injustice it does to the passion for concrete and constructive achievement which was a consistent feature, perhaps the dominating one, in Lloyd George's life. This is, even for his severest critics, the redeeming feature of his career. His skilful improvisation and evident enjoyment of the game of politics did not reflect an empty pursuit of prestige or power. His penchant for identifying precise solutions to precise problems may be contrasted with the languid cynicism of, for example, A. J. Balfour, for whom politics really was a game. Temperamentally Lloyd George shared a good deal with Joseph Chamberlain, and perhaps Churchill. Chamberlain in particular, displayed a powerful vision and a capacity for diagnosing the ills of society. All these big men are vulnerable to charges of inconsistency and opportunism because of their characteristic refusal to allow anything to obstruct their frenetic search for solutions. Only in the most literal sense may Lloyd George be considered an opportunist; he was second to none in recognising what could be attained and when. Indeed his endless pursuit of remedies often blinded him to broader party and personal interest; had he been a conventional opportunist he would have held even more power than he did.

An alternative approach to Lloyd George has been to see him as rather firmly rooted in late Victorian, Welsh, Nonconformist society, and to interpret his career as an assault, mounted from that base, on the British Establishment. The culmination of this interpretation has come in the shape of Dr Morgan's study of the 1918–22 administration in which he develops his defence of Lloyd George as a consistent, reforming Liberal on some highly unpromising ground.[5] As with the 'rooted in nothing' approach, this clearly has some validity. Its strength lies in the solidity and in the enduring character of Lloyd George's reforming achievements. The adoption of the broad principle that governments should tax their citizens according to ability to pay, pulled Britain out of the nineteenth-century pattern of taxation in which the very poor paid as high a proportion of their income in tax as the very rich. The Edwardian system has remained broadly the basis of British taxation up to the present day in spite of some attempts to undermine it in the 1980s. Though there is room for argument about how far the Edwardian innovations in social welfare represent a first instalment of what, after 1945, has been known as the 'Welfare State', it is beyond dispute that many of the underlying principles – such as national insurance – are enduring, and that much of the social reform since 1914 has been an extension of Lloyd George's work.

However, this view of Lloyd George is, ultimately a shade romantic; it represents essentially *one* facet of him and overlooks the complications. He simply cannot be fitted neatly into a Liberal scheme of things. As we have seen, he was, from the start, detached, freelance, something of a buccaneer in politics. In the second place, he was deficient in some of the attitudes that, in the twentieth century, go to make up the quintessential Liberal. His lack of interest in matters of individual rights and freedoms, in constitutional reforms, and in the rights of subject peoples to self-determination, cuts him off from the central stream of British Liberal principles from the early nineteenth century to the present day. Thirdly, and most obviously, he had an instinctive scepticism about shibboleths and dogma, religious and political. A. G. Gardiner described this, not unfairly:

> He is, indeed, the least doctrinaire of men .... No anchor of theory holds him, and he approaches life as if it were a new problem .... He is unconscious of the roads and fences of his forefathers. His maxims are his own, coined out of the metal quarried from his direct contact with life. He is not modern: he is momentary. There is no past: only the living present; no teachers: only the living facts.[6]

Yet if Gardiner saw all too clearly the gulf separating Lloyd George from the orthodox party regulars, he also appreciated that he was not simply an untethered bundle of talents; he fitted into a pattern – the question was, which one? Unavoidably, Gardiner could glimpse only a little of it from his standpoint in the Edwardian period. We can appreciate more readily that Lloyd George, though indeed no doctrinaire, was a surprisingly consistent politician; on free trade, on social reform, on imperialism, there is not the weaving and bobbing that many a jaundiced commentator suggests. It is too easy to equate the undoctrinaire with the inconsistent.

But if Lloyd George can be caught out being consistent on certain topics, what, if anything, did his consistency amount to in total? Did it make him a Liberal, a Nationalist, a Centrist? Unfortunately British politics has always suffered from an inadequate terminology, especially on the left. Useful terms, such as social democratic, which would serve to describe significant parts of the political spectrum in Britain, disappeared from use until quite recently. Terms like socialist, that are used rather sparingly and accurately on the Continent, have in Britain been applied loosely to large parts of the spectrum.[7] Since Lloyd George can hardly be labelled in conventional party terms, it is tempting to use an alternative like centrist. This reflects a wide feeling that, though Britain has had no centrist party, she has had an extensive centrist tradition. Dr Harrison has argued that the great majority of politicians, Conservative, Liberal, and Labour, are centrist.[8] By this, however, he really means the practical tendency for men of government to trim towards a moderate position; centrism here describes a *practice* rather than a coherent or distinct ideological position. Nor should centrism be confused with the migration of certain breakaway groups and parties – Whigs, Liberal Unionists, National Liberals – from the left to a position on the right of politics. On the other hand, a coherent and enduring centrist tradition is discernible in Britain. This is clear enough if one considers why certain politicians in *both* parties have been uncomfortable, whether in the period of Liberal–Conservative hegemony or under Labour–Conservative dominance. Centrists are not moderates, but people with a foot in both camps. On the right, for example, there exists a well-established tradition which regards the State in a positive light, as a beneficent force capable of regulating social and economic life for the benefit of the less advantaged members of society. This sometimes surfaces as 'Toryism', but by and large during the nineteenth and twentieth centuries it has tended to be submerged by Peelite Conservatism, by the preference for individual enterprise, and by the fatalistic view that little can ever be accomplished through politics. Then on the left – both in Victorian–Edwardian Liberal and in twentieth-century Labour politics – there have always been those who are troubled by the prevalent views on external affairs – by opposition to colonial expansion, to wars, and to expenditure on armaments, especially among the rank-and-file activists. Just as on the Conservative side, their view does, of course, prevail from time to time; under a Palmerston, a Rosebery, or an Attlee they feel reassured. But there remains an underlying feeling that a strong, patriotic external policy is unduly difficult to pursue within the existing party framework.

Much of the time the resulting tensions remain latent on both left and right; but occasionally they burst to the surface, and create splits in the old parties, sometimes lead to new groupings and eventually to the retirement or the reabsorption of the rebels into one of the major groupings. This behaviour underlines the long-term basis for a centrist position among those politicians whose political creed combines a belief in the positive application of state power for social purposes with the need to adopt a strong, nationalist line in matters of defence, empire, and foreign policy. Their attitudes are not original, but the *blend* of attitude is distinctive and frequently cannot be accommodated satisfactorily within either of the main parties. This was best articulated in the career of Joseph Chamberlain.

During the 1870s Chamberlain emerged, along with Charles Dilke, as the foremost 'constructive radical', but he realised in the 1880s that Gladstone still exercised a great hold over radical Liberalism because of his approach to *external* affairs; Liberal activists tended to share his, not Chamberlain's, view on the colonies or Ireland. As a result, his bid to take over the party had failed by 1885-86. Subsequently, Chamberlain found a measure of fulfilment in the Conservative ranks as an apostle of empire and old-age pensions. But in 1903 he 'came out' clearly as a centrist once again with his tariff reform campaign, which combined the patriotic external policy with state responsibility for social welfare and employment in a most satisfying way. This initiative finally submerged a similarly centrist strategy by Lord Rosebery which he had pursued from an increasingly detached position in Liberal circles since the late 1890s.

Despite his youthful political apprenticeship within orthodox Gladstonianism, Lloyd George found Chamberlain's approach highly appealing, so much so that he came within inches of joining him in 1886. Unavoidably adrift from Chamberlain during the 1890s, he seems to have regarded Rosebery as the natural alternative within Liberalism. So strong was this conviction that it survived the Boer War. This is underlined by his sympathetic view of the 1902 Education Act – typical of the 'national efficiency' school which included Liberals like Richard Haldane. The Edwardian period brought to a climax internal policies of state interventionism, combined with a reorientation of external policy towards rearmament and the continental commitment designed to maintain France as a Great Power. It was, thus, one of those periods in which a centrist could function effectively within a straight party context. During the war years it became much easier to pursue the centrist line, given the disruption of parties, the external crisis, and the temporary diminution of resistance to state interventionism. Despite being blown off course by the coupon election and the post-war coalition, Lloyd George nevertheless reverted to the twin pillars of his creed later in the inter-war years; this manifests itself in, on the one hand, his approach to empire and nationalist movements, and, on the other, in his espousal of a bold, Keynesian vision of social and economic reconstruction.

On the Conservative side of politics centrism continued to be well represented, even after the withdrawal of Chamberlain from active campaigning. Lord Milner, J. L. Garvin, F. E. Smith and L. S. Amery were among those who believed that they glimpsed in Lloyd George, the natural heir to the Chamberlain–Rosebery tradition. War drew this element into much greater prominence and generated further support from a variety of figures including Waldorf and Nancy Astor, Eric Geddes, Lord Beaverbrook, and Sir Arthur Lee, as well as more of Milner's disciples. It was during this period that the prevalent belief in the irrelevancy of the old parties – comparable to the mood of 1900–02, but stronger – seemed almost certain to facilitate the birth of a centrist party.

On the left, too, centrists succeeded in making their mark. In the late Victorian and Edwardian period the most articulate centrists were those dedicated advocates of 'national efficiency', Sidney and Beatrice Webb, detached from party, interventionist at home, and notably patriotic in both the Boer War and the First World War. Then there were the patriotic trade-union leaders, of whom J. H. Thomas is perhaps the best example. Centrist impulses also manifested themselves in another rash and doomed enterprise – Sir Oswald Mosley's New Party in 1931. During the inter-war period Labour showed itself to be divided, just as the Liberals had always been, between an 'imperialist' and a 'Little Englander' tendency; this was reflected in the struggle between the supporters of 'pacifism' and 'collective security'. The gradual establishment of the latter policy, and ultimately of rearmament, in official Labour thinking during the 1930s reflected the growing influence of Hugh Dalton and Ernest Bevin. With their highly patriotic, even chauvinistic, view of foreign and imperial affairs, and their firm grasp of the idea of the State as economic manager, Dalton and Bevin were conspicuous examples of centrist politicians in the twentieth century. After 1945 the Attlee administration adhered so closely to the twin pillars of centrism that they found little difficulty, ideologically, in operating within the orthodox party framework.

Thus, as Lloyd George's own career gradually lost momentum, other centrists struggled to come to terms with the same dilemma, often with considerable success. Among Conservatives the tradition was preserved by Winston Churchill, Harold MacMillan, Edward Heath, and, most recently, Mr Michael Heseltine. In the Labour Party the era of Dalton and Bevin was followed by that of Hugh Gaitskell, and, from the 1960s onwards, by a whole series of centrist breakaways. In the 1980s the centrist approach to politics has found its most articulate expression in the ideas of Dr David Owen; for he encapsulates the classic dilemma of the centrist in finding neither the Labour nor Conservative Parties an entirely natural resting-place, and in seeking to combine the humanity of one with the patriotism of the other.

In this light it would indeed be a travesty to characterise Lloyd George as a politician rooted in nothing; on the contrary he seems to have been rooted only too well in a distinct and coherent ideological tradition with a century-long history from the time of Joseph Chamberlain to the present day. Prone to the same tactical weaknesses as most politicians of his type, Lloyd George must be counted luckier than most centrists; for, having kept to the straight and narrow path of party orthodoxy in 1886, he eventually enjoyed an immensely long period of high office, during which he managed to leave his mark upon the fortunes of his country, both at home and abroad, to a degree which has been equalled by no other modern statesman.

. . .

NOTES AND REFERENCES

1. Gardiner A G 1914 *Prophets, Priests and Kings*, J M Dent, p. 129.
2. Mallet Sir Charles 1930 *Mr Lloyd George: a study*. E. Benn, p. v.
3. F S Oliver to Austen Chamberlain 4/6/15, Austen Chamberlain Papers, Birmingham University, 14/6.
4. Keynes J M 1933 *Essays in Biography*. Macmillan, pp. 36-7.
5. Morgan K O 1979 *Consensus and Disunity: the Lloyd George Coalition 1918-22*. Oxford University Press.
6. Gardiner 1914, p. 134.

7. Clarke P F, The Social Democratic theory of the class struggle, in Winter J M (ed.) 1983 *The Working Class in Modern British History*. Cambridge University Press.
8. Harrison Brian 1982 *Peaceable Kingdom*. Oxford University Press, pp. 321–6.

BIBLIOGRAPHICAL ESSAY

. . .

SOURCES

Lloyd George's marked preference for the spoken over the written word is as irritating to the historian today as it was to the civil servants with whom he worked. One must, indeed, bear in mind that, despite the quantity of material which has survived, Lloyd George himself is often silent in the primary sources; what we hear is others commenting to him, or about him, or about the matters with which he was involved. This is particularly the case with the main collection of political papers which passed via Frances Stevenson to Lord Beaverbrook and eventually to the House of Lords Record Office. These papers are sparse on the period before 1912 when Frances began to introduce some order to his affairs. They are, however, complemented by the other main collection at the National Library of Wales in which there is a greater emphasis on personal and family matters. Fortunately, these papers are still being added to by deposits, made by members of Lloyd George's family, of material pertaining to his earlier life.

Down the decades contemporaries have put their own recollections and diaries into print quite freely. Since oratory was a major weapon in his career it is worth noting one or two splendid collections of Lloyd George's speeches: 1910 *Better Times: speeches on the social question*, Hodder and Stoughton, and 1929 *Slings and Arrows*, Cassell, which includes the Queen's Hall speech. Lloyd George's own vigorous volumes of self-defence are not quite as biased as might have been expected: 1933–36 *War Memoirs*, 6 vols, Nicholson & Watson, 1938 *The Truth About The Peace Treaties* 2 vols, Gollancz. An easily overlooked volume of prime importance for his ideas on economics is 1928 *Britain's Industrial Future*, Ernest Benn. A good deal of information about Lloyd George's early life may be found in the books by his younger brother, William George 1958 *My Brother and I*, Faber & Faber; his nephew, W R P George 1976 *The Making of Lloyd George*, Faber & Faber; his daughter, Lady Olwen Carey Evans 1986 *Lloyd George Was My Father*, Gomer Press; and by Herbert du Parcq 1913 *The Life of Lloyd George*, Caxton. For his relations with Margaret, K O Morgan (ed.) 1973 *Lloyd George: family letters 1885–1936*, University of Wales Press, is invaluable. In 1967 Frances Stevenson published her autobiography *The Years That Are Past*, Hutchinson. Her diary provides us with a vivid view on events as seen from inside the Lloyd George camp: A J P Taylor (ed.) 1971 *Lloyd George: a diary by Frances Stevenson*, Hutchinson; and the depth of their love and mutual dependence is clear in their published letters: A J P Taylor (ed.) 1975 *My Darling Pussy* Weidenfeld & Nicolson. A J Sylvester was also more than a mere typist for Lloyd George and nearly succeeded him as MP for Caernarfon. Since he worked with Lloyd George from the war onwards he presents a more autocratic impression of his subject, and is naturally much less sympathetic than Frances; A J Sylvester 1947 *The Real Lloyd George*, Cassell, and Colin Cross (ed.) 1975 *Life With Lloyd George: the diary of A J Sylvester*, Macmillan; Trevor Wilson (ed.) 1970 *The Political Diaries of C P Scott 1911–28*, Collins, is a valuable source for the radical Liberal element in Lloyd George's career – and his steady separation from it. Several of the men who worked closely with Lloyd George in an official capacity give a good idea of his unusual methods of operating: Sir H Bunbury (ed.) 1957 *Lloyd George's Ambulance Wagon*, Methuen, is useful on the National Insurance Act, though its author, W J Braithwaite, had a chip on his shoulder as he felt that Lloyd George had neglected him after 1912; Lucy Masterman 1939 *C F G Masterman* Nicolson & Watson seems to be a mixture of diary and memory; Lord Riddell 1933 *War Diary 1914–18* Nicholson & Watson; Lord Hankey 1961 *The Supreme Command*, 2 vols, Allen & Unwin; Stephen Roskill (ed.) 1970–72 *Hankey: man of secrets*, 2 vols, Collins; Joseph Davies 1951 *The Prime Minister's Secretariat 1916–20*, R H Johns; Thomas Jones 1969 *Whitehall Diary*, vol. I, Oxford University Press.

. . .

BIOGRAPHIES

From the Edwardian period onwards a stream of sympathetic works on Lloyd George began to appear, presenting his career in heroic terms as the progressive advance of a radical Nonconformist Welshman. The best of the traditional biographies, and more perceptive than most, is Frank Owen 1954 *Tempestuous Journey*, Hutchinson. The short, scholarly study by K O Morgan 1974 *Lloyd George*, Weidenfeld & Nicolson, was a great improvement in that it took account of new material, but it is still within the traditional interpretative framework. Don Cregier 1976 *Bounder From Wales*, University of Missouri Press, covers his career up to 1914. Peter Rowland's huge 1975 volume, *Lloyd George*, Barrie & Jenkins, is much less sympathetic to Lloyd George personally than most biographers, while Donald McCormick 1976 *The Mask of Merlin*, MacDonald, is so hostile and inaccurate in its attacks on Lloyd George that it seems almost a throwback to the 1920s. Much the most stimulating and original contribution came in 1973 with John Grigg's *The Young Lloyd George*, Metheun. With a politician's perception Grigg challenged the conventional emphasis on the Welshness of Lloyd George and argued that from adolescence he had been attuned to *British* politics and British patriotic causes. This was the first of a multi-volume work of which two more volumes have appeared: 1978 *Lloyd George: the People's Champion 1902-11*, Metheun, and 1985 *Lloyd George: from peace to war 1912-16*, Methuen. Meanwhile the somewhat neglected phase of Lloyd George's career between 1922 and 1931 has been examined afresh: John Campbell 1977 *Lloyd George: the goat in the wilderness*, Cape. This is a readable and sympathetic treatment which emphasises Lloyd George as a prophet of Keynesianism. Bentley B. Gilbert 1987 *David Lloyd George: a political biography*, Batsford, is the first instalment (to 1912) of another multi-volume work; it tends to become bogged down in the detail and lacks the perception of Grigg.

. . .

ASPECTS

A stimulating attempt to set Lloyd George in an interpretative framework other than the traditional one is R J Scally 1975 *The Origins of the Lloyd George Coalition: the politics of social imperialism 1900-18*, Princeton University Press. This has been criticised for exaggerating the coherence and significance of social imperialism, but the author undoubtedly reveals one important facet of the truth about Lloyd George. On a similar theme is the excellent discussion on Lloyd George's proposal for a coalition government in 1910 in G R Searle 1971 *The Quest For National Efficiency*, Blackwell. B K Murray 1980 *The People's Budget 1909-10*, Oxford University Press, is a fine, detailed analysis; and there are some useful chapters by H V Emy, M L Dockrill, Peter Lowe, K O Morgan, and others in A J P Taylor (ed.) 1971 *Lloyd George: twelve essays*, Hamish Hamilton. M G Fry 1977 *Lloyd George and Foreign Policy*, vol. I, *1890-1916*, McGill-Queen's University Press examines a neglected area. On the war period see Cameron Hazelhurst 1971 *Politicians at War*, Cape; the somewhat dated but still valuable essay by A J P Taylor 'Lloyd George: rise and fall', A J P Taylor (ed.) 1964 *Politics in Wartime*, Hamish Hamilton; and, for a very hostile view of Lloyd George, Trevor Wilson 1966 *The Downfall of the Liberal Party 1914-35*, Collins. On his methods of government there are three excellent critical studies: John Turner 1980 *Lloyd George's Secretariat*, Cambridge University Press; K O Morgan 1970 'Lloyd George's premiership' *Historical Journal*, 13; and J Erhman 1961 'Lloyd George and Churchill as war leaders', *Transactions of the Royal Historical Society*, 11. C J Wrigley 1976 *David Lloyd George and the British Labour Movement*, Harvester, is much narrower than the title suggests, being essentially a study of wartime industrial relations. A Lentin 1985 *Guilt at Versailles: Lloyd George and the pre-history of appeasement*, Methuen, is a readable and perceptive analysis of Lloyd George's role in peacemaking in 1919. A sustained and detailed defence of the record of his post-war administration from a liberal perspective is K O Morgan 1979 *Consensus and Disunity: the Lloyd George Coalition 1918-22*, Oxford University Press. His fall from power in 1922 has been analysed by Michael Kinnear 1973 *The Fall of Lloyd George* Macmillan.

CHRONOLOGY

1915   The 'Treasury Agreement', 17 March; appointed Minister of Munitions

1916   Appointed Secretary of State for War; Succeeded to the premiership, 7 December

1917   The Calais Conference; creation of the Supreme War Council

1918   The Maurice Debate; won the 'coupon' election

1919   The Paris Peace Conference; the Sankey Commission on the coal industry

1920   The Irish Treaty

1921   Retirement of Bonar Law

1922   Chanak Crisis; Carlton Club Meeting, 19 October; resigned premiership

1923   Rejoined Liberal Party

1924   *Coal and Power* published

1925   *Land and the Nation* (the Green Book) published

1926   Became Liberal Party Leader; Liberal Industrial Inquiry established

1928   *Britain's Industrial Future* (the Yellow Book) published; birth of Jennifer

1931   Operation for removal of the prostate gland, July; opposed National Government

1933   Publication of first volume of memoirs

1935   Set up Council of Action for Peace and Reconstruction

1936   Visited Hitler at Berchtesgaden in September

1938   Celebrated golden wedding anniversary at Cannes

1940   Denounced Neville Chamberlain in Norweigan Campaign Debate, 8 May

1941   Death of Margaret

1943   Married Frances Stevenson

1945   Died at Ty Newydd, 26 March

INDEX